My Life AMONG THE INDIANS

My Life
AMONG
THE INDIANS

By
GEORGE CATLIN

Edited with Biographical Sketch by
MARY GAY HUMPHREYS

WITH SIXTEEN ILLUSTRATIONS FROM THE
AUTHOR'S ORIGINAL DRAWINGS

NEW YORK
CHARLES SCRIBNER'S SONS
1915

Copyright, 1909, by
CHARLES SCRIBNER'S SONS

— — —

Published September, 1909

ISBN: 978-1-6673-0661-2 paperback
ISBN: 978-1-6673-0662-9 hardcover

IN THE SAME SERIES
Published by CHARLES SCRIBNER'S SONS

Beyond the Old Frontier. Adventures of Indian Fighters, Hunters, and Fur Traders. By GEORGE BIRD GRINNELL.

Missionary Explorers Among the American Indians. Edited by MARY GAY HUMPHREYS.

True Tales of Arctic Heroism in the New World. By A. W. GREELY.

The Boy's Catlin. My Life Among the Indians, by George Catlin. Edited by MARY GAY HUMPHREYS.

The Boy's Hakluyt. English Voyages of Adventure and Discovery, retold from Hakluyt by EDWIN M. BACON.

The Boy's Drake. By EDWIN M. BACON.

Trails of the Pathfinders. By GEORGE BIRD GRINNELL.

Zebulon M. Pike. Edited by MARY GAY HUM- PHREYS.

Each Volume Illustrated. 12mo. Net $1.50

PREFACE

The two large volumes from which this book has been mainly taken were compiled, as Mr. Catlin himself states, from letters written at the time to the Commercial Advertiser of New York City, and his notes made during the successive journeys they record.

These letters were written under the shade of some neighboring tree, from the bed in his wigwam, and always among the scenes he transcribes. To this immediateness is due the value which belongs to first impressions, the wealth of detail, accuracy of statement, and that engaging buoyancy of spirit which pervades the two big books. Elsewhere there are no such data concerning the North American Indian in his primitive state either for the ethnologist or those who love romantic adventure, the charm of the untamed landscape, and life in the open.

But Mr. Catlin writes as a painter, susceptible to moods and pictorial impressions, rather than as a trained writer. This has obliged much condensation, the bringing together of widely separated material into chronological order, and large excisions in order to get into one book the wealth of material lavished on two large volumes.

This has been done unsparingly in the interest of a less leisurely world of readers, perhaps, than that for which Catlin wrote. It has required change of tenses, of periods substituted for commas and semicolons, the elision of clauses, and even the suppression of paragraphs. But in every case care has been taken to cling to the words of the author; for these are a large part of the picture-making for which he has used the pen instead of the brush.

This narrative has also been re-enforced from a small book published by Sampson Low & Co., London, and from the catalogue prepared by Catlin for his Indian gallery. These extracts have been introduced wherever they have tended to add to the information contained in the main work. Moreover, this has been done without recourse to foot-notes or any interruption of the course of his experiences. The only consideration has been to add facts and observations, and to preserve the generous and persuasive attitude of the author. In this the editor has been aided and encouraged by Miss Elizabeth Catlin and Mrs. Ernest Kinney, the daughters of Mr. Catlin.

M. G. H.

August, 1909

CONTENTS

Preface 7

Contents 8

Illustrations 10

THE BOY'S CATLIN

CHAPTER I. The Missouri River In The Thirties 19

CHAPTER II. A Studio Among The Guns 26

CHAPTER III. Indian Aristocrats: The Crows And Blackfeet 35

CHAPTER IV. Painting An Indian Dandy 42

CHAPTER V. Canoeing With Bogard And Batiste 49

CHAPTER VI. Mandans: The People Of The Pheasants 60

CHAPTER VII. Social Life Among The Mandans 67

CHAPTER VIII. The Artist Becomes A Medicine-Man 73

CHAPTER IX. A Mandan Feast 82

CHAPTER X. The Mandan Women 91

CHAPTER XI. Mandan Dances And Games 99

CHAPTER XII. O-Kee-Pa – A Religious Ceremony 108

CHAPTER XIII. Dances Of The O-Kee-Pa 115

CHAPTER XIV. The Making Of Braves 121

CHAPTER XV. Mandan Legend Of The Deluge 129

CHAPTER XVI. Corn Dance Of The Minatarees 135

CHAPTER XVII. The Attack On The Canoe 147

CHAPTER XVIII. The Death Of Little Bear: A Sioux Tragedy 152

CHAPTER XIX. The Dances And Music Of The Sioux 157

CHAPTER XX. A Dog Feast 166

CHAPTER XXI. The Buffalo Chase 173

CHAPTER XXII. A Prairie Fire 184

CHAPTER XXIII. Songs And Dances Of The Iowas 193

CHAPTER XXIV. Painting Black Hawk And His Warriors 200

CHAPTER XXV. With The Army At Fort Gibson 204

CHAPTER XXVI. Lassoing Wild Horses 211

CHAPTER XXVII. Visiting The Camanches 221

CHAPTER XXVIII. The Stolen Boy 227

CHAPTER XXIX. A Cruel March 233

CHAPTER XXX. A Choctaw Ball Game 237

CHAPTER XXXI. Alone With Charley 245

CHAPTER XXXII. Canoeing On The Upper Mississippi................253

CHAPTER XXXIII. Painting The Portrait Of Keokuk 259

CHAPTER XXXIV. The Land Of The Red-Pipe Stone.....................263

CHAPTER XXXV. The Sad Fate Of Osceola 271

CHAPTER XXXVI. The Indian As An All-Around Man 274

GEORGE CATLIN

ILLUSTRATIONS

Buffalo Hunt. Accidents Of The Chase .... Frontispiece
                                                                    FACING PAGE
Antelope Shooting 58
"Game Of The Arrow" or Archery or The Mandans 107
Buffalo Dance 117
The Bear Dance 160
A Buffalo Chase 175
Buffalo Hunt on Snow-Shoes 178
Buffalo Hunt. With Wolf-Skin Mask 182
Buffalo Hunt. Approaching in a Ravine 187
Wild Horses at Play 213
Catching The Wild Horse 219
Dance Before The Ball-Play 240
An Indian Ball-Play 243
Three Distinguished Ball-Players.
Portraits from Life, in The Ball-Play Dress 255

SKETCH OF CATLIN'S LIFE

The career of George Catlin, the Indian painter, was that of one crying in the wilderness. The prophetic voice, however, was bound up with the fibre of a healthy American boy, who whiled away the time with "books held reluctantly in one hand, and a rifle and fishing-rod affectionately grasped in the other."

It is interesting to pick up the early threads of this unique life and see the weaving of the web that finally enmeshed him. George Catlin was born July 26, 1796, at Wilkesbarre, Pa., in the romantic valley of the Wyoming. His maternal grandfather was one of the few who saved their lives by swimming the river in the Indian massacre of 1778. His grandmother and mother, then a child of seven, were captured by the Indians at the surrender of Forty Fort, but were subsequently released.

In 1797 his family removed to a farm in Broome County, New York, his mother carrying him, a year-old baby, before her on a horse for forty miles over the Indian trail to their new home. To this valley, shut in between high mountains, Brant, the Mohawk chief, retired after the massacre of Wyoming, and here he was subsequently routed by the Pennsylvania militia. Thus the boy grew up with his mind fed on stories of Indian life and traditions. At the hospitable fireside of Putnam Catlin, his father, trappers and Indian fighters exchanged Indian experiences during the long winter nights. During the day the ploughs on his father's farm turned up Indian skulls, arrow-heads, and beads, which he preserved in a little cabinet; and to his death he bore the scar made by an Indian tomahawk, which he found, thrown by another boy while playing Indians.

In 1817, having received all the education his surroundings were able to give him, an education overseen by his father, and especially by his mother, from whom he seems to have inherited his out-door tastes and love of art, George Catlin was sent to the law school of Reeve & Gould at Litchfield, Conn., where his father before him had studied law, and was admitted to the bar. Here he remained one year, making for himself the reputation of an amateur artist, at least. During this time he painted the portrait of Judge Tapping Reeve, the only portrait in existence of the founder of the first law school in this country. Of his brief career as a lawyer between the years 1819 and 1823 Mr. Catlin says that he was chiefly occupied in covering the table in front of him with sketches of the judge, jurors, and culprit. At last his love of art overcame him, and he deliberately turned his law library into paint pots and brushes, and went to Philadelphia to set up a studio.

The next year the young artist was admitted to the Pennsylvania Academy of Fine Arts, and entered into friendly association with Thomas Sully, Rembrandt Peale, Charles Wilson, and John Nagle, the leading artists of that day. The following year he went to Washington, and painted a number of portraits of public men. There he was a guest at the White House, and painted Mrs. Madison in her turban, a portrait that has been frequently reproduced. Going on to Richmond, he painted the Virginia Constitutional Convention, then in session, a picture that contained one hundred and fifteen portraits, accompanied by a key. He is afterward found painting portraits in Albany, one of which, that of Governor De Witt Clinton, now hangs in the City Hall, New York. Meanwhile he had esLouis Philippe was then on the throne. As Duke of Orleans he had been in this country, threaded the bayous and streams of Mississippi and Ohio, and profited by the hospitality of the Indians in their wigwams. Eager as any old trapper for the delights of reminiscence, he hastened to bring Mr. Catlin and the Indians, then re-enforced by a band of Iowas, to court, where he presented them to his family, and talked with them in that human way which is the prerogative of kings.

Subsequently Mr. Catlin was invited to Saint Cloud with the King of Belgium, and the Indians gave a regatta on the lake. This was the beginning of much royal intercourse, and talks over old times. The king ordered fifteen paintings from Indian themes of Mr. Catlin. These were afterward executed at Brussels, for the Revolution of 1848, which cost Louis Philippe his throne, caused Mr. Catlin to take the Indian gallery and the Indians back to London.

But the happiest result of this visit to Paris was the friendship of Alexander von Humboldt, who became a determining factor in Mr. Catlin's career. So impressed was the scientist with the value of Mr.

Catlin's work to comparative ethnology that he urged him to go to South America and make the same study of the tribes of the southern part of the continent that he had made of the North American Indians. Accordingly in 1852 Mr. Catlin set sail for Venezuela, where he ascended the Essequibo, and crossing the mountains, descended into the valley of the Amazon. For six years he explored South America by pack mule and pirogue, making a détour from Lima to the Aleutian Islands, visiting all the tribes on the Pacific slope, and back again to Yucatan, where he painted the Mayas hovering about the ruins of Uxmal, which by this time had become part of Mr. Catlin's speculative conclusions about the aborigines of this continent.

This itinerary was now broken by a visit to Humboldt at Potsdam, where he was presented to the King and Queen of Prussia at Sans Souci. With a letter of introduction to M. Bompland, the French scientist in South America, from Humboldt, Mr. Catlin sailed for Buenos Ayres. From there he ascended the Parana, and crossing over to the head-waters of the Uruguay, descended by pirogue with his own paddle seven hundred miles down that river. From Buenos Ayres he coasted the entire length of Patagonia, and through the Straits of Magellan, visiting all the Indians of that region, and up the western coast to Panama, on his way back to Caracas to study the effect of the cataclysm that had broken the chain of the Andes, and separated the Antilles from the mainland.

The accumulation of data, that had been heaping up through many years of close observation, had now begun to stimulate theories concerning the presence of the Indian on this continent. To these theories this study of geological formations was to contribute. Mr. Catlin was now a veteran, but the fire of his enthusiasm was still aflame, and his zest as a sportsman as keen as in his youth. With rifle and rod he was as expert as ever, and the forests of the Amazon, and the waterways of South America afforded him constant sport. During this period Mr. Catlin was entirely lost to his family and friends, and at length the government sent out to its consuls and agents for traces of the wanderer.

In 1860 Mr. Catlin went back to Europe, where he began that series of paintings known as the cartoon collection. This was by the advice of Humboldt, who considered that, for the study of comparative ethnology, it would be advisable to paint characteristic groups of the different tribes on one canvas, and of the size that museums had found most expedient. These canvases were to be hung on folding screens, not only for economy of space, but that they might be placed on a level with the eye, and easily studied. This work occupied him eight years, when he returned to this country and exhibited them in New York City, and afterward in the Smithsonian Institution, where they remained until Mr. Catlin's death in 1872.

While on his first visit to England, Mr. Catlin brought out his *Notes and Observations on the North American Indians*. Its success was immediate. Not only was the subject popular, but from its stirring adventure and interesting detail it was as readable to all classes and ages as Robinson Crusoe. For the first time the Indian was seriously written of as a member of the human family, for Cooper's novels were still regarded as founded on fiction. It was neither as hero, warrior, nor wild man that Mr. Catlin wrote of him. We see the Indian in his daily life, eating, sleeping, hunting, at his games and at his prayers, attacking and defending himself from his enemies, but pre-eminently as a family man and among social influences.

One tribe is not as another tribe. Mr. Catlin does not deal in generalities, nor set down theories, and in ranging over the entire field of Indian life, he includes the Indian's own point of view. His style is direct, almost conversational, but when his emotions are stirred it acquires an almost poetical elevation.

These books, to which two others were afterward added, it is estimated brought him in fifty thousand dollars. But the money earned was at once spent in further researches. Notwithstanding a disastrous experience he had in England, he earned substantial sums, and it was his boast that in all his travels he never ate a meal at the expense of the government, while he usually had two men, trappers or natives, to assist him in transportation.

Unconsciously during these wanderings certain prepossessions arose in Mr. Catlin's mind concerning the origin of the Indian, and his relation to this continent. He was familiar with the various theories, and one may trace in his writings how details in favor of now one and now the other came up to confront him. His own conclusions did not admit any theory of immigration from another continent, and these he supports by a large amount of interesting facts, which it is impossible to do more than allude to here. These retrospective observations are indeed of less consequence than the foresight that led him to undertake these journeys. In 1832 he clearly foresaw the fate of the buffalo as he saw that of the Indian, and pleaded as earnestly for the one as for the other.

A suggestion then made by Mr. Catlin it is pertinent to recall. This was that the government should set aside a great National Park in the Yellowstone region. The Yellowstone Park is now an accomplished fact, and it seems that now, in laying out the great bison range contemplated by the government to rescue the fast-expiring species of the noblest animal of the plains, some recognition should be made of the man who first pleaded its cause, and who in 1832 wrote:

"I would ask no other monument to my memory, nor any other enrolment of my name among the famous dead, than the reputation of having been the founder of such an institution."

THE BOY'S CATLIN

CHAPTER I
THE MISSOURI RIVER IN THE THIRTIES

THE BOILING, turbid current of the Missouri River sweeps from its falls unresistingly to the Mississippi, into which it empties. In the early part of the century it presented the fascinating peril of the unknown. Half the twenty-six hundred miles to the mouth of the Yellowstone was strewn with the dangerous trunks of the lofty cotton-wood trees it had torn from the heavily timbered banks and tossed about on its shifting sands.

In the upper half it had cut its way through the rich, alluvial soil of the prairie, swinging from bluff to bluff, that here rose precipitously several hundred feet high, and then, sloping to the water's edge, was carpeted with deepest green. Over these fertile slopes roamed herds of buffaloes, elks, antelopes, mountain goats, and wolves. Where verdure failed rose graceful and fantastic shapes – ramparts, turrets, domes, citadels, castles – fashioned by centuries of rain and frost, glowing with color, and sparkling with crystals of gypsum amid the play of light and shadow in the level rays of the sun.

Such was this wild and strange country, almost unknown to the white man, when, in 1832, a little steamer, the "Yellowstone," made its way up the upper half of the navigable length of the Missouri River. Its passengers were Major John Sanford, the government Indian agent, Mr. Pierre Chouteau, one of the owners of the boat, and, at his courteous invitation, myself. Our destination was the Fort erected by the American Fur Trading Company at the mouth of the Yellowstone River.

If the dangerous stream involved peril to the adventurers, it also carried terror to the wild animals and the Indian tribes that roamed along its banks. For defence the boat was armed with a twelve-pounder cannon and several small swivel guns. These, fired in rapid succession, sent the wild herds in frightened confusion over the prairie, and the Indians prostrate to the ground with cries to the Great Spirit, who spoke to them in his wrath from the "big thunder canoe," whose eyes found the deep water in the channel and flashed lightning from its sides. Even the playful discharge of the steam-pipe, when the boat landed at their villages, caused men, women, children, and dogs to tumble over one another in flight. Accompanied by such scenery and scenes, the intrepid little steamer made its way, and after a journey of three months reached the Fort.

The Fort was situated in a beautiful prairie near the junction of the Missouri and the Yellowstone Rivers. As the head-quarters of the Fur Company it was the largest and best-equipped fort in that region. It consisted of eight or ten log houses and stores within a stockade; and, as large quantities of goods were kept in exchange for furs from the Indians, it was built to withstand assaults from a possible enemy, and manned by a force of fifty men under Mr. McKenzie, the company's Scotch agent, a kind-hearted, high-minded man.

He treated me with the same generous hospitality and politeness as Mr. Chouteau in my passage up the river. His table groaned under the luxuries of the country. There was neither bread, butter, nor coffee, to be sure, but there was an abundance of buffalo tongues, beaver tails, and marrow fat, and, curiously enough, plenty of Madeira and port. This company of three bons-vivants was increased by a fourth, an Englishman named Hamilton, a gentleman of many accomplishments, thus forming a group whose conversation, customs, and manner of life were in striking contrast to the rude, wild world about them.

There could be no more fortunate entrance into a life that an artist desired to paint. The Crows, Blackfeet, Assinniboines, the Knisteneaux, Ojibbeways, and Man- dans are the best-equipped and the most beautifully costumed of any Indians on the Continent, and these were then in camp outside the Fort for the purposes of trade. Living in a country well stocked with buffaloes and wild horses, which furnish them with an excellent and easy livelihood, they carried their good fortune in their independent bearing, perfection of form, and grace of movement in the chase and at their games. I have always held the theory that in the wilderness were models for the painter as perfect as those the Greek sculptors transferred to marble. I now found them in their state of primitive wildness, handsome and picturesque beyond description. Nothing in the world, of its kind, can possibly surpass in beauty and grace some of their games and amusements – their gambols and parades, of which I shall speak and paint hereafter.

No man's imagination, with all the aids of description that can be given to it, can ever picture the beauty and wildness of scenes that may be daily witnessed in this romantic country: of hundreds of these graceful youths, without a care to wrinkle, or a fear to disturb the full expression of pleasure and enjoyment that beams upon their faces – their long black hair mingling with their horses' tails, floating in the wind, while they are flying over the carpeted prairie, and dealing death, with their spears and arrows, to a band of infuriated buffaloes; or their splendid procession in a war-parade, arrayed in all their gorgeous colors and trappings, moving with most exquisite grace and manly beauty.

This confirms my former predictions that those Indians living most nearly to a state of nature, and with the least knowledge of civilized society, would be found most cleanly in their persons, elegant in their dress and manners, and enjoying life with the keenest satisfaction. Of such tribes the Crows and Blackfeet stand first, the richness and the elegance of their dress and the taste displayed being a revelation and a delight. Daily I have accompanied the Indians in their buffalo hunts, studying their methods, attitudes, and expressions, sometimes on a horse, but often running by their sides on foot.

The Indian rarely hunts the deer, elk, or antelope unless a skin is wanted for clothing. But the buffalo not only furnishes flesh for food, but provides horns, hoofs, hide, and bones for the Indian's bows, shields, wigwam, covering, and tools. Almost without exception they are killed by the Indians with arrows while riding at full speed. As the buffalo bull, when excited to resistance, is one of the most formidable and ferocious animals in appearance, with his long, shaggy mane almost sweeping the ground, a more pictorial and spirited sporting scene for the pencil of an artist could scarcely be found.

I have mentioned that McKenzie's table groans under the weight of beaver tails and buffalo tongues, and other luxuries of this Western land. He has within the Fort a spacious ice-house in which he preserves his meat. When the larder runs low he leads a party on his favorite buffalo horse to supply it. In one of these hunts I was privileged to join.

As we were mounted and ready to start, McKenzie called up some four or five of his men and told them to follow immediately on our trail, with as many one- horse carts, which they were to harness up, to bring home the meat. "Ferry them across the river in the scow," said he, "and following our trail through the bottom, you will find us on the plain yonder, between the Yellowstone and the Missouri Rivers, with meat enough to load you home. My watch on yonder bluff has just told us by his signals that there are cattle a- plenty on that spot, and we are going there as fast as possible." We all crossed the river and galloped away a couple of miles or so, when we mounted the bluff; and to be sure, as was said, there was in full view of us a fine herd of some four or five hundred buffaloes, perfectly at rest, and in their own estimation (probably) perfectly secure. Some were grazing and others were lying down and sleeping. We advanced within a mile or so of them, in full view, and came to a halt. Monsieur Chardon "tossed the feather" (a custom always observed to try the course of the wind), and we commenced "stripping," as it is termed (i. e., every man strips himself and his horse of every extraneous and unnecessary appendage of dress, etc., that might be an incumbrance in running): hats are laid off, and coats – and bullet pouches; sleeves are rolled up, a handkerchief tied tightly around the head and another around the waist – cartridges are prepared and placed in the waistcoat pocket, or a half-dozen bullets "thrown into the mouth," etc., etc., all of which takes up some ten or fifteen minutes, and is not, in appearance or in effect, unlike a council of war. Our leader lays the whole plan of the chase, and preliminaries all fixed, guns charged and ramrods in our hands, we mount and start for the onset. The horses are all trained for this business, and seem to enter into it with as much enthusiasm, and with as restless a spirit, as the riders themselves. While "stripping" and mounting they exhibit the most restless impatience; and when "approaching" (which is, all of us abreast, upon a slow walk, and in a straight line toward the herd, until they discover us and run) they all seem to have caught entirely the spirit of the chase, for the laziest nag amongst them prances with an elasticity in his step – champing his bit – his ears erect – his eyes strained out of his head, and fixed upon the game before him, whilst he trembles under the saddle of his rider. In this way we carefully and silently marched until within some forty or fifty rods, when the herd, discovering us, wheeled and laid their course in a mass. At this instant we started (and all *must* start, for no one could check the fury of those steeds at that moment of excitement) ! and away all sailed, and over the prairie flew, in a cloud of dust which was raised by their trampling hoofs. McKenzie was foremost in the throng, and soon dashed off amidst the dust and was out of sight – he was after the fattest and the fastest. I had discovered a huge bull whose shoulders towered above the whole band, and I picked my way through the crowd to get him. What I wanted was not meat but his head and horns. I dashed along through the thundering mass, as it swept over the plain, scarcely knowing whether I was on a buffalo's back or that of my horse, so hit, hooked, and jostled about as I was. At length I found myself alongside of my game, and gave him a shot as I passed. At this moment Monsieur Chardon, one of our number, had wounded a stately bull, and while they were both at full speed, the bull turned, and receiving the horse on his horns sent poor Chardon a frog's leap of twenty feet or more over the bull's back and almost under my horse's heels. I wheeled my horse to rescue poor Chardon, who was raising himself on his hands and feeling for his gun, for his eyes and mouth were full of dirt, and who then promptly fainted. When we were all on our legs again I turned my eyes in the direction the herd had gone, and nothing could be seen of them but a cloud of dust.

However, at a little distance on the right was my bull making what headway he ' could on three legs. I galloped up to him when he wheeled around and bristled for battle. He seemed to know perfectly well that he could not escape, and resolved to meet his enemy as bravely as possible. I found my shot had entered a little too far forward, and, lodging in his breast, his great weight would make it impossible to do me harm. I rode within a few paces of him, and with my gun across my lap drew my sketch-book from my pocket and took his likeness.

No man on earth can imagine what is the look and expression of such a subject before him as this was. I defy the world to produce another animal that can look so frightful as a huge buffalo bull, when wounded as he was, turned around for battle, and swelling with rage – his eyes bloodshot and his long, shaggy mane hanging to the ground – his mouth open and his horrid rage hissing in streams of smoke and blood from his mouth and through his nostrils, as he is bending forward to spring upon his assailant.

After I had had the requisite time and opportunity for using my pencil, McKenzie and his companions came walking their exhausted horses back from the chase, and in our rear came four or five carts to carry home the meat. The party met from all quarters around me and my buffalo bull, whom I then shot in the head and finished. And being seated together for a few minutes, each took a smoke of the pipe, and recited his exploits, and his "coups" or deaths; when all parties had a hearty laugh at me, as a novice, for having aimed at an old bull, whose flesh was not suitable for food, and the carts were escorted on the trail, to bring away the meat. I rode back with Mr. McKenzie, who pointed out five cows which he had killed, and all of them selected as the fattest and slickest of the herd. This astonishing feat was all performed within the distance of one mile – all were killed at full speed, and every one shot through the heart. In the short space of time required for a horse, under "full whip," to run the distance of one mile, he had discharged his gun five and loaded it four times – selected his animals, and killed at every shot! There were six or eight others killed at the same time, which altogether furnished, as will be seen, abundance of freight for the carts; which returned, as well as several pack-horses, loaded with the choicest parts which were cut from the animals, and the remainder of the carcasses left a prey for the wolves.

Such is the mode by which white men live in this country – such the way in which they get their food, and such is one of their delightful amusements – at the hazard of every bone in one's body, to feel the fine and thrilling exhilaration of the chase for a moment, and then as often to upbraid and blame himself for his folly and imprudence.

From this scene we commenced leisurely wending our way back; and dismounting at the place where we had stripped, each man dressed himself again, or slung his extra articles of dress, etc., across his saddle, astride of which he sat; and we rode back to the Fort, reciting as we rode and for twenty-four hours afterward, deeds of chivalry and chase, and hair's-breadth escapes which one another had fought and run on other occasions. McKenzie, with all the true character and dignity of a leader, was silent on these subjects, but smiled while those in his train were reciting for him the astonishing and almost incredible deeds of his sinewy arms which they had witnessed in similar scenes; from which I learned, as also from my own observations, that he was reputed, and actually was, the most distinguished of all the white men who have flourished in these regions in the pursuit and death of the buffalo.

On our return to the Fort, a bottle or two of wine were set forth upon the table, a half-dozen parched throats were moistened, and good cheer ensued. Ba'-tiste; Defonde, and Chardon had retired to their quarters, enlarging smoothly upon the events of our morning's work to their wives and sweethearts, when the gates of the Fort were thrown open, and the procession of carts and pack-horses laden with buffalo meat made its entrée, gladdening the hearts of a hundred women and children, and tickling the noses of as many hungry dogs and puppies, who were stealing in and smelling at the tail of the procession. The door of the ice-house was thrown open, the meat was discharged into it, and I, being fatigued, went to sleep.

CHAPTER II
A STUDIO AMONG THE GUNS

ONE OF the bastions of the Fort was set apart for a studio. The breech of a twelve-pounder, whose muzzle looked out a port-hole, served as a seat in front of the easel. To the chiefs were first disclosed the mysteries of the brush, which they decided were "great medicine." In consequence none but the most worthy were permitted to enter the "medicine" room, and none but the most distinguished they permitted to be painted. Outside the door the curious throng pressed, but guards were placed at the door by the chiefs, who determined all these matters. The regulations of the Fort required all Indians to leave their weapons in the arsenal.

The Crows and Blackfeet were hereditary and deadly enemies. The Assinniboines were foes of the Blackfeet. The chiefs of these tribes were now for the first time brought together unarmed, and smoking their pipes peacefully sat and lay around the room relating to each other the battles they had fought, pointing to the scalp-locks fringing their shirts and leggings as proofs of their prowess, while they watched the painting of the head chief of the Blackfeet, and anticipated their own turns. The peaceable mission of art had never a more signal, if brief, triumph; for once again on the plains the war-cry would be raised and the bows drawn.

The name of this chief of the Blackfeet was Stu-mick- a-suck (the buffalo's back fat), a good-looking, dignified man of fifty and magnificently dressed. There is no tribe on the Continent, except perhaps the Crows, that dresses more superbly than the Blackfeet. In general appearance there is no great difference in the dress of the tribes. But each has a distinctive method of stitching and ornamenting with porcupine quills that furnish the principal decoration in all their dresses of ceremony, which any one familiar with the Indians will at once recognize as peculiar to this or that tribe. This brave wore a shirt of finely dressed deerskins, so placed that the necks of the skins and the skins of the hind legs were stitched together, with the seam running down on each arm from the neck to the knuckles of the hand. This seam was covered with a band two inches wide, of beautiful porcupine-quill embroidery, and under this, from shoulder to hand, hung a fringe of black hair taken from the heads of enemies slain in battle. The leggings were also of deerskin, and outside the leg, from hip to foot, ran a similar band of ornament fringed with scalp-locks. The scalp is the evidence that the foe is dead. After having been formally "danced," that is to say, held up on a pole by an old woman, and the warriors have danced around it at intervals for two or three weeks, it is separated into small locks and used as a fringe.

The moccasins of Stu-mick-a-suck were of buckskin wrought with porcupine quills. Over this dress he wore a robe made of the skin of the young buffalo bull with the hair left on, which on the flesh side was rudely pictured with the different battles he had fought. In his hand he carried a pipe with a handle over four feet long, the stem wound with different-colored braids made from porcupine quills and the bowl of red pipe stone ingeniously carved by himself.

Much like this were the dresses of Pe-toh-pee-kiss (the eagle's rib), Mix-ke-mote-skin-na (the iron horse), of Wu-nes-tou (the white buffalo), Toha-aes-sa-ko- mah-pe (the bear's child), including the little grandson of the sachem, all of whom I painted. This child, a boy of six, was too young to have earned a name. In his raccoon dress, with his bow and arrow slung, he stood up like a tried warrior before me. As he has twice been stolen by the Crows, and twice recaptured by the Blackfeet, he is now under the protection of the Fort until he is old enough to look after himself. When he is of age he will be the hereditary chief of the Blackfeet.

I was also permitted to paint the youngest of the bevy of wives of the Blackfeet chief. She had the pretty name of Eeh-nis-kin (the crystal stone). This young woman was smiled upon and guarded as the apple of his eye, and exempt from all the drudgery of the tribe. The Eagle's Rib, mentioned above, was one of the distinguished men of the tribe. Although not a chief, he proudly wore eight scalps taken from the heads of trappers, as he frankly admitted, and his splendid dress was covered with the scalp-locks of white men and red. His head-dress was made entirely of ermine skins surmounted by the polished horns of the buffalo. This custom of wearing horns is permitted only to the bravest of the brave, or to men distinguished for some extraordinary feat.

All these braves in full dress carry bow, quiver, lance, and shield, and some their medicine-bag, of which something more is to be said. The North American tribes are all armed with bow and lance, and are protected by a shield or arrow fender, which is carried outside of the left arm, exactly as the shield of the Roman and Greek soldier was borne, and for the same reason. The clypeus or small shield of the ancients was made of bull's hide, sometimes single, sometimes double and triple, but was always small and light, and a means of defence on horseback only. Such was Hector's shield and of others of the Homeric heroes, worn as a defence against darts, javelins, and lances, these, too, being exactly like those carried by the Indians of our Continent to-day.

There is an appearance purely classic in the plight and equipment of these warriors and "knights of the lance." They are almost literally always on their horses' backs, and they wield these weapons with desperate effect upon the open plains, where they kill their game while at full speed, and contend in like manner in battles with their enemy. There is one prevailing custom in these respects among all the tribes who inhabit the great plains or prairies of these western regions. These plains afford them an abundance of wild and fleet horses, which are easily procured; and on their backs, at full speed, they can come alongside of any animal, which they easily destroy.

The bow with which they are armed is small, and apparently an insignificant weapon, though one of great and almost incredible power in the hands of its owner, whose sinews have been from childhood habituated to its use and service. The length of these bows is generally about three feet, and sometimes not more than two and a half. They have, no doubt, studied to get the requisite power in the smallest compass possible, as it is more easily and handily used on horseback than one of greater length. The greater number of these bows are made of ash, or of "bois d'arc" (as the French call it), and lined on the back with layers of buffalo or deer's sinews, which are inseparably attached to them, and give them great elasticity. There are very many also (among the Blackfeet and the Crows) which are made of bone, and others of the horn of the mountainsheep. Those made of bone are decidedly the most valuable, and cannot in this country be procured of a good quality short *of* the price of one or two horses. About these there is a mystery yet to be solved, and I advance my opinion against all theories that I have heard in the country where they are used and made. I have procured several very fine specimens, and when purchasing them have inquired of the Indians what bone they were made of, and in every instance the answer was, "That's medicine," meaning that it was a mystery to them, or that they did not wish to be questioned about them. The bone of which they are made is certainly not the bone of any animal now grazing on the prairies, or in the mountains between this place and the Pacific Ocean; for some of these bows are three feet in length, of a solid piece of bone, and that as close-grained – as hard – as white, and as highly polished as any ivory; it cannot, therefore, be made from the elks' horn (as some have supposed), which is of a dark color and porous; nor can it come from the buffalo. It is my opinion, therefore, that the Indians on the Pacific coast procure the bone from the jaw of the sperm whale, which is often stranded on that coast, and bringing the bone into the mountains, trade it to the Blackfeet and Crows, who manufacture it into these bows without knowing any more than we do from what source it has been procured.

One of these little bows in the hands of an Indian, on a fleet and well-trained horse, with a quiver of arrows slung on his back, is a most effective and powerful weapon in the open plains. No one can easily credit the force with which these missiles are thrown, and the sanguinary effects produced by their wounds, until he has ridden by the side of a party of Indians in chase of a herd of buffaloes, and witnessed the apparent ease and grace with which their supple arms have drawn the bow, and seen these huge animals tumbling down and gushing out their hearts' blood from their mouths and nostrils.

Their bows are often made of bone and sinews, and their arrows headed with flints or with bones, of their own construction, or with steel, as they are now chiefly furnished by the Fur Traders quite to the Rocky Mountains. The quiver, which is uniformly carried on the back, and made of the panther or otter skins, is a magazine of these deadly weapons, and generally contains two varieties. the one to be drawn upon an enemy, generally poisoned, and with long flukes or barbs, which are designed to hang the blade in the wound after the shaft is withdrawn, in which they are but slightly glued; the other to be used for their game, with the blade firmly fastened to the shaft, and the flukes inverted, that it may easily be drawn from the wound and used on a future occasion.

Such is the training of men and horses in this country, that this work of death and slaughter is simple and easy. The horse is trained to approach the animals on the *right* side, enabling its rider to throw his arrows to the left; it runs and approaches without the use of the halter, which is hanging loose upon its neck, bringing the rider within three or four paces of the animal, when the arrow is thrown with great ease and certainty to the heart; and instances sometimes occur where the arrow passes entirely through the animal's body.

An Indian, therefore, mounted on a fleet and well-trained horse, with his bow in his hand, and his quiver slung on his back, containing a hundred arrows, of which he can throw fifteen or twenty in a minute, is a formidable and dangerous enemy. Many of them also ride with a lance of twelve or fourteen feet in length, with a blade of polished steel; and all of them (as a protection for their vital parts) with a shield or arrowfender made of the skin of the buffalo's neck, which has been smoked, and hardened with glue extracted from the hoofs. These shields are arrow-proof, and will glance off a rifle-shot with perfect effect by being turned obliquely, which they do with great skill.

In addition to these portraits was that of an old chief who combined with his high office that of mystery or medicine man – that is to say, doctor, magician, soothsayer, high-priest. The name of this oracle was Wan-nis-tou (the white buffalo), and he was painted carrying on his left arm his mystery drum, in which are hidden the sacred mysteries of his calling. The word medicine comes from the French fur traders and was easily transmitted to the English and Americans. The Indians, however, do not use the word themselves. The artist's art may be great medicine, his pistols and guns great medicine, and the white man's weapons of war be great medicine; but for themselves each tribe constructs a word of its own synonomous with mystery and mystery man.

The medicine-bag is a mystery bag, and its importance may be said to furnish the key to the Indian character. It comes about in a curious manner: A boy, at the age of fourteen or fifteen years, is said to be making or "forming his medicine" when he wanders away from his father's lodge, and absents himself for the space of two or three, and sometimes even four to five, days; lying on the ground in some remote or secluded spot, crying to the Great Spirit, and fasting the whole time. During this period of peril and abstinence, when he falls asleep, the first animal, bird, or reptile of which he dreams (or pretends to have dreamed, perhaps) he considers the Great Spirit has designated for his mysterious protector through life. He then returns home to his father's lodge and relates his success; and after allaying his thirst and satiating his appetite, he sallies forth with weapons or traps until he can procure the animal or bird, the skin of which he preserves entire, and ornaments it according to his own fancy, and carries it with him through life for "good luck" (as he calls it). It is his strength in battle – and in death, as his guardian *Spirit,* it is buried with him, that it may conduct him safe to the beautiful hunting-grounds, which he contemplates in the world to come.

These bags are, as it happens, made of the skin of the otter, beaver, musk-rat, polecat, snake, frog, toad, bat, mole, mouse, eagle, magpie, or sparrow, sometimes of an animal as large as a wolf, and again of an animal so small that it can scarcely be found in the dress. These bags are ornamented according to the taste or freak of the wearer. They are then stuffed with grass or moss, and as they are religiously sealed, are rarely opened. The Indian offers his medicine-bag a sort of idolatry. Feasts are made for it and dogs and horses sacrificed to it. Even weeks of fasting and penance are undergone to appease it, for a medicine-bag may also be offended.

The value of the medicine-bag to the Indian is beyond all price; for to sell it, or give it away, would subject him to such signal disgrace in his tribe that he could never rise above it; and again, his superstition would stand in the way of any such disposition of it, for he considers it the gift of the Great Spirit. An Indian carries his *medicine-bag* into battle, and trusts to it for his protection; and if he loses it thus, when fighting ever so bravely for his country, he suffers a disgrace scarcely less than that which occurs in case he sells or gives it away; his enemy carries it off and displays it to his own people as a trophy; while the loser is cut short of the respect that is due to other young men of his tribe, and forever subjected to the degrading epithet of "a man without medicine," or "he who has lost his medicine," until he can replace it again, which can only be done by rushing into battle and plundering one from an enemy whom he slays with his own hand. This done, his medicine is restored, and he is reinstated again in the estimation of his tribe; and even higher than before, for such is called the best of medicine, or *"medicine honorable."*

It is a singular fact that a man can institute his mystery, or medicine, but once in his life; and equally singular that he can reinstate himself by the adoption of the medicine of his enemy; both of which regulations are strong and violent inducements for him to fight bravely in battle: the first, that he may protect and preserve his medicine; and the second, in case he has been so unlucky as to lose it, that he may restore it, and his reputation also, while he is desperately contending for the protection of his community.

During my travels thus far, I have been unable to buy a medicine-bag of an Indian, although I have offered them extravagant prices for them; and even on the frontier, where they have been induced to abandon the practice, though a white man may induce an Indian to relinquish his medicine, yet he cannot *buy* it of him – the Indian in such case will bury it, to please a white man, and save it from his sacrilegious touch; and he will linger around the spot and at regular times visit it and pay it his devotions as long as he lives.

Such is the medicine-bag – such its meaning and importance, and when its owner dies it is buried with him. Pe-toh-pee-kiss, the extraordinary Blackfoot, carried two medicine-bags, which were proudly displayed in his portrait. One of these he had "formed" himself; the other he had taken from an enemy in battle. But the medicine-bag is the simplest form of this superstition, as will appear.

The Knisteneaux – a tribe known in later days as the Crees – are the natural enemies of the Blackfeet. For two weeks they had camped at the Fort in apparent or compulsory good-fellowship – since their arms were stored in the arsenal – with the Blackfeet. Having completed their trade, after much delay they got their packs ready, and, bidding friends and foes a hearty farewell, started away. As they left the Fort, one of them, unobserved, loitered behind, and poking the muzzle of his gun between the pickets took aim at a Blackfoot chief talking with Mr. McKenzie, who fell with two bullets in his body. The Frenchmen of the Fort seized their guns and followed with the Blackfeet in pursuit. In a skirmish that lasted half an hour, they drove the Knisteneaux over the bluff and wounded one man.

Meanwhile the dying chief lay in agony on the ground. Although there was not the slightest hope of his recovery, the medicine-man, Wun-nes-tou (the white buffalo) was sent for. The several hundred spectators were required to form a ring about forty feet in diameter around the dying chief, leaving a space through which the medicine-man could pass without touching any one. His arrival was announced by a whispered "Hush-sh" through the crowd. Nothing was heard but the light and casual tinkling of the rattles on his dress, and these scarcely perceptible to the ear, as he came into the ring in which his victim lay.

His body and head were entirely covered with the skin of a yellow bear, the head of which, enclosing his own head, served as a mask, while the huge claws dangled on his wrists and ankles. In one hand he shook a frightful rattle, and in the other he brandished his medicine-spear or magic wand. To the din and discord of all this he added the wild and startling jumps and yelps of the Indian, the appalling grunts, snarls, and growls of the grizzly bear, in his guttural incantations to the Good and Bad Spirits in behalf of his patient, who lay in his death agonies while the medicine-man was dancing around him, jumping over him, and rolling him in every direction. This horrible scene lasted a half-hour in death-like stillness before the large audi- ence until the chief died. The medicine-man then danced off to his quarters, where he took off and hid his mystery dress and equipment.

This dress, in all its parts, is one of the greatest curiosities in the whole collection of Indian manufactures which I have yet obtained in the Indian country. It is the strangest medley and mixture, perhaps, of the mysteries of the animal and vegetable kingdoms that ever was seen. Besides the skin of the yellow bear (which, being almost an anomaly in that country, is out of the regular order of nature, and, of course, great medicine, and converted to a medicinal use), there are attached to it the skins of many animals, which are also anomalies or deformities, which render them, in their estimation, *medicine;* and there are also the skins of snakes and frogs and bats; beaks and toes and tails of birds; hoofs of deer, goats, and antelopes; and, in fact, the "odds and ends," and fag ends and tails and tips of almost everything that swims, flies, or runs in this part of the wide world.

Such is the medicine-man or a physician, and such is one of his wild and ridiculous manœuvres, which I have just witnessed in this strange country.

CHAPTER III
INDIAN ARISTOCRATS: THE CROWS AND BLACKFEET

THE CROWS and the Blackfeet are the aristocrats of this Western world. The Blackfeet are the largest as they are the most warlike of all the tribes. They number, including the tribes of their confederacy, about sixty thousand, according to the estimate of the government agent. The Blackfeet proper are divided into four bands – the Piegans, the Blackfeet band, the Blood band, and the Small Robes – numbering in all sixteen hundred and fifty lodges. The other members of the confederacy are the Gros Ventres des Praries, the Circées, and the Cotonnés. These hunt, eat, fight and intermarry with the Blackfeet, but each speaks its own language and retains its own customs.

The Blackfeet occupy all the country about the sources of the Missouri to the base of the Rocky Mountains. Being the most powerful of the tribes, they are fully conscious of their strength, and not only roam the prairie fearlessly, making war with other tribes, but have steadily resisted the efforts of the fur traders to establish profitable relations with them. The country abounds in buffalo, beaver, and almost all of the fur-bearing animals of this northern country. The American Fur Company has . pushed its trappers up the streams and rivers of the Blackfoot country, and has almost destroyed the beaver. The Blackfeet, accordingly, have persistently warned the traders that if their men continue trapping the beavers they will kill them wherever found. This threat they carry out, and the Fur Company annually loses from fifteen to twenty men, killed by the Blackfeet in defence of what they believe to be their property and their rights.

The Blackfeet have therefore held aloof from the traders, and are consequently less known than any other tribe.

It is interesting to compare this tribe with the Crows, who, although they are deadly enemies on the plains, are here sitting and smoking quietly together with dignified reserve. The Crows live on the head-waters of the Yellowstone, which also extend to the Rocky Mountains, and, like the Blackfeet, find their chief occupation in seeking and fighting their enemies. The Crows are, however, a much smaller tribe than the Blackfeet, from whom they have greatly suffered, and by whom they will probably be finally exterminated. At present the Crow nation does not number over seven thousand, with a fighting force of not over eight hundred braves.

I have just been painting a number of Crows, fine- looking, noble gentlemen. They are as handsome and as well-formed a set of men as could be found in any part of the world, and their grace and dignity of manner would distinguish them anywhere. They are almost all over six feet high, and many of these have cultivated their hair until it sweeps the ground. I have frequently seen a foot or more trailing over the grass, giving a singular grace to their movements. They are accustomed almost every morning to oil their hair with bear's grease, but this cannot be said to be the cause of its extraordinary length, for other tribes use bear's grease without the same results.

The present chief of the Crows is called Long Hair, having received both his office and his name from having the longest hair in his tribe. This, I am assured by two gentlemen who lived in his hospitable lodge for months, and measured it, was ten feet and seven inches long. On ordinary occasions he wore it wound on a broad leather strap a foot long, either under his arm or in the folds of his robe. But on great occasions he let it drag three feet behind him on the ground, shining with bear's grease like a raven's wing.

It is the custom among some of these Northern tribes to splice on several lengths of hair and fasten them with glue, probably in imitation of the Crows, on whom alone Nature seems to have bestowed so signal an ornament. Among the Crows of distinction at the Fort I have painted several who exhibit striking peculiarities. Among these is Chah-ee-shopes (the four wolves), a fine-looking fellow, six feet high, whose natural hair sweeps the ground as he walks. He is beautifully clad and carries himself in graceful and manly fashion. He is in mourning for his brother, and according to custom has cut off a number of locks of his long hair, which is a sacrifice of some consideration since he has spent the greater part of his life cultivating it. I have also painted Pa-ris-ka-roo-pa (two crows), one of the most extraordinary men in the Crow nation, not only from the distorted form of his head, but from his sagacity as a counsellor and orator from his youth. The semi-lunar outline of the Crow head, with a low and retreating forehead, is a peculiar and striking characteristic, although rarely so strongly marked as in this subject.

Neither the Crow or Blackfeet women are as handsome as their lords. As other Indian women they are the slaves of their husbands. They perform all the domestic duties and drudgeries of their tribes, and are not allowed to join in the religious rites and ceremonies, nor in the dances and other amusements. As all the women of these Northern tribes they are decently dressed, and often with great beauty and taste. Their dresses are of deer and goat skins, and extend from their chins quite down to their feet. These dresses are frequently trimmed with ermine and ornamented with porcupine quills and beads. The Crow and Blackfeet women, as in all the tribes I have seen, part their hair in the middle and streak the crease with vermilion or red earth. In mourning they are obliged to cut their hair short, and may cease mourning as the hair approaches its former length.

The men of the Blackfeet tribe part their hair in two places on the forehead, leaving a lock between an inch or two wide, which is carefully straightened down to the nose where it is cut square off. This is apparently their defence against the possible charge of effeminacy. These two tribes, which I associate together, speak two distinct and entirely dissimilar languages, and each of these is radically different from the other tribes about them. As they are always at war with each other, time out of mind, they have never intermarried or held any converse together by which any knowledge of each other's language could be acquired

The Crows, like the Blackfeet, are beautifully costumed, and perhaps with somewhat more taste and elegance. A Crow is known everywhere by the whiteness of his dress and his tall, elegant figure. The Blackfeet, on the other hand, are more Herculean in figure, being of middling stature, with broad shoulders and great expanse of chest;

and the skins, of which their dresses are made, are for the most part black or dark brown in color. They also wear black leggings and moccasins, and I assume that it is these that have given the tribe its name. The art of dressing skins belongs to the Indians of all countries. But the Crows surpass all in the beauty of their skin-dressing. The usual mode of dressing the buffalo and other skins is by immersing them for a few days under a lye from ashes and water, until the hair can be removed, when they are strained upon a frame or upon the ground, with stakes or pins driven through the edges into the earth, where they remain for several days, with the brains of the buffalo or elk spread upon and over them, and at last finished by "graining," as it is termed, by the squaws, who use a sharpened bone, the shoulder-blade or other large bone of the animal, sharpened at the edge, somewhat like an adze, with the edge of which they scrape the fleshy side of the skin, bearing on it with the weight of their bodies, thereby drying and softening the skin, and fitting it for use.

The greater part of these skins, however, go through still another operation afterward, which gives them a greater value, and renders them much more serviceable – that is, the process of smoking. For this a small hole is dug in the ground and a fire is built in it with rotten wood, which will produce a great quantity of smoke without much blaze; and several small poles of the proper length are stuck in the ground around it, and drawn and fastened together at the top, around which a skin is wrapped in the form of a tent, and generally sewed together at the edges to secure the smoke within it. Within this the skins to be smoked are placed, and in this condition the tent will stand a day or so, enclosing the heated smoke, and by some chemical process, which I do not understand, the skins thus acquire a quality which enables them to dry, no matter how often wet, as soft and pliant as before. . . . An Indian dress of deerskins, which is wet a hundred times upon his back, dries soft; and his lodge also, which stands in the rains, and even through the severity of winter, is taken down as soft and clean as when it was first put up.

The Crows, of all the tribes in this region, make the most beautiful lodges. They construct them as do the Sioux, the Blackfeet and the Assinniboines. This is by sewing the dressed buffalo skins into the form of a tent, and supporting them by twenty or thirty poles twenty-five feet long, with an aperture at the top through which the smoke escapes and the light is admitted. But the Crows dress these skins until they are almost as white as linen, and ornament them with porcupine quills and paint in a variety of ways that are always picturesque and agreeable to the eye. I have procured a fine one, highly ornamented and fringed with scalplocks, large enough for forty men to dine under. There are thirty poles supporting it that were cut in the Rocky Mountains and have been in use about a hundred years. When erected, the tent displays the Good Spirit painted on one side and the Evil Spirit on the other. If I can ever succeed in transporting it to New York it will be found to be a beautiful and interesting specimen of the Indian's work.

The manner in which an encampment of Indians strike their tents and transport them is curious, and to the traveller in this country a very novel and unexpected sight when he first beholds it. While ascending the river to this place, I saw an encampment of Sioux, consisting of six hundred of these lodges, struck, and all things packed and on the move in a very few minutes. The chief sends his runners or criers (for such all chiefs keep in their employment) through the village, a few hours before they are to start, announcing his determination to move, and the hour fixed upon, and the necessary preparations are in the meantime making and at the time announced, the lodge of the chief is seen flapping in the wind, a part of the poles having been taken out from under it. This is the signal, and in one minute six hundred of them (on a level and beautiful prairie), which before had been strained tight and fixed, were seen waving and flapping in the wind, and in one minute more all were flat upon the ground. Their horses and dogs, of which they had a vast number, had all been secured upon the spot, in readiness, and each one was speedily loaded with the burden allotted to it and ready to fall into the grand procession.

For this strange cavalcade preparation is made in the following manner: the poles of a lodge are divided into two bunches, and the little ends of each bunch fastened upon the shoulders or withers of a horse, leaving the butt ends to drag behind on the ground on either side. Just behind the horse, a brace or pole is tied across, which keeps the poles in their respective places; and then upon that and the poles behind the horse is placed the lodge or tent, which is rolled up, and also numerous other articles of household and domestic furniture, and on the top of all, two, three, and even (sometimes) four women and children! Each one of these horses has a conductress, who sometimes walks before and leads it, with a tremendous pack upon her own back; and at others she sits astride of its back, with a child, perhaps, at her breast, and another astride of the horse's back behind her, clinging to her waist with one arm, while it affectionately embraces a sneaking dog-pup in the other.

In this way five or six hundred wigwams, with all their furniture, may be seen drawn out for miles, creeping over the grass-covered plains of this country; and three times that number of men, on good horses, strolling along in front or on the flank; and, in some tribes, in the rear of this heterogeneous caravan, at least five times that number of dogs, which fall into the rank, and follow in the train and company of the women, and every cur of them who is large enough, and not too cunning to be enslaved, is encumbered with a car or sled (or whatever it may be better called) on which he patiently drags his load – a part of the household goods and furniture of the lodge to which he belongs. Two poles about fifteen feet long are placed upon the dog's shoulder, in the same manner as the lodge poles are attached to the horses, leaving the larger ends to drag upon the ground behind him, on which is placed a bundle or wallet which is allotted to him to carry, and with which he trots off amid the throng of dogs and squaws, faithfully and cheerfully dragging his load until night, and by the way loitering and occasionally

"Catching at little bits of fun and glee
That's played on dogs enslaved by dog that's free."

At St. Louis I was told that the Crows were a thieving set of "vagabonds," "highway robbers," and other names of pleasant import. These people, I find, have in some instances plundered and robbed the trappers and traders and driven away their horses. This they call "capturing," and consider it a species of summary justice that it is right and honorable for them to administer. Why not ? These mercenary white men are committing unlicensed trespass in their country in catching the beaver and other fur-bearing animals without rendering an equivalent, although they have been warned of their danger if they persist. My experience with the Indian has taught me to regard him as belonging to the most honest race of people I have ever lived among. In his native state it is only necessary to trust to his honor to find him perfectly honest.

It is, indeed, a part of the system of jurisprudence among all savages to revenge themselves upon the persons who give offence. If they cannot find the offender the punishment falls upon the first of his kind who comes in their way. So I should not be surprised if I were yet robbed of my horse by reason of some other person's guilt.

CHAPTER IV
PAINTING AN INDIAN DANDY

BESIDE THE Crows and Blackfeet assembled at the Fort are now the Knisteneaux, or Crees, as they are commonly called, the Ojibbeways, and the Assinniboines. The Crees are a pretty and pleasing tribe about three thousand strong, living in the country north-west of the Yellowstone and into the British possessions, where they commonly trade. The Crees are small in stature but of wonderful prowess for their number, since they wage unceasing war with the powerful Blackfeet who are their neighbors in the West, and these are rapidly thinning out the ranks of their warriors. They are a very primitive people, civilization having as yet left them untouched. Among the most renowned of their warriors is Bro-cas-sie (the broken arm), whose portrait I have painted in his handsome dress, with that of his wife, a handsome, comely woman.

The Ojibbeways number about six thousand and occupy the country north-east of the Yellowstone, extending to Lake Winnipeg, where they trade principally with the British Company. This tribe is undoubtedly a part of the Chippewas, who live on the southern shores of Lake Superior and with whom we are better acquainted. Although these two tribes live hundreds of miles apart, and have no knowledge of each other, and there exists no tradition of the time or manner of their separation, their language is the same. This is very significant, since tribes living side by side will speak radically dissimilar languages. Not the slightest resemblance can be traced between the Blackfeet, Cheyenne, Crow, Circée, Cotonné, and Mandan tongues, while the Sioux is equally distinct from all these. This seems to dispose of the idea that some learned gentlemen entertain of tracing all the languages of the North American Indians back to two or three roots.

The chief of this tribe is Cho-co-pay (the six), a man of huge size, with dignity of manner and pride and vanity in proportion to his bulk. He sat for his portrait in a most beautiful dress fringed profusely with scalplocks that he had snatched from his enemies in battle, and wore a shirt of buckskin lavishly embroidered and painted with curious hieroglyphics, which related the history of his battles and pictured the chart of his life. Each article of his dress had been made by his wives, and one, although not the most agreeable, I had the honor to paint.

The Assinniboines, Ojibbeways and the Crees are neighbors, and live, at least for a time, on terms of friendship. The Assinniboines are undoubtedly a branch of the Dacotahs, or Sioux, for their personal appearance and their language are similar. How these nations- strayed away from one another is a mystery.

However, one may conjecture that in hunting or at war a large party may have been intercepted by their enemy and run off to a distant region, where they established a residence and became a nation. Their name, Assinniboinnes, or Stone Boilers, they have received from their neighbors from a curious custom which obtains among them. When they kill meat, a hole is dug in the ground about the size of a common pot, and a piece of the rawhide of the animal is taken from the back, put over the hole, and with the hands is pressed down close to the sides and filled with water. The meat to be boiled is then placed in the water. Meanwhile, near by a fire is built in which several large stones are heated red hot. These are successfully held in the water until the meat is cooked. The custom is awkward and tedious, and could have been used only by a tribe too rude and ignorant to construct a pot. The traders have recently provided these Stone Boilers with pots, and previously the Mandans had taught them how to make good earthen pots, but, as others of the human family, the Assinniboines like to perpetuate this custom at all of their public festivals.

As a tribe the Assinniboines are a noble-looking race of Indians, and, as I have said, bear a striking resemblance to the Sioux. The men are tall and graceful in their movements, and wear their pictured robes of buffalo-skins with fine effect. They are good hunters and tolerably well supplied with horses. Living in a country well supplied with buffaloes and all the necessaries of Indian life, they are very comfortable. They are especially fond of games and amusement and are generally at them. These are the games of moccasins, horse-racing, dancing, and playing ball, at which they excel. Their dances are frequent and varied, and very like those of the Sioux.

One of these scenes, however, that I witnessed the other day, appeared to me to be peculiar to this tribe, and is exceedingly picturesque in its effect. This is described to me as the *pipe-dance,* and was as follows: On a hard-trodden pavement in front of their village, which place is used for all their public meetings and many of their amusements, the young men, who were to compose the dance, had gathered themselves around a small fire, and each one seated on a buffalorobe spread upon the ground. In the centre and by the fire was seated a dignitary, who seemed to be a chief (perhaps a doctor or medicine-man), with a long pipe in his hand, which he lighted at the fire and smoked incessantly, grunting forth at the same time, in half-strangled gutturals, a sort of song, which I did not get translated to my satisfaction, and which might have been susceptible of no translation. While this was going on, another grim-visaged fellow in another part of the group commenced beating on a drum or tambourine, accompanied by his voice, when one of the young men, seated, sprang instantly to his feet, and commenced singing in time with the taps of the drum, and leaping about on one foot and the other in the most violent manner imaginable. In this way he went several times around the circle, bowing and brandishing his fists in the face of each one who was seated, until at length he grasped one of them by the hands and jerked him forcibly up on his feet This man joined in the dance for a moment, leaving the one who had pulled him up to continue his steps and his song in the centre of the ring, while he danced around in a similar manner, jerking up another, and then joining his companion in the centre, leaving the third and the fourth, and so on, to drag into the ring, each one his man, until all were upon their feet, and at last joined in the most frightful gesticulations and yells that seemed almost to make the earth quake under our feet. This strange manoeuvre, which I did but partially understand, lasted for half or three quarters of an hour, to the great amusement of the gaping multitude who were assembled around, and broke up with the most piercing yells and barks, like those of so many affrighted dogs.

I have painted the portrait of a very distinguished young man, the son of a chief. His name is Wi-jun-jon (the pigeon's-egg head). This brave travelled with us on our journey in the steamer "Yellowstone." He was returning, after an absence of a year or more, from Washington city, where he had been with Major Sanford in the polished and fashionable circles of the Capital. There he was presented by the President with the uniform of a colonel. I enjoyed the pleasure of seeing this young man step ashore in a beaver hat and feather, gold epaulets, sash, belt, and broadsword, high-heeled boots, a jug of whiskey under one arm and a blue umbrella in his hand.

Thus metamorphosed, he took a position on the bank in the midst of his parents, wife, and little children, as well as his friends, and for a half-hour or more not one showed a gleam of recognition, although they knew perfectly well who he was. On his part he gazed at them as if they were strangers with whom he had nothing in common.

After a time a gradual but cold and exceedingly formal acquaintance began, which ultimately, without the least apparent emotion, resolved itself into their accustomed mutual intercourse as if nothing had ever intervened to check it.

This is an instance of the stoic customs of the North American Indians, and one of the most striking traits of their character. At present Wi-jun-jon is creating a sensation in his tribe. Daily and nightly he is surrounded by a gaping, listless crowd to whom he relates his wonderful and to them incomprehensible adventures. But it is apparent that already they are beginning to regard him as a liar and an impostor. Far from envying him his fashionable tour, he is in disgrace among the chiefs and spurned by the leading men among the tribe. What disasters his incredible narrations will yet subject him to time will only develop. Meanwhile, I have been painting his wife, Chin-cha-pee (the fire-bug that creeps), a fine-looking squaw in a handsome dress of the mountain-elk skin, holding in her hand a stick curiously carved such as every woman in this country carries. These are used in digging up the "pommes blanches," or prairie turnip, which is used in great quantities by the Indians for food, and is found in great abundance on these prairies.

A traveller in this country has but little time to moralize. It is as much as he can do to "look out for his scalp" and get "something to eat." But to the mind susceptible to impressions, what a web of fascinations its allurements spread over the soul! To paint the vast panorama of a world entirely different from anything ever seen or painted before; to paint a vast country of green fields, where the men are red, where meat is the staff of life, where the oak and pine give way to the cotton-wood and the pecan, where the buffaloes range, and the elk and mountain-sheep and the fleet-bounding antelope, where the magpie and chattering parroquets supply the place of the red-breast and the bluebird, where wolves are white and bears grizzly, where pheasants are hens of the prairie and frogs have horns, where the rivers are yellow and white men are turned savages in looks. Through the whole of this strange land the dogs are all wolves, women all slaves, men all lords. The *sun* and *rats* alone (of all the list of old acquaintance) could be recognized in this country of strange metamorphose. The former shed everywhere his familiar rays, and Monsieur Ratapon was hailed as an old acquaintance which it gave me pleasure to meet, though he had grown a little more *savage* in his look.

To reach this country one must pass through the different grades of civilization down to the pitiable misery of savage degradation along the frontier, where one sees the natural liberty and independence of the Indian destroyed by the contaminating vices of the worst elements of the white civilization. From the first settlements of the Atlantic Coast to the present day, the frontier has swept like the blasts of prairie fires over Indian life. There are many who believe that the numerous tribes of the Atlantic States fled and are to be found in the Far West. This is not the case. They were blasted by this frontier fire that passed over them; they are in their graves, and nothing remains of them but their names.

The distinctive character of the Western Indians, as well as the traditions relating to their past, indicate that they have lived, beyond the memory of man, on the soil they now possess. It is these unoffending people, yet unvisited by the vices of civilized society, that I desire to make known. We have taken from them territory enough, and the country they now inhabit is too barren of timber for the use of the white man; it affords them, however, the means and the luxuries of savage life, and it is hoped that our government will not permit the wilful destruction of these happy people.

I have been taking many rambles about this beautiful country of green fields, and in a few days will begin my voyage down the river in a canoe. I will take with me two men, Bogard, a Yankee, and Batiste, a jolly, dauntless semi-barbarian.

"Batiste, you say you trade with the Indians and trap beavers; you are in the employment of the American Fur Company, I suppose?"

"Non, Monsieur, not quite éxact; mais, suppose, I am 'free trappare,' free, Monsieur, free."

"Free trapper! What's that? I don't understand you, Batiste."

"Well, Monsieur, sùppose he is easy pour understand – you shall know all. In de first place, I am enlist for tree year in de Fur Comp in St. Louis – for bounté – pour bounté, eighty dollare (understand, ha ?); den I am go for wages, et I ave come de Missouri up, et I am trap castors putty much for six years, you see, until I am learn very much; and den you see, Monsieur, McKenzie is give me tree horse – one pour ride, et two pour pack (mais he is not buy, him not give, he is lend), and he is lend twelve trap; and I ave make start into de Rocky Montaigne, et I am live all alone on de leet rivares pour prendre les castors. Sometime six months – sometime five month, and I come back to Yelstone, et Monsieur McKenzie is give me coot price pour all."

"So Mr. McKenzie fits you out, and takes your beaver of you at a certain price ?"

"Oui, Monsieur, oui."

"What price does he pay you for your beaver, Batiste ?"

"Ha! súppose one dollare pour one beavate."

"A dollar per skin, ah ?"

"Oui."

"Well, you must live a lonesome and hazardous sort of life; can you make anything by it ?"

"Oh! oui, Monsieur, putty coot, mais if it is not pour for de dam rascalité Riccaree, et de dam Pieds Noirs, de Blackfoot Ingin, I am make very much monnair, mais (sacré), I am rob – rob – rob too much!"

"What! Do the Blackfeet rob you of your furs ?"

"Oui, Monsieur, rob, suppose, five time! I am been free trappare seven year, et I am rob five time – I am someting left not at all – he is take all; he is take all de horse – he is take my gun – he is take all my clothes – he is takee de castors – et I am come back with foot. So in de Fort, some cloths is cost putty much monnair, et some whiskey is give sixteen dollares pour gall; so you see I am owe de Fur Comp six hundred dollare, by Gar ! "

"Well, Batiste, this, then, is what you call being a free trapper, is it ?"

"Oui, Monsieur, 'free trappare,' free!"

"You seem to be going down toward the Yellowstone, and probably have been out on a trapping excursion."

"Oui, Monsieur, c'est vrai."

"Have you been robbed this time, Batiste?"

"Oui, Monsieur, by de dam Pieds Noirs – I am loose much; I am loose all – very all – eh bien – pour le dernier – c'est la dernière fois, Monsieur. I am go to Yelstpne – I am go le Missouri down, I am go to St. Louis."

"Well, Batiste, I am to figure about in this part of the world a few weeks longer, and then I shall descend the Missouri from the mouth of Yellowstone, to St. Louis, and I should like exceedingly to employ just such a man as you are as a voyageur with me. I will give you good wages and pay all your expenses. What say you ?"

"De tout mon cœur, Monsieur, remercie, remercie."

"It's a bargain, then, Batiste; I will see you at the mouth of Yellowstone."

"Oui, Monsieur, in de Yelstone, bon soir, bon soir, Monsieur."

CHAPTER V
CANOEING WITH BOGARD AND BATISTE

WHEN I had completed my rambles and sketches, and when Bogard and Batiste had taken their last spree, fought their last battles, and forgotten them in the final affectionate embrace, as is the custom with these game fellows when settling up their long-standing accounts with their brother trappers of these mountain streams, we launched the little craft that was to waft us down the mighty torrent.

Mr. McKenzie had provided me with this canoe, which, built of green timber, was heavy and awkward, but our course being with the current, it promised a fair and successful voyage. Ammunition was laid in in abundance, and our larder consisted of a stock of buffalo tongues, a dozen or two of beaver tails, and a good supply of pemmican, to which we added several pounds of fresh buffalo meat. Besides these and its crew, which consisted of Bogard and Batiste in the middle and bow with their paddles, and I in the stern with my steering oar, our craft carried several packs of Indian dresses I had bought, and our kitchen, which consisted of three tin cups, a coffee-pot, one tin plate, and a tin kettle. Thus fitted out we took our leave one fine morning of the Fort and our friends, and of the green fields and dales and prairie bluffs that encompass the enchanting shores of the Yellowstone. We swept off at a rapid rate amid the shouts of the Indians and the cheers of our friends, who lined the banks until we were out of sight. Soon nothing intervened between us and St. Louis, over two thousand miles distant, but the wide-spread and wild region and the roaming savage.

At the end of our first day's journey we found ourselves handily encamping with several thousand Assinniboines, who had pitched their tents upon the bank of the river, and received us with every mark of esteem and friendship.

In the midst of this group was my friend Wi-jun-jon (the pigeon's-egg head), still lecturing on the manners and customs of the "palefaces," continuing to relate, without any appearance of exhaustion, the marvellous scenes which he had witnessed among the white people on his tour to Washington city.

Many were the gazers who seemed to be the whole time crowding around him to hear his recitals; and the plight which he was in rendered his appearance quite ridiculous. His beautiful military dress, of which I before spoke, had been so shockingly tattered and metamorphosed that his appearance was truly laughable.

His keg of whiskey had dealt out to his friends all its charms; his frock-coat, which his wife had thought was of no earthly use below the waist, had been cut off at that place, and the nether half of it supplied her with a beautiful pair of leggings; and his silver-laced hatband had been converted into a splendid pair of garters for the same. His umbrella the poor fellow still affectionately held on to, and kept spread at all times. As I before said, his theme seemed to be exhaustless and he, in the estimation of his tribe, to be an unexampled liar.

Of the village of Assinniboines we took leave on the following morning, and rapidly made our way down the river. The rate of the current being four or five miles per hour, through one continued series of picturesque, grass-covered bluffs and knolls, which everywhere had the appearance of an old and highly-cultivated country with houses and fences removed.

On the second day of our journey we discovered a number of mountain-sheep. These are much like our goats, except in the horns, which resemble those of a ram. Sometimes these make entire circles in their coils, and at the root of each horn measure from five to six inches in breadth. These sheep skip along the sides of the precipice, always keeping equidistant from the top and bottom of the ledge, where they leap and vault from point to point, seeming actually to cling to the sides of the wall, where neither man nor beast can follow them.

We landed our canoe and endeavored to shoot one of these sagacious animals. After he had led us a long and fruitless chase among the cliffs, we thought we had fairly entrapped him. At least we had brought him within command of our rifles. Suddenly he bounded from his narrow foothold in the ledge, and tumbled down a distance of more than a hundred feet among the fragments of rocks and clay.

There I thought we would certainly find his carcass without further trouble, when, to my great surprise, I saw him bounding off and he was almost instantly out of sight.

Bogard, who is an old hunter, and intimately acquainted with these creatures, shouldered his rifle and said to me:

"The game is up. You now see the use of those big horns. When they fall by accident, or find it necessary to quit their foothold in the crevices, they fall upon their heads at a great distance unharmed, even though it be on the solid rock."

Being on shore and our canoe securely landed, we whiled away the greater part of the day among these wild and rugged cliffs. Part of the day we spent in vain pursuit of a war eagle. This noble bird is the one which the Indians value so highly for its tail feathers, which they use for decorating the heads and dresses of their warriors. The Indians tell me that it conquers all other variety of eagles; for this reason they hold it in high esteem. I am unable to say to what variety it belongs, but I am sure it is not in any of our museums, nor is it to be found in America, in my opinion, until one gets near the base of the Rocky Mountains. This bird is often called the calumet eagle, presumably from the fact that the Indians almost invariably ornament their calumets, or pipes of peace, with its quills.

Our day's loitering brought us through many a wild scene: occasionally across the tracks of the grizzly bear, and in sight merely of a band of buffaloes, "which got the wind of us," and were out of the way, leaving us to return to our canoe at night, with a mere speck of good luck. Just before we reached the river, I heard the crack of a rifle, and in a few moments Bogard came in sight, and threw down from his shoulders a fine antelope, which added to our larder, and we were ready to proceed. We embarked and travelled until nightfall, when we encamped on a beautiful little prairie at the base of a series of grass-covered bluffs, and the next morning cooked our breakfast and ate it, and rowed on until late in the afternoon, when we stopped at the base of some huge clay bluffs forming one of the most curious and romantic scenes imaginable. At this spot the river expands itself into the appearance somewhat of a beautiful lake; and in the midst of it, and on and about its sand-bars, floated and stood hundreds and thousands of white swans and pelicans.

Though the scene in front of our encampment at this place was placid and beautiful – with its flowing water, its wild fowl, and its almost endless variety of gracefully sloping hills and green prairies in the distance – yet it was not less wild and picturesque in our rear, where the rugged and various-colored bluffs were grouped in all the wildest fancies and rudeness of Nature's accidental varieties.

The whole country behind us seemed to have been dug and thrown up into huge piles, as if some giant mason had been there mixing his mortar and paints, and throwing together his rude models for some sublime structure of a colossal city, with its walls, its domes, its ramparts, its huge porticos and galleries, its castles, its fosses and ditches, and as if in the midst of his progress he had abandoned his works to the destroying hand of time, which had already done much to tumble them down, and deface their noble structure, by jostling them together, with all their vivid colors, into an unsystematic and unintelligible mass of sublime ruins.

During the day I loitered about this strange scene, rifle and sketchbook in hand, leaving the men stretched on the grass by the canoe. While endeavoring to find a possible crater, I suddenly came upon the enormous tracks of a grizzly bear, travelling in the same direction, and evidently but a few moments before me. My ardor suddenly cooled and I hastily retraced my steps.

In the morning and before sunrise, as usual, Bogard (who was a Yankee, and a "wide-awake fellow," just retiring from a ten years' siege of hunting and trapping in the Rocky Mountains) thrust his head out from under the robe, rubbing his eyes open, and exclaiming as he grasped for his gun, "By darn, look at old Cale, will you!" Batiste, who was more fond of his dreams, snored away, muttering something that I could not understand, when Bogard seized him with a grip that instantly shook off his iron slumbers. I rose at the same time, and all eyes were turned at once upon *Caleb* (as the grizzly bear is familiarly called by the trappers in the Rocky Mountains – or more often "Cale," for brevity's sake), who was sitting up in the dignity and fury of her sex, within a few rods, and gazing upon us, with her two little cubs at her side. Here was a *"fix,"* and a subject for the painter; but I had no time to sketch it – I turned my eyes to the canoe, which had been fastened at the shore a few paces from us, and saw that everything had been pawed out of it, and all eatables had been without ceremony devoured. My packages of dresses and Indian curiosities had been drawn out upon the bank and deliberately opened and inspected. Everything had been scraped and pawed out, to the bottom of the boat, and even the rawhide thong, with which it was tied to a stake, had been chewed, and no doubt swallowed, as there was no trace of it remaining. Nor was this peep into the secrets of our luggage enough for her insatiable curiosity – we saw by the prints of her huge paws, that were left in the ground, that she had been perambulating our humble mattresses, smelling at our toes and our noses, without choosing to molest us, verifying a trite saying of the country that "Man lying down is *medicine* to the grizzly bear," though it is a well-known fact that man and beast, upon their feet, are sure to be attacked when they cross the path of this grizzly and grim monster, which is the terror of all this country, often growing to the enormous size of eight hundred or one thousand pounds.

Well, while we sat in the dilemma which I have just described, each one was hastily preparing his weapons for defence, when I proposed the mode of attack, by which means I was in hopes to destroy her – capture her young ones, and bring her skin home as a trophy.

My plans, however, entirely failed, though we were well armed, for Bogard and Batiste both remonstrated with a vehemence that was irresistible, saying that the standing rule in the mountains was "never to fight Caleb, except in self-defence." I was almost induced, however, to attack her alone, with my rifle in hand, and a pair of heavy pistols, a tomahawk and scalpingknife in my belt, when Batiste suddenly thrust his arm over my shoulder, and, pointing in another direction, exclaimed in an emphatic tone, "Voilà! voilà un corps de reserve – Monsieur Cataline – voilà son mari! allons – allons! descendons la rivière, toute de suite! toute de suite! Monsieur," to which Bogard added, "These darned animals are too much for us, and we had better be off"; at which my courage cooled, and we packed up and re-embarked as

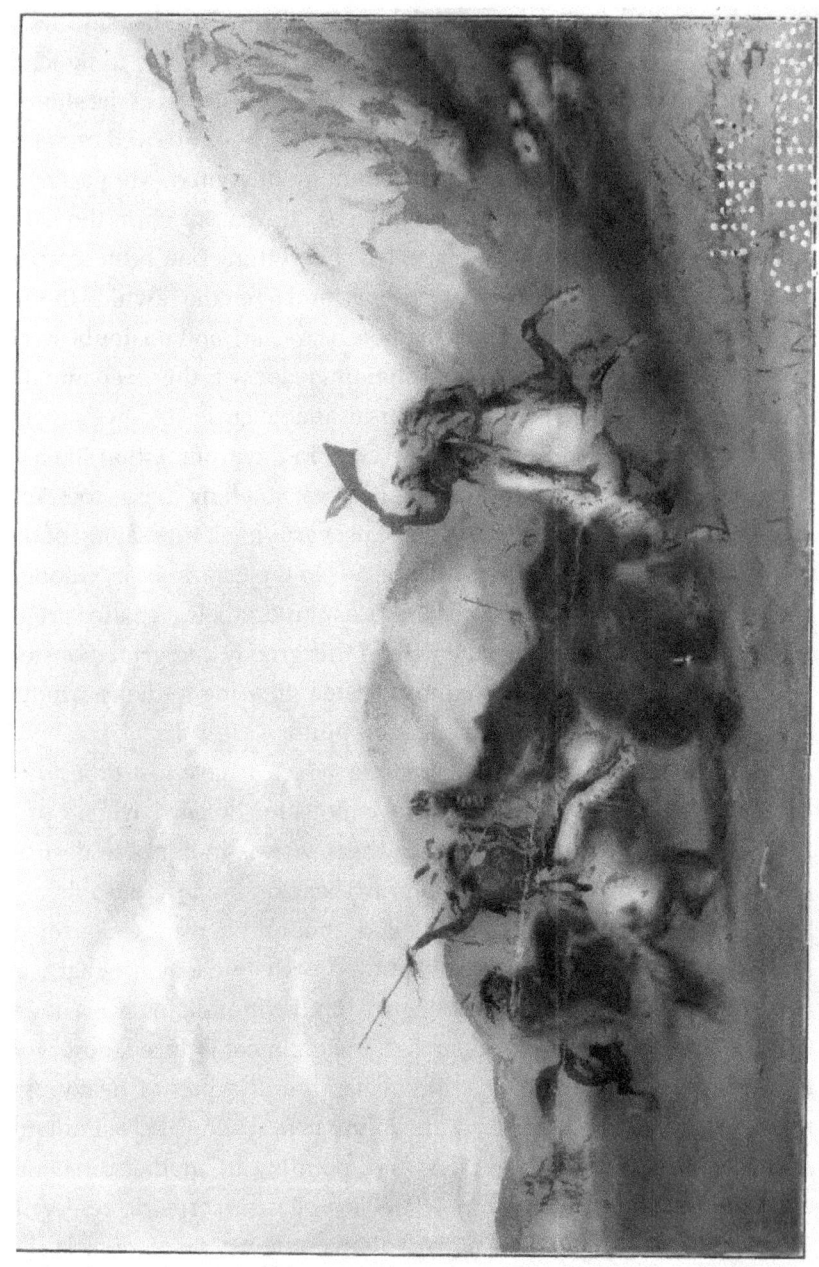

ATTACK OF THE GRIZZLY BEAR

fast as possible, giving each one of them the contents of our rifles as we drifted off on the current, which brought the she monster in all her fury to the spot we had just prudently quitted.

Our conversation was now chiefly about grizzly bears and hair-breadth escapes of which my companions had a store. Our breakfast we took about five o'clock in the afternoon, our empty larder being replenished by an antelope that the unerring rifle of Bogard had brought down, as it was innocently gazing at us from the banks of the river. We landed our boat and took in our prize, but there being no wood for a fire, we shoved off and soon ran upon the head of an island covered with immense piles of driftwood. Here we kindled a huge fire and ate our meal from a clean-peeled log, astride of which we comfortably sat, making it admirably answer the double purpose of chair and table. After our meal was finished we plied our paddles and went several miles further on our course, leaving our fire burning. In the dark, and in a wild and unknown spot, we silently dragged our canoe on shore, and spread our buffalo-robes for sleeping. This it is not considered prudent to do by the side of our fires, since it might lead some prowling war-party upon us.

The scenery, as I have said, was one of enchantment. Frequently we ran our canoe ashore to admire the wild flowers and the abundance of delicious fruits about us. Sun-flowers and voluptuous lilies were constantly taunting our faces in the high grass, and everywhere were copses of plum-trees, gooseberry and wild currant bushes laden with fruit. To add to the effect were wild rose bushes that seemed to be planted in beds and hedges, adding aroma to every breath of air that passed over them. We also had service berries without stint, and the buffalo bush, which is peculiar to this region, sometimes lining the banks of the rivers for miles. These formed an almost impassable hedge and were weighted to the ground with berries.

The buffalo bush, or *Shepperdia,* is the most beautiful ornament that decks the wild prairies. From the blue tint of its leaves it is in striking contrast to the rest of the foliage and can be distinguished for miles. The fruit that hangs in clusters to every limb and every twig is about the size of ordinary currants, and is not unlike them in color and flavor.

After the berries are touched by the frost they have something of the flavor of the grape, and I am sure would make excellent wine. I made some such suggestion to Bogard and Batiste, and they were so taken with the idea I did not know but that I should lose my men. Several times we took a large mackinaw blanket, and, spreading it on the ground, struck the stalks with a club. Instantly the entire bush would discharge its fruit and the boughs, relieved of their burden, spring back into position. Of this beautiful native, which I think would form one of the loveliest ornamental shrubs for a gentleman's park or pleasure grounds, I took with me a number of roots, but lost them all in the many accidents of our unlucky bark on the river.

On the fifth day of our journey from the Yellowstone we landed our canoe that I might paint the magnificent scene that spreads out at the Grand Détour, or Big Bend, as it is called by the voyagers. There are few things in nature more picturesque than the wonderful manner in which the gorges of the river have cut out its deep channel through these walls of clay on either side, of two or three hundred feet in elevation. The imposing features of the high table-lands in distance, standing as a perpetual anomaly in the country, and producing the indisputable though astounding evidence of the fact that there has been at some ancient period a *super* surface to this country, corresponding with the elevation of these tabular hills, whose surface, for half a mile or more, on their tops, is perfectly level. Being covered with a green turf, and yet one hundred and fifty or two hundred feet elevated above what may now be properly termed the summit level of all this section of country, it will be seen stretching off at their base, without furnishing other instances, in hundreds of miles, of anything rising one foot above its surface excepting this solitary group.

Batiste and Bogard having carried my canvas and easel to the top of a huge mound, left me at my work while they amused themselves in decoying antelopes to replenish our larder. The antelope of this country I believe to be different from all other varieties, and it is one of the most pleasing living ornaments of this Western world. They are seen in great numbers playing over the hills and dales, and will often follow the boat for hours together, at a safe distance, as they gallop up and down the hills, snuffing their noses and stamping their feet, as if to remind the traveller that he is trespassing on their hallowed ground. This little animal, as many other gentle, sweet-breathing creatures, has a curiosity that often leads to its own destruction. The hunter need not trouble himself to follow them. He has only to put his red or yellow handkep chief on the top of his gun rod, so that it can be seen above the grass, when they will advance with great caution. Meanwhile the hunter, lying on the ground at a little distance, finds it an easy matter to make sure of two or three at one shot.

Several times we stopped in this manner, once that I might paint the Grand Dome, whose huge domes, turrets, and towers are so perfectly formed and precisely placed that it is one of the most wonderful formations on this mighty river. After my painting was made we wandered back to the plains in toilsome pursuit of a herd of buffaloes. Although our chase was futile we found amusement in a prairie-dog village. The prairie- dog of the American prairie is undoubtedly a variety of the marmot, and probably not unlike those that inhabit the vast steppes of Asia. It bears no resemblance to any variety of dogs, except in the sound of its voice when excited by the approach of danger, which is something like that of a very small dog, and still much more resembling the barking of a gray squirrel.

The size of these curious little animals is not far from that of a very large rat, and they are not unlike in their appearance. As I have said, their burrows are uniformly built in a lonely desert, and away from the proximity of both timber and water. Each individual, or each family, digs its hole in the prairie to the depth of eight or ten feet, throwing up the dirt from each excavation in a little pile, in the form of a cone, which forms the only elevation for them to ascend, where they sit, to bark and chatter when an enemy is approaching their village. These villages are sometimes of several miles in extent, containing (I would almost say) myriads of their excavations and little dirt hillocks, and to the ears of their visitors the din of their barkings is too confused and too peculiar to be described.

In the present instance we made many endeavors to shoot them, but found our efforts to be entirely in vain. As we were approaching

ANTELOPE SHOOTING

them at a distance, each one seemed to be perched up on his hind feet, on his appropriate domicile, with a significant jerk of his tail at every bark, positively disputing our right of approach. I made several attempts to get near enough to "draw a bead" upon one of them, and just before I was ready to fire (and as if they knew the utmost limits of their safety), they sprang down into their holes, and instantly turning their bodies, showed their ears and the ends of their noses, as they were peeping out at me, which position they would hold until the shortness of the distance subjected their scalps to danger again from the aim of a rifle, when they instantly disappeared from our sight, and all was silence thereafter about their premises, as I passed them over, until I had so far advanced by them that their ears were again discovered, and at length themselves, at full length, perched on the tops of their little hillocks and threatening as before, thus gradually sinking and rising like a wave before and behind me.

Such were some of the incidents of our voyage which came to an end on the evening of the seventh day out from the Fort on the Yellowstone, when our little boat landed in front of the Mandan village. Here hundreds came to the banks to greet us, and among them Mr. Kipp, the agent of the American Fur Company, who carried me to his quarters, where I am now reaping the benefits of his politeness and enjoying the pleasures of his society.

CHAPTER VI
MANDANS: THE PEOPLE OF THE PHEASANTS

HERE I find myself surrounded by subjects and scenes worthy the pens of Irving or Cooper – of the pencils of Raphael or Hogarth. I am in a country so rich in romances and legends that no imagination is needed for book or picture.

The Mandans, or See-pohs-kah-nu-mah-kah-kee, (people of the pheasants), are perhaps one of the oldest tribes in our country. Their origin is lost in mystery, but their traditions assert that they were the first people created on the earth. They have not always been in this region. They contend that they were once a large and powerful nation, but continual warfare has reduced them to their present number. The tribe now has but two thousand members, living in two villages about two miles distant from each other. These villages are on the west bank of the Missouri about eighteen hundred miles above St. Louis. The site of the lower and principal town is in the centre of a vast valley with a thousand graceful swells of interminable green changing to blue in the distance, in which not a tree or bush can be seen. The construction of the Mandan lodges, so different from that of the other tribes, seems to indicate another origin and a peculiar history.

The ground on which the Mandan village is at present built was admirably adapted for defence, being on a bank about fifty feet above the bed of the river. The greater part of this bank is nearly perpendicular and of solid rock. The river suddenly changing its course at right angles protects the village, which is built on a promontory at this angle, on two sides. The other is protected by a strong picket and a ditch four feet deep inside. The picket is composed of timbers a foot or more in diameter and eighteen feet high. These are set firmly in the ground sufficient distance apart to allow guns and other missiles to be fired between them. The ditch, unlike that of civilized modes of fortification, is placed inside the picket that the warriors may screen their bodies from the view and the weapons of their enemies, while they are reloading and discharging their weapons through the pickets.

The Mandans have evidently nothing to fear from their enemies in their village. This has a most novel appearance to the eye of the stranger. The lodges are closely grouped together, leaving just room enough to walk and ride between them, and appear from without to be built entirely of dirt. But one is surprised on entering to see the neatness, comfort, and spaciousness of these domed, earth-covered dwellings. They are all circular and are from forty to sixty feet in diameter. Their foundations are prepared by digging about two feet in the ground and forming the floor by levelling the requisite site for the lodge.

These floors or foundations are all perfectly circular, and varying in size in proportion to the number of inmates, or of the quality or standing of the families which are to occupy them. The superstructure is then produced by arranging, inside of this circular excavation, firmly fixed in the ground and resting against the bank, a barrier or wall of timbers, some eight or nine inches in diameter, of equal height (about six feet), placed on end and resting against each other, supported by a formidable embankment of earth raised against them outside; then, resting upon the tops of these timbers or piles, are others of equal size and equal in number, of twenty or twenty-five feet in length, resting firmly against each other, and sending their upper or smaller ends toward the centre and top of the lodge, rising at an angle of forty-five degrees to the apex, or skylight, which is about three or four feet in diameter, answering as a chimney and a skylight at the same time. The roof of the lodge, being thus formed, is supported by beams passing around the inner part of the lodge about the middle of these poles or timbers, and themselves upheld by four or five large posts passing down to the floor of the lodge. On the top of and over the poles forming the roof is placed a complete mat of willow-boughs, of half a foot or more in thickness, which protects the timbers from the dampness of the earth with which the lodge is covered from bottom to top, to the depth of two or three feet, and then with a hard or tough clay, which is impervious to water, and which with long use becomes quite hard, and a lounging-place for the whole family in pleasant weather – for sage, for wooing lovers, for dogs and all; an airing-place, a look-out, a place for gossip and mirth, a seat for the solitary gaze and meditations of the stern warrior, who sits and contemplates the peaceful mirth and happiness that is breathed beneath him, fruits of his hard-fought battles on fields of desperate combat with bristling red men.

The floors of these dwellings are of earth, but so hardened by use, and swept so clean and tracked by bare and moccasined feet, that they have almost a polish and would scarcely soil the whitest linen. In the centre, and immediately under the skylight is the fireplace, a hole of four or five feet in diameter, of a circular form, sunk a foot or more below the surface, and curbed around with stone. Over the fireplace, and suspended from the apex of diverging props or poles, is generally seen the pot or kettle, filled with buffalo meat; and around it are the family, reclining in all the most picturesque attitudes and groups, resting on their buffalo-robes and beautiful mats of rushes. These cabins are so spacious that they hold from twenty to forty persons – a family and all their connections. They all sleep on bedsteads similar in form to ours, but generally not quite so high, made of round poles rudely lashed together with thongs. A buffalo-skin, fresh stripped from the animal, is stretched across the bottom poles, and about two feet from the floor, which, when it dries, becomes much contracted and forms a perfect sacking-bottom. The fur side of this skin is placed uppermost, on which they lie with great comfort, with a buffalo-robe folded up for a pillow, and others drawn over them instead of blankets. These beds, as far as I have seen them (and I have visited almost every lodge in the village), are uniformly screened with a covering of buffalo or elk skins, oftentimes beautifully dressed and placed over the upright poles or frame, like a suit of curtains, leaving a hole in front sufficiently spacious for the occupant to pass in and out, to and from his or her bed. Some of these coverings or curtains are exceedingly beautiful, being cut tastefully into fringe, and handsomely ornamented with porcupine's quills and picture writings or hieroglyphics.

To accommodate the great number of inmates in these lodges, they are necessarily very spacious and the number of beds is considerable. It is no uncommon thing to see these lodges fifty feet in diameter inside (which is an immense room), with a row of these curtained beds extending quite around their sides, being some ten or twelve of them, placed four or five feet apart, and the space between them occupied by a large post, fixed quite firm in the ground, and six or seven feet high, with large wooden pegs or bolts in it, on which are hung and grouped, with a wild and startling taste, the arms and armor of the respective proprietor, consisting of his whitened shield, embossed and emblazoned with the figure of his protecting *medicine* (or mystery), his bow and quiver, his war-club or battle-axe, his dart or javelin, his tobacco-pouch and pipe, his medicine-bag, and his eagle – ermine or raven head-dress; and over all, and on the top of the post (as if placed by some conjuror or Indian magician, to guard and protect the spell of wildness that reigns in this strange place), stands forth and in full relief the head and horns of a buffalo, which is, by a village regulation, owned and possessed by every man in the nation, and hung at the head of his bed, and which he uses as a mask when called upon by the chiefs to join in the buffalo-dance, of which I shall say more in a future epistle.

This arrangement of beds, of arms, etc., combining the most vivid display and arrangement of colors, of furs, of trinkets – of barbed and glistening points and steel – of mysteries and hocus-pocus, together with the sombre and smoked color of the roof and sides of the lodge, and the wild and rude and red, the graceful (though uncivil), conversational, garrulous story-telling, and happy, though ignorant and untutored, groups that are smoking their pipes, wooing their sweethearts, and embracing their little ones about their peaceful and endeared firesides, together with their pots and kettles, spoons, and other culinary articles of their own manufacture around them, presents altogether one of the most picturesque scenes to the eye of a stranger that can be possibly seen, and far more wild and vivid than could ever be imagined.

Of all the erroneous ideas concerning the Indians in which the civilized world indulges there is none more untrue than that the Indian is morose, reserved, and taciturn. In all my travels among the Indian tribes. and particularly among these unassuming people, I have found them more talkative than the civilized races. No one can look into the lodges of these people, or into any little momentary group, without being convinced that small talk, garrulity, gossip, and story-telling are the leading passions with them. One has but to walk or ride about this little town and its environs for a few hours on a pleasant day, and overlook the numerous games and gambols, and hear their notes and yelps of exultation, or peep into their wigwams and watch the glistening fun that is beaming from the noses, cheeks, and chins, of the crouching, cross-legged, prostrate groups around the fire, where the pipe is passed and the jokes and laughter immoderate, to become confident that it is natural to laugh and be merry. Why,* indeed, should these people not be merry. They live in a country where it is not necessary to look into the future with concern, and where their faculties and inclinations are solely directed toward the present day. If the uncultivated condition of their minds curtails the number of their enjoyments, they are free from the many cares and jealousies of our more mercenary world, and in my opinion are far ahead of us in the real, natural enjoyment of their faculties.

The groups of lodges around me, resembling nothing so much as inverted potash-kettles, present a very curious appearance. They are used outside quite as much as within. On the tops of these are to be seen groups standing and reclining, whose wild and picturesque appearance it would be difficult to transcribe. Stern warriors, like statues, stand in dignified groups wrapped in their painted robes, with their heads decked and plumed with quills of the war eagle, extending their arms to the east and the west, recounting the scenes of their battles. In another direction, the wooing lover softening the heart of his fair Taih-nah-tai-a with the notes of his lute. On other lodges groups are engaged in the game of "moccasin," or "platter." Some seem to be making robes and dresses, others have stretched their limbs in the luxury of sleep while basking in the sun. With all this varied and wild medley of living beings are the dogs, which are so near to the Indian heart that they are a part of his life. Besides these groups of the living are buffalo heads, skin canoes, pots and pottery, sleds and sledges, and displayed on poles twenty feet above the lodges hang the scalps of warriors kept as trophies. In other parts are poles on which hang the white shields and quivers of the warriors, with their medicine-bags attached, and here and there a sacrifice of red cloth or other costly stuff, offered up to the Great Spirit, over the door of some benignant chief, in humble gratitude for the blessings which he is enjoying. Such is a part *of* the strange medley that is before and around me; and amid them and the blue streams of smoke that are rising from the tops of these hundred "coal-pits" can be seen, in the distance, the green and boundless, treeless, bushless prairie; and on it, and contiguous to the piquet which encloses the village, a hundred scaffolds on which their "dead live," as they term it.

These people never bury the dead, but place the bodies on slight scaffolds just above the reach of human hands, and out of the way of wolves and dogs, and they are there left to moulder and decay. This cemetery, or place of deposit for the dead, is just back of the village, on a level prairie, and with all its appearances, history, forms, ceremonies, etc., is one of the strangest and most interesting objects to be described in the vicinity of this peculiar race.

Whenever a person dies in the Mandan village, and the customary honors and condolence are paid to his remains, and the body dressed in its best attire, painted, oiled, feasted, and supplied with bow and quiver, shield, pipe, and tobacco, knife, flint, and steel, and provisions enough to last him a few days on the journey which he is to perform, a fresh buffalo's skin, just taken from the animal's back, is wrapped around the body and tightly bound and wound with thongs of rawhide from head to foot. Then other robes are soaked in water till they are quite soft and elastic, which are also bandaged around the body in the same manner, and tied fast with thongs, which are wound with great care and exactness so as to exclude the action of the air from all parts of the body.

There is then a separate scaffold erected for it, constructed of four upright posts a little higher than human hands can reach, and on the tops of these are small poles passing around from one post to the others, across which are a number of willow-rods just strong enough to support the body, which is laid upon them on its back, with its feet carefully presented toward the rising sun.

There are a great number of these bodies resting exactly in a similar way, excepting in some instances where a chief, or medicine-man, may be seen with a few yards of scarlet or blue cloth spread over his remains, as a mark of public respect and esteem. Some hundreds of these bodies may be seen reposing in this manner in this curious place, which the Indians call "the village of the dead"; and the traveller who visits this country to study and learn will not only be struck with the novel appearance of the scene, but if he will give attention to the respect and devotions that are paid to his sacred place, he will draw many a moral deduction that will last him through life; he will learn, at least, that filial, conjugal, and paternal affection are not necessarily the results of civilization, but that the Great Spirit has given them to man in his native state. There is not a day on which one may not see here most touching scenes. Fathers, mothers, wives, and children lie prostrate before these scaffolds with piteous and heartbroken cries, tearing their hair and cutting their flesh with knives, and doing other penance to appease the spirits of the dead, whom they fancy they have offended.

When these scaffolds decay and fall to the ground, the nearest relations, having buried the other bones, take the skulls, which are perfectly bleached and purified, and place them, a hundred or more, not quite a foot apart in circles on the prairie. In the centre of these circles is a little mound several feet high, which rests on two buffalo skulls, male and female; and in the centre of this mound is a medicine-pole, twenty feet high, supporting many curious articles of mystery and superstition that are supposed to guard and protect its circle. Each skull of the circle rests upon a bunch of wild sage. As soon as the sage begins to decay a fresh piece is gathered and replaces it. Each wife knows the skull of her husband or child, and there is not a day that she does not visit it with a dish of her choicest food. Here are always, on pleasant days, to be seen several women sitting by the skulls of husband and children talking affectionately to them. Not infrequently a woman takes out her needle-work and spends the greater part of the day by some skull, embroidering and chattering, until, fatigued, she falls asleep with her arms encircling it and remains for hours.

CHAPTER VII
SOCIAL LIFE AMONG THE MANDANS

THE MANDANS are most pleasing in personal appearance and manners. Both in looks and customs they differ from all the other tribes.

They are not a warlike people – that is to say, they do not carry war into the enemy's country, but when invaded their valor equals that of any tribe. Being a small nation, they are unable to contend on the prairie with Sioux or other roaming tribes; accordingly, they have judiciously intrenched themselves in a permanent fortified village. This has enabled them to cultivate manufactures of different kinds, and their lodges are better supplied with comforts than those of any other nation. This also seems to account for the fact that they are far ahead of other tribes in manners and refinement, if one may use this word in connection with Indian life. The traders always speak of them as "the polite and friendly Mandans."

A stranger in a Mandan village is immediately struck by the ease and elegance of this people, with the diversity of their complexions, the varying shades of their hair, the singularity of their language, and their peculiar and unaccountable customs. At first one is disposed, on seeing them, to exclaim, "These are not Indians. The Indian is copper-colored, with jet-black hair." Many of these people, especially the women, are as light as half-breeds. Their skins are almost white; their features are symmetrical and pleasing; their eyes are gray, hazel, even blue; their expression is sweet, and their demeanor exceedingly modest.

The diversity in the color of hair is also as great as that in the complexion; for in a numerous group of these people (and more particularly among the females, who never take pains to change its natural color, as the men often do) there may be seen every shade and color of hair that can be seen in our own country, with the exception of red or auburn, which is not to be found.

And there is yet one more strange and unaccountable peculiarity, which can probably be seen nowhere else on earth, nor on any rational grounds accounted for, other than that it is a freak or order of nature for which she has not seen fit to assign a reason. There are very many, of both sexes and of every age, from infancy to manhood and old age, with hair of a bright silvery gray, and in some instances almost perfectly white.

This singular and eccentric appearance is much oftener seen among the women than it is with the men, for many of the latter who have it seem ashamed of it, and artfully conceal it by filling their hair with glue and black and red earth. The women, on the other hand, seem proud of it, and display it often in an almost incredible profusion, which spreads over their shoulders and falls as low as the knee. I have ascertained, on a careful inquiry, that about one in ten or twelve of the whole tribe are what the French call "cheveux gris," or gray-hairs, and that this strange and unaccountable phenomenon is not the result of disease or habit, but is unquestionably a hereditary character which runs in families and indicates no inequality in disposition or intellect. And by passing this hair through my hands, as I often have, I have found it uniformly to be as coarse and harsh as a horse's mane, differing materially from the hair of other colors, which, among the Mandans, is generally as fine and as soft as silk.

The stature of the Mandans is rather below the ordinary size of man, with beautiful symmetry of form and proportion, and wonderful suppleness and elasticity; they are pleasingly erect and graceful, both in their walk and their attitudes, and the hair of the men, which generally spreads over their backs, falling down to the hams, and sometimes to the ground, is divided into plaits or slabs of two inches in width, and filled with a profusion of glue and red earth or vermilion, at intervals of an inch or two, which, becoming very hard, remains in and unchanged from year to year.

This mode of dressing the hair is curious, and gives to the Mandans the most singular appearance. The hair of the men is uniformly all laid over from the forehead backward, carefully kept above and resting on the ear, and thence falling down over the back in these flattened bunches, and painted red, extending oftentimes quite on to the calf of the leg, and sometimes in such profusion as almost to conceal the whole figure from the person walking behind them.

The hair of the women is also worn as long as they can possibly cultivate it, oiled very often, which preserves on it a beautiful gloss and shows its natural color. They often braid it in two large plaits, one falling down just back of the ear, on each side of the head; and on any occasion which requires them to "put on their best looks" they pass their fingers through it, drawing it out of braid and spreading it over their shoulders. The Mandan women observe strictly the same custom which I have observed among the Crows and Blackfeet (and, in fact, all other tribes I have seen, without a single exception) of parting the hair on the forehead and always keeping the crease or separation filled with vermilion or other red paint. This is one of the very few little (and apparently trivial) customs which I have found among the Indians, without being able to assign any cause for it other than that "they are Indians" and that this is an Indian fashion.

The art of swimming is known to all the American Indians, and perhaps no people on earth have taken more pains to learn it, nor any who turn it to better account. There certainly are no people whose vocations more often call for the use of their limbs in this way, as many of the tribes spend their lives on the shores of our vast lakes and rivers, paddling about from their childhood in their fragile bark canoes, which are liable to continual accidents and often throw the Indian upon his natural resources for the preservation of his life.

Among the Mandans as among all tribes there are different grades of society. There are those who care little for their looks and those who take great care of their appearance. Such are the chiefs, braves, men of distinction, and their families, who pay strict regard to decency, cleanliness, and elegance of dress. There are few races who pay more attention to personal cleanliness. A half-mile above the village on the river is the bathing-place of the women. Here they go every morning in summer by hundreds at sunrise to bathe. About a quarter of a mile from this place is a semi-circular terrace in the prairie, and here are stationed sentinels with bows and arrows to protect the bathers from the approach of men or boys. But at this distance one can see them leaping into the water, and their bodies glistening in the sun as they gambol on the beautiful beach. The poorest swimmer among them will dash into the boiling current of the Missouri and cross with perfect ease.

The bathing-place of the boys and men is below the village. After the morning bath they return to the village, wipe their limbs, and anoint their bodies and hair with bear's grease.

During their long marches, in the prosecution of their almost continuous warfare, it often becomes necessary to plunge into and swim across the wildest streams and rivers when they have neither canoes nor other craft in which to cross them. I have as yet seen no tribe which neglects the art of swimming, which is learned at a very early age by both sexes, and enables even the women and children to plunge into and swim across the turbulent streams. The hardy sqaws will take their children on their backs and cross any river that comes in their path. The Indian does not part his hands under his chin and make his stroke outward and horizontally, thus throwing the burden on the chest. He throws his body alternately upon the right and the left side, raising one arm entirely above the water, and reaching as far forward as he can to dip it in again, while the force and weight of his body is spent upon the arm that is under him, and like a paddle is propelling him along. While this arm is making a halfcircle beneath him, the opposite arm is describing a similar arc overhead. In this manner he lessens the strain on breast and spine.

In addition to these morning baths, the Mandans have another and greater luxury. This is the vapor bath, which is resorted to not only by the sick, but as a means of hardening their bodies for the exposure and vicissitudes of life to which they are constantly liable. These sudatories, of which each village has several, are public, and accessible to all ages and both sexes. In every Mandan lodge is a crib, or basket, curiously woven of willow boughs, and large enough to hold any member of the family lying down. When any one desires to take a bath this basket is carried to the sudatory and is brought back after it has been used. These baths are built near the river, and generally of skins, resembling in form a Crow or Sioux lodge. Over it is thrown buffalo-skins sewed tight together, with a kind of furnace in the centre; or, in other words, in the centre of the lodge are two walls of stone about six feet long and two and a half apart, and about three feet high; across and over this space, between the two walls, are laid a number of round sticks, on which the bathing-crib is placed. Contiguous to the lodge, and outside of it, is a little furnace something similar, in the side of the bank, where the woman kindles a hot fire and heats to a red heat a number of large stones, which are kept at these places for this particular purpose, and having them all in readiness, she goes home or sends word to inform her husband or other one who is waiting that all is ready, when he makes his appearance, entirely naked, though with a large buffalo-robe wrapped around him. He then enters the lodge and places himself in the crib or basket, either on his back or in a sitting posture (the latter of which is generally preferred), with his back toward the door of the lodge, when the squaw brings in a large stone, red hot, between two sticks (lashed together somewhat in the form of a pair of tongs), and, placing it under him, throws cold water upon it, which raises a profusion of vapor about him. He is at once enveloped in a cloud of steam, and a woman or child will sit at a little distance and continue to dash water upon the stone, while the matron of the lodge is out and preparing to make her appearance with another heated stone; or he will sit and dip from a wooden bowl, with a ladle made of the mountain-sheep's horn, and throw upon the heated stones, with his own hands, the water which he is drawing through, his lungs and pores, in the next moment, in the most delectable and exhilarating vapors, as it distils through the mat of wild sage and other medicinal and aromatic herbs, which he has strewed over the bottom of his basket, and on which he reclines.

During all this time the lodge is shut perfectly tight, and he quaffs this delicious and renovating draught to his lungs with deep-drawn sighs, and with extended nostrils, until he is drenched in the most profuse degree of perspiration that can be produced, when he makes a kind of strangled signal, at which the lodge is opened, and he darts forth with the speed of a frightened deer and plunges headlong into the river, from which he instantly escapes again, wraps his robe around him, and "leans" as fast as possible for home. Here his limbs are wiped dry and wrapped close and tight within the fur of the buffalo-robes, in which he takes his nap, with his feet to the fire; then he oils his limbs and hair with bear's grease, dresses and plumes himself for a visit – a feast, a parade, or a council – or slicks down his long hair and rubs his oiled limbs to a polish with a piece of soft buckskin, prepared to join in games of ball or Tchung-kee.

Such is the sudatory or the vapor bath of the Man- dans, and, as I before observed, it is resorted to both as an every-day luxury by those who have the time and energy or industry to indulge in it, and also used by the sick as a remedy for nearly all the diseases which are known among them.

CHAPTER VIII
THE ARTIST BECOMES A MEDICINE-MAN

PERHAPS NOTHING ever more completely astonished these people than the work of my brush. Portrait-painting, of course, they knew nothing of, so that my appearance here has begun a new era in the arcana of mystery. Soon after arriving I began the portraits of the two principal chiefs. These were done without exciting any curiosity among the villagers, who did not know what I was doing. Even the chiefs did not fully understand. No one was admitted to my lodge until the pictures were completed. It was very amusing to see them mutually recognizing each other's likeness, and assuring each other of the resemblance. For a time they pressed their hands over their mouths in dead silence, a custom among the tribes when greatly astonished, all the time looking at the portraits, then at myself, and on the palette and colors which had produced these unaccountable effects.

They then walked up to me in the most gentle manner, taking me in turn by the hand with a firm grip, with head and eyes inclined downward, and in a tone a little above a whisper pronounced the words "te-ho-pe-nee Wash-ee!" and walked off.

At that moment I was christened with a new and a great name – one by which I am now familiarly hailed and talked of in this village, and no doubt will be as long as traditions last in this strange community.

After I had finished the portraits of the two chiefs, and they had returned to their wigwams and deliberately seated themselves by their respective firesides and silently smoked a pipe or two (according to a universal custom), they gradually began to tell what had taken place; and at length crowds of gaping listeners, with mouths wide open, thronged their lodges, and a throng of women and girls were about my house, and through every crack and crevice I could see their glistening eyes, which were piercing my hut in a hundred places, from a natural and restless propensity, a curiosity to see what was going on within. An hour or more passed in this way, and the soft and silken throng continually increased, until some hundreds of them were clung and piled about my wigwam like a swarm of bees hanging on the front and sides of their hive.

During this time not a man made his appearance about the premises; after awhile, however, they could be seen, folded in their robes, gradually *siding* up toward the lodge with a silly look upon their faces, which confessed at once that curiosity was leading them, reluctantly, where their pride checked and forbade them to go. The rush soon after became general, and the chiefs and medicine-men took possession of my room, placing *soldiers* (braves with spears in their hands) at the door, admitting no one but such as were allowed by the chiefs to come in.

Monsieur Kipp (the agent of the Fur Company, who has lived here eight years, and to whom, for his politeness and hospitality, I am much indebted) at this time took a seat with the chiefs, and, speaking their language fluently, he explained to them my views and the objects for which I was painting these portraits, and also expounded to them the manner in which they were made, at which they seemed all to be very much pleased. The necessity at this time of exposing the portraits to the view of the crowds who were assembled around the house became imperative, and they were held up together over the door, so that the whole village had a chance to see and recognize their chiefs. The effect upon so mixed a multitude, who as yet had heard no way of accounting for them, was novel and really laughable. The likenesses were instantly recognized, and many of the gaping multitude commenced yelping; some were stamping off in the jarring dance, others were singing, and others again were crying; hundreds covered their mouths with their hands and were mute; others, indignant, drove their spears frightfully into the ground, and some threw a reddened arrow at the sun and went home to their wigwams.

The pictures seen, the next curiosity was to see the man who made them, and I was called forth. I stepped forth and was instantly hemmed in in the throng. Women were gaping and gazing, and warriors and braves were offering me their hands, – while little boys and girls, by dozens, were struggling through the crowd to touch me with the ends of their fingers; and while I was engaged from the waist upward in fending off the throng and shaking hands, my legs were assailed (not unlike the nibbling of little fish when I have been standing in deep water) by children, who were creeping between the legs of the by-standers for the curiosity or honor of touching me with the end of a finger. The eager curiosity and expression of astonishment with which they gazed upon me plainly showed that they looked upon me as some strange and unaccountable being. They pronounced me the greatest *medicine-man* in the world, for they said I had made *living beings;* they said they could see their chiefs alive in two places; those that I had made were a *little* alive – they could see their eyes move, could see them smile and laugh, and that if they could laugh they could certainly speak, if they should try, and they must therefore have *some life* in them.

But we had not counted on the squaws, who insisted that my "medicine was too great for the Mandans." I had put life into the picture; they could see it move. I must then have taken some life from the subject. A person with such power could only do harm to the community. I must be a dangerous man. Bad luck would follow those who were painted, for I would carry away with me the portraits and with them a part of their lives, and they could never rest quietly in their graves.

They then set up a mournful chant, with weeping and wailing through the village, saying that if I could make living things by looking at them, I could destroy life in the same way if I chose. In this way, with the aid of some quack medicine-men, they aroused a general panic, and so successfully that the chiefs who had agreed to sit for me held a grave council for several days and my work was at a complete stand-still.

At length I got admitted to the secret conclave and assured them that I was but a man like themselves, and that my art held no mystery, but could be learned by any of them if they tried. Moreover, that I lived in a country where brave men never allowed their squaws to frighten them with foolish whims and stories. Whereupon they rose and immediately dressed for their pictures. Afterward the squaws were silent and my painting-room was a resort for chiefs, braves, and medicinemen waiting the completion of each picture, interested in the likeness as it came from the brush, when they would laugh, yell, sing, and smoke a fresh pipe to the health and success of him who had just been safely delivered from the mystic operation of the white medicine.

But I observed that as each portrait was begun a pipe or two was filled and that the chiefs and braves passed the pipe around, and continued to smoke until the portrait was completed, doubtless smoking for the safe deliverance of the sitter from harm. Then I, too, occasionally, stopped as if something was wrong, and taking a tremendous puff or two at the pipe, and letting the smoke stream through my nostrils, would give evidence of immense relief, enabling me to proceed with greater facility. Thus by complimenting each one on his good looks, taking them according to their rank, and making it a matter of honor with them, I succeeded in giving my art and myself a certain standing.

After this signal success I was taken by the chiefs and led to their several lodges and feasted in the best manner the country affords. To be led by the arm, it must be understood, is a high honor. I was also waited upon by the medicine-men, who presented me with a she-shee-quoi, or doctor's rattle, a magic wand strung with the claws of the grizzly bear, the hoofs of the antelope, ermine, wild sage, and bat's wings, all of which were perfumed with the savory odor of the polecat. A dog was then sacrificed and hung by the legs over my lodge, and I was thereby considered as a Fellow of the Extraordinary Society of the Conjurati.

Things went on pleasantly after this for some time. There was some altercation among the braves concerning their rank, of which they are very jealous, and a few still feared premature death if they were painted, or when painted, that the picture, which would go on living after they were dead, might prevent them sleeping quietly in their graves. But now and then an extraordinary occurrence would take place. Several times some of the aspiring young men came into my lodge, and after looking at the portraits would put their hands up before their eyes and walk to the right or left of the lodge where they could take a side look at the portrait, since it is an unpardonable offence to look a chief full in the face. But having taken this position from which they could look freely at the painting, they have thrown their robes over their heads and bolted out of the wigwarn, filled equally with astonishment and indignation, averring, as they always will in a sullen mood, that they "saw the eyes move" – that as they walked around the room "the eyes of the portrait followed them." With these unfortunate gentlemen repeated efforts have been made by the traders, and also by the chiefs and doctors, who understand the illusion, to convince them of their error by explaining the mystery; but they will not hear to any explanation whatever, saying that "what they see with their eyes is always evidence enough for them"; that they always "believe their own eyes sooner than a hundred tongues," and all efforts to get them a second time to my room, or into my company in any place, have proved entirely unsuccessful.

I had trouble brewing also the other day from another source: one of the *"medicines"* commenced howling and haranguing around my domicile, among the throng that was outside, proclaiming that all who were inside and being painted were fools and would soon die, and very materially affecting thereby my popularity. I, however, sent for him and called him in the next morning, when I was alone, having only the interpreter with me, telling him that I had had my eye upon him for several days and had been so well pleased with his looks that I had taken great pains to find out his history, which had been explained by all as one of a most extraordinary kind, and his character and standing in his tribe as worthy of my particular notice, and that I had several days since resolved that as soon as I had practised my hand long enough upon the others, to get the stiffness out of it (after paddling my canoe so far as I had) and make it to work easily and successfully, I would begin on his portrait, which I was then prepared to commence on that day, and that I felt as if I could do him justice. He shook me by the hand, giving me the "Doctor's grip," and beckoned me to sit down, which I did, and we smoked a pipe together. After this was over he told me that "he had no inimical feelings toward me, although he had been telling the chiefs that they were all fools, and all would die who had their portraits painted; that although he had set the old women and children all crying, and even made some of the young warriors tremble, yet he had no unfriendly feelings toward me nor any fear or dread of my art."

"I know you are a good man," said he; "I know you will do no harm to any one; your medicine is great and you are a great medicine-man. I would like to see myself very well, and so would all of the chiefs, but they have all been many days in this medicine-house, and they all know me well, and they have not asked me to come in and be *made alive* with paints. My friend, I am glad that my people have told you who I am; my heart is glad. I will go to my wigwam and eat, and in a little while I will come, and you may go to work." Another pipe was lit and smoked, and he got up and went off. I prepared my canvas and palette, and whistled away the time until twelve o'clock, before he made his appearance, having used the whole of the fore part of the day at his toilet, arranging his dress and ornamenting his body for his picture.

At that hour, then, bedaubed and streaked with paints of various colors, with bear's grease and charcoal, with medicine-pipes in his hands and foxes' tails attached to his heels, entered Mah-to-he-hah (the old bear), with a train of his own profession, who seated themselves around him; and also a number of boys, whom it was requested should remain with him, and whom I supposed it possible might have been pupils, whom he was instructing in the mysteries of *materia medica* and *hoca poca*. He took his position in the middle of the room, waving his eagle calumets in each hand, and singing his medicine-song, which he sings over his dying patient, looking me full in the face until I completed his picture, which I painted at full length. His vanity has been completely gratified in the operation; he lies for hours together, day after day, in my room, in front of his picture, gazing intensely upon it, lights my pipe for me while I am painting, shakes hands with me a dozen times on each day, and talks of me, and enlarges upon my *medicine* virtues and my talents wherever he goes, so that this new difficulty is now removed, and instead of preaching against me he is one of my strongest and most enthusiastic friends and aids in the country.

In addition to these chiefs, braves, and doctors, there is another celebrity of whom each tribe seems to possess at least one. This is the Indian dandy, who may be seen strutting through the village always dressed in his best clothes, unadorned, however, with such honorable trophies as scalps and the claws of the grizzly. The dandy never puts his life in peril; he stays about the wigwams to take care of the women. His dress is made of such animals as he can easily kill. He adorns himself with swan's down and duck quills, and with braids of sweet-scented grass and other meaningless decorations. These elegant gentlemen are held in little estimation by the chiefs and braves, who call them "faint hearts" and "old women." But these names do not seem to trouble them. For the most part they seem to enjoy the admiration of the women and children, and enjoy their lives as men of leisure.

These gay and tinselled bucks may be seen on a pleasant day in all their plumes, astride of their pied or dappled ponies, with a fan in the right hand, made of a turkey's tail; with whip and a fly-brush attached to the wrist of the same hand, and underneath them a white and beautiful and soft pleasure-saddle, ornamented with porcupine quills and ermine, parading through and lounging about the village for an hour or so, when they will cautiously bend their course to the suburbs of the town, where they will sit or recline upon their horses for an hour or two, overlooking the beautiful games where the braves and the young aspirants are contending in manly and athletic amusements. When they are fatigued with this severe effort, they wend their way back again, lift off their fine white saddle of doeskin, which is wadded with buffalo's hair, turn out their pony, take a little refreshment, smoke a pipe, fan themselves to sleep, and doze away the rest of the day.

While I have been painting from day to day, there have been two or three of these fops continually strutting and taking their attitudes in front of my door, decked out in all their finery, without receiving other benefit or other information than such as they could discover through the cracks and seams of my cabin. The chiefs, I observed, passed them by without notice, and of course without inviting them in, and they seemed to figure about my door from day to day in their best dresses and best attitudes, as if in hopes that I would select them as models for my canvas. It was natural that I should do so, for their costume and personal appearance was entirely more beautiful than anything else to be seen in the village. My plans were laid, and one day when I had got through with all of the head men who were willing to sit to be painted, and there were two or three of the chiefs lounging in my room, I stepped to the door and tapped one of these fellows on the shoulder, who took the hint and stepped in, well pleased and delighted with the signal and honorable notice I had at length taken of him and his beautiful dress. Readers, you cannot imagine what was the expression of gratitude which beamed forth in this poor. fellow's face, and how high his heart beat with joy and pride, at the idea of my selecting him to be immortal, alongside of the chiefs and worthies whose portraits he saw arranged around the room, and by which honor he undoubtedly considered himself well paid for two or three weeks of regular painting, and greasing, and dressing, and standing alternately on one leg and the other at the door of my premises.

Well, I placed him before me, and a canvas on my easel, and "chalked him out" at full length. He was truly a beautiful subject for the brush, and I was filled with enthusiasm – his dress from head to foot was of the skins of the mountain-goat, dressed so neatly that they were almost as soft and as white as Canton crape; around the bottom and the sides it was trimmed with ermine, and porcupine quills of beautiful dyes garnished it in a hundred parts; his hair which was long and spread over his back and shoulders, extending nearly to the ground, was all combed back and parted on his forehead like that of a woman. He was a tall and fine figure, with ease and grace in his movements that were well worthy of a man of better caste. In his left hand he held a beautiful pipe, and in his right hand he plied his fan, and on his wrist was still attached his whip of elk's horn and his fly-brush made of the buffalo's tail.

I was painting my subject with the greatest pleasure when the two or three chiefs seated in my lodge, and whose portraits I had previously painted, arose suddenly and, wrapping themselves tightly in their robes, crossed the room with a quick, heavy step and took an informal leave. I was apprehensive of their displeasure, although I continued my work. In a few moments the interpreter came furiously into my room.

"My God, sir, this will never do. You have given great offence to the chiefs. They have complained to me of your conduct. They tell me this is a worthless fellow, a man of no account in their nation, and if you paint his picture you must instantly destroy theirs. You have no alternative, my dear sir. The quicker this chap is out of your lodge the better."

The matter was explained to my sitter by the interpreter. Picking up his robe, he wrapped himself in it and, plying his fan about his face, walked out of the lodge in silence but with a consequential smile. He took his old position in front of the door for a time, when he walked quietly away. It was interesting to me to note how highly the Mandan braves esteem the honor of being painted, and also to observe how little they value a man who has not the pride and noble bearing of the warrior.

CHAPTER IX
A MANDAN FEAST

MAH-TO-TOH-PAH (THE four bears), whose portrait was one of the first I painted, deserves something more than this statement. Although the second in office, he is the first and most popular man in the nation. I have found him to be not only a high-minded and gallant warrior, but a polished gentleman. Mah-to-toh-pah had agreed to stand for his portrait early in the morning. I had my palette prepared, and waited until noon. Mah-to-toh- pah was dressing. At length the word came that "Mah-to-toh-pah was coming in full dress."

I looked out of the door and saw him approaching with a firm, elastic step, accompanied by a crowd of women and children, who were gazing on him with admiration and escorting him to my wigwam. No tragedian ever trod the stage or gladiator entered the Roman Forum with more grace and manly dignity than did Mah-to-toh-pah my wigwam where I received him. He took his attitude before me with the sternness of a Brutus and the stillness of a statue. There he stood before me until the darkness of night fell on our silence. His dress, which was a very splendid one, was complete in all its parts, and consisted of a shirt or tunic, leggings, moccasins, head-dress, necklace, shield, bow and quiver, lance, tobacco-sack and pipe, robe, belt, and knife, medicine-bag, tomahawk, and warclub, or *po-ko-mo-kon*.

The shirt, of which I have spoken, was made of two skins of the mountain-sheep beautifully dressed, and sewed together by seams which rested upon the arms, one skin hanging in front, upon the breast, and the other falling down upon the back, the head being passed between them, and they falling over and resting on the shoulders. Across each shoulder, and somewhat in the form of an epaulet, was a beautiful band, and down each arm from the neck to the hand was a similar one, of two inches in width (and crossing the other at right angles on the shoulder), beautifully embroidered with porcupine quills worked on the dress and covering the seams. To the lower edge of these bands the whole way, at intervals of half an inch, were attached long locks of black hair, which he had taken with his own hand from the heads of his enemies whom he had slain in battle, and which he thus wore as a trophy and also as an ornament to his dress. The front and back of the shirt were curiously garnished in several parts with porcupine quills and paintings of the battles he had fought, and also with representations of the victims that had fallen by his hand. The bottom of the dress was bound or hemmed with ermine skins, and tassels of ermines' tails were suspended from the arms and the shoulders.

The leggings, which were made of deerskins beautifully dressed and fitting tight to the leg, extended from the feet to the hips, and were fastened to a belt which was passed around the waist. These, like the shirt, had a similar band, worked with porcupine quills of richest dyes, passing down the seam on the outer part of the leg, and fringed also the whole length of the leg with the scalp-locks taken from his enemies' heads.

The moccasins were of buckskin, and covered in almost every part with the beautiful embroidery of porcupine quills.

The head-dress, which was superb and truly magnificent, consisted of a crest of war-eagles' quills gracefully falling back from the forehead over the back part of the head, and extending quite down to his feet, set the whole way in a profusion of ermine, and surmounted on the top of the head with the horns of the buffalo shaved thin and highly polished.

The necklace was made of fifty huge claws or nails of the grizzly bear, ingeniously arranged on the skin of an otter, and worn, like the scalp-locks, as a trophy.

His shield was made of the hide of the buffalo's neck and hardened with the glue that was taken from its hoofs; its boss was the skin of a pole-cat, and its edges were fringed with rows of eagles' quills and hoofs of the antelope.

His bow was of bone and as white and beautiful as ivory.

The quiver was made of a panther's skin and hung upon his back charged with its deadly arrows; some were poisoned and some were not; they were feathered with hawks' and eagles' quills; some were clean and innocent and pure, and others were stained all over with animal and human blood that was dried upon them. Their blades or points were of flint, and some of steel, and altogether were a deadly magazine.

The lance or spear was held in his left hand; its blade was two-edged and of polished steel, and the blood of several human victims was seen dried upon it, one over the other; its shaft was of the toughest ash, and ornamented at intervals with tufts of war-eagles' quills.

His tobacco-sack was made of the skin of an otter and tastefully garnished with quills of the porcupine. In it was carried his *k'nick-k'neck* (the bark of the red willow, which is smoked as a substitute for tobacco). It contained also his flint and steel and punk for lighting.

His pipe was ingeniously carved out of the red steatite, or pipe-stone, the stem of which was three feet long and two inches wide, made from the stalk of the young ash; about half its length was wound with delicate braids of the porcupine's quills, so ingeniously wrought as to represent figures of men and animals upon it. It was also ornamented with the skins and beaks of woodpeckers' heads and the hair of the white buffalo's tail. The lower half of the stem was painted red, and on its edges it bore the notches he had recorded for the snows (or years) of his life.

His robe was made of the skin of a young buffalo bull, with the fur on one side, and the other finely and delicately dressed, with all the battles of his life emblazoned on it by his own hand.

His belt, which was of a substantial piece of buckskin, was firmly girded around his waist, and in it were worn his tomahawk and scalping-knife.

His medicine-bag was the skin of a beaver curiously ornamented with hawks' bills and ermine. It was held in his right hand, and his *po-ko-mo-kon* (or war-club), which was made of a round stone tied up in a piece of rawhide and attached to the end of a stick, somewhat in the form of a sling, was laid with others of his weapons at his feet.

The horns of the head-dress are allowed only to a chief or warrior of extraordinary renown. Mah-to-toh-pah, although second in rank, was the only man in his tribe permitted to wear them. They are made of about a third part of the horns of the buffalo bull, split from end to end, shaved thin and light, and highly polished. These two pieces are attached to the head-dress on each side in the same place that they rise on the head of the buffalo, and from a mass of ermine skins and tails hanging over the top of the head-dress to resemble the locks of hair that hang over the head of the buffalo bull.

This custom seems to belong to all the Northern tribes of Indians, and is no doubt of ancient origin and has some classic meaning. One is impressed with its resemblance to the horns worn by the Abyssinian chiefs and the Hebrews as a symbol of power and command.

"The false prophet Zedekiah made him horns of iron." (I Kings 22 : 2.)

"Lift not your horns on high; speak not with a stiff neck." (Psalms 75: 5.)

The horns on these head-dresses are loosely attached at the bottom so that they can fall backward and forward, and by an ingenious movement of the head, so slight as to be almost imperceptible, they are made to balance to and fro, like a horse's ears, giving an appearance of force and character to the person wearing them. This head-dress with horns is worn only on great formal occasions such as the visit of foreign chiefs, Indian agents, or at the celebration of victories and great public festivals. A chief, however, who determines to lead his warriors to battle, will decorate his head with this symbol of power to stimulate his men, and thus invite the enemy to concentrate their shafts on him. Such, then, was the dress of Mah-to-toh-pah when he entered my wigwam. Much of this ornament I was forced to reject, since it interfered with the grace and simplicity of the figure.

About a week after the portrait was painted he came into my room at noon again in full dress, and passing his arm through mine led me through the village to his own lodge where a fine feast awaited us. His lodge was a room of immense size, circular, about fifty feet in diameter and twenty feet high, with a sunken curb of stone in the centre five feet across and a foot deep. In the centre of this was a fire and a pot boiling. I was led near the edge of the curb and seated on a handsome robe, ingeniously ornamented and painted with hieroglyphics. At a little distance from me Mah-to-toh- pah seated himself gracefully on another. A beautiful rush mat was placed between us, and on this the dishes were served.

Our feast consisted of three dishes only, two of which were contained in wooden bowls, and the third in an earthen vessel of Mandan manufacture and resembling in form our own bread-tray. This dish held a quantity of pemmican and marrow *fat;* and one of the former held a fine brace of buffalo ribs delightfully roasted, and the other was filled with a kind of paste or pudding, made of the flour of the *"pomme blanche"* as the French call it, a delicious turnip of the prairie, finely flavored with the buffalo-berries, which are collected in great quantities in this country, and used with divers dishes in cooking, as we in civilized countries use dried currants, which they very much resemble.

A handsome pipe and a tobacco-pouch made of the otter-skin, filled with k'nick-k'neck (Indian tobacco), lay by the side of the feast; and when we were seated mine host took up his pipe and deliberately filled it, and instead of lighting it by the fire, which he could easily have done, he drew from his pouch his flint and steel, and raised a spark with which he kindled it. He drew a few strong whiffs through it, and presented the stem of it to my mouth, through which I drew a whiff or two while he held the stem in his hands. This done, he laid down the pipe, and drawing his knife from his belt cut off a very small piece of the meat from the ribs, and pronouncing the words "Ho-pe-ne-chee wa-pa-chee" (meaning a *medicine* sacrifice), threw it into the fire.

He then, by signals, requested me to eat, and I commenced, after drawing out from my belt my knife (which it is supposed that every man in this country carries about him, for at an Indian feast a knife is never offered to a guest). Be not astonished that I sat and ate my dinner *alone,* for such is the custom of this strange land. In all tribes in these Western regions it is an invariable rule that a chief never eats with his guests invited to a feast; but while they eat he sits by, at their service, and ready to wait upon them, deliberately charging and lighting the pipe which is to be passed around after the feast is over. Such was the case in the present instance, and while I was eating, Mah-to-toh-pa sat cross-legged before me, cleaning his pipe and preparing it for a cheerful smoke when I had finished my meal. For this ceremony I observed he was making unusual preparation, and I observed as I ate, that after he had taken enough of the k'nick-k'neck, or bark of the red willow, from his pouch, he rolled out of it also a piece of the *"castor,"* which it is customary among these folks to carry in their tobacco-sack to give it a flavor, and, shaving off a small quantity of it, mixed it with the bark with which he charged his pipe. This done, he drew also from his sack a small parcel containing a fine powder which was made of dried buffalo dung, a little of which he spread over the top (according also to custom), which was like tinder, having no other effect than that of lighting the pipe with ease and satisfaction. My appetite satiated, I straightened up, and with a whiff the pipe was lit, and we enjoyed together for a quarter of an hour the most delightful exchange of good feelings, amid clouds of smoke and pantomimic signs and gesticulations.

The dish of "pemmican and marrow fat," of which I spoke, was thus: The first, an article of food used throughout this country as familiarly as we use bread in the civilized world. It is made of buffalo meat dried very hard, and afterward pounded in a large wooden mortar until it is nearly as fine as sawdust. When packed in this dry state in bladders, it may be easily carried to any part of the world in good order. Marrow fat is collected by the Indians from buffalo bones, which, broken in pieces, yield an immense amount of marrow. This is boiled out and put into buffalo bladders, which have been distended. When this fat cools it is as hard as tallow, but has the appearance, and much of the taste, of the richest yellow butter.

At a feast chunks of this marrow fat are cut off and placed in a bowl with the pemmican, and the two are eaten together. We civilized people in this region think these a very good substitute for bread and butter. In this dish, at our feast, lay a spoon made of buffalo horn beautifully polished. In one of the other dishes was a spoon of even more ingenious workmanship, made of the horn of the mountain-sheep, or *gros corne,* as the French trappers call them. This was large enough to hold several pints and was almost entirely transparent.

While sitting at this feast the wigwam was as silent as death, although we were not alone in it. This chief, as most of the others, has a number of wives, and all of them, some six or seven, were seated around the sides of the lodge on robes or mats on the ground, and not allowed to speak, although ready to obey his orders, which were given by manual signs and executed in the neatest and most silent manner.

When I rose to leave, the pipe through which we had smoked was presented to me, and the robe on which I had sat he raised by the corners and offered me, explaining that on it were the representations of the battles of his life in which he had killed with his own hand fourteen of his enemies. He had been two weeks painting it and had made this occasion to present it to me.

Some days after Mah-to-toh-pah called upon me with Mr. Kipp, who is the trader and interpreter of the Mandans, and I had from his own lips the story of these battles, which I wrote down, and accept as historical fact, since the Indians are very jealous of their honor and standing, and in so small a community each man's deeds are known, and it would not be even safe for a warrior to wear on his robe battles he had never fought.

The sixth of the rude pictures represented the most extraordinary of these exploits, and gives an interesting view not only of this man but of the Indian character. In a skirmish with the Ricarees, Mah-to-toh-pah found the body of his brother, and in it a handsome spear which had pierced his heart. At the Mandan village this spear was recognized as belonging to a noted Ricaree brave named Won-ga-tap. With the blood on the spear, Mah-to-toh-pah swore that he would yet revenge the death of his brother with the same spear. He kept it in his wigwam for four years, when one day he ran through the village brandishing the spear, exclaiming that the blood of his brother on its blade was yet fresh and called loudly for revenge. "Let every Mandan," said he, "be silent, and let no one sound the name of Mah-to-toh-pa – let no one ask for him, nor where he has gone, until you hear him sound the war-cry in front of the village, when he will enter it and show you the blood of Won-ga-tap. The blade of this lance shall drink the heart's blood of Won-ga-tap, or Mah-to-tohpa mingles his shadow with that of his brother."

With this he sallied forth from the village and over the plains, with the lance in his hand. His direction was toward the Riccaree village, and all eyes were upon him, though none dared to speak till he disappeared over the distant grassy bluffs. He travelled the distance of two hundred miles entirely alone, with a little parched corn in his pouch, making his marches by night and lying secreted by days, until he reached the Riccaree village, where, being acquainted with its shapes and its habits, and knowing the position of the wigwam of his doomed enemy, he loitered about in disguise, mingling himself in the obscure throng, and at last, silently and alone, observed through the rents of the wigwam the last motions and movements of his victim, as he retired to bed with his wife: he saw him light his last pipe and smoke it "to its end"; he saw the last whiff and saw the last curl of blue smoke that faintly steeped from its bowl; he saw the village awhile in darkness and silence, and the embers that were covered in the middle of the wigwam gone nearly out, and the last flickering light which had been gently playing over them; when he walked softly, but not slyly, into the wigwam and seated himself by the fire, over which was hanging a large pot, with a quantity of cooked meat remaining in it, and by the side of the fire the pipe and tobacco-pouch which had just been used; and knowing that the twilight of the wigwam was not sufficient to disclose the features of his face to his enemy, he very deliberately turned to the pot and completely satiated the desperate appetite, which he had got in a journey of six or seven days with little or nothing to eat, and then, as deliberately, charged and lighted the pipe, and sent (no doubt in every whiff that he drew through its stem) a prayer to the Great Spirit for a moment longer for the consummation of his design. While eating and smoking, the wife of his victim, while lying in bed, several times inquired of her husband what man it was who was eating in their lodge, to which he as many times replied, "It's no matter; let him eat, for he is probably hungry."

Mah-to-toh-pa knew full well that his appearance would cause no other reply than this from the dignitary of the nation; for, from an invariable custom among these Northern Indians, any one who is hungry is allowed to walk into any man's lodge and eat. While smoking his last gentle and tremulous whiffs on the pipe, Mah-to-toh-pa (leaning back and turning gradually on his side, to get a better view of the position of his enemy, and to see a little more distinctly the shapes of things) stirred the embers with his toes (readers, I had every word of this from his own lips, and every attitude and gesture acted out with his own limbs) until he saw his way was clear, at which moment, with his lance in his hands, he rose and drove it through the body of his enemy, and snatching the scalp from his head, he darted from the lodge, and quick as lightning, with the lance in one hand and the scalp in the other, made his way to the prairie! The village was in an uproar, but he was off, and no one knew the enemy who had struck the blow. Mah-to-toh-pa ran all night and lay close during the days, thanking the Great Spirit for strengthening his heart and his arm to this noble revenge, and prayed fervently for a continuance of his aid and protection till he should get back to his own village. His prayers were heard, and on the sixth morning, at sunrise, he descended the bluffs, and entered the village amid deafening shouts of applause, while he brandished and showed to his people the blade of lance, with the blood of his victim dried upon it, over that of his brother, and the scalp of Won-ga-tap suspended from its handle.

Such was the story that Mah-to-toh-pa had represented on his robe. As he stood for his portrait he held in his left hand a lance. Its blade was two-edged and of polished steel, and the blood of his victims was dried on its surface. Its shaft was of the toughest ash, and ornamented at intervals with the tufts of war-eagle's quills. Balanced on the hilt of the lance was an eagle's quill severed from the others and loose on the weapon. When he came for the portrait he had the quill in his hand and carefully balanced it, telling me he wished me to be very exact in painting it, as he wished the spot of blood on it to show. I did as he desired, and he then gave me his reason. "That quill," said he, "is great *medicine;* it belongs to the Great Spirit, and not to me. When I was running out of the lodge of Won-go-tap, I looked back and saw that quill hanging to the wound in his side. I ran back, and pulling it out, brought it home in my left hand, and I have kept it for the Great Spirit to this day!"

"Why do you not then tie it on to the lance again, where it came off?"

"Hush-sh," said he, "if the Great Spirit had wished it to be tied on in that place, it never would have come off; he has been kind to me, and I will not offend him."

CHAPTER X
THE MANDAN WOMEN

THE MANDAN women are both pretty and modest, and, among the better families of the tribe, as unapproachable as in society anywhere. At the same time, a chief may marry a dozen women if he pleases, and so may a white man. The most desirable maiden in the tribes may be secured for two horses, a gun with powder and ball for a year, five or six pounds of beads, a couple of gallons of whiskey, and a handful of awls.

Polygamy is practised among all the North American Indians. But those who avail themselves of this privilege are the chiefs and medicine-men. While there is no law preventing a poor or obscure man from taking more than one wife, he does not do so because either his position in the tribe would not satisfy the father, or because he has not enough worldly goods. Wives in this country are bought and sold, and the bargain is conducted always by the father as a purely mercenary contract, in which he stands out for the highest possible price. This does not prevent mutual fondness, the exchange of vows, and other assurances of affection as in the civilized world among the young people. But the marriage is not consummated without the necessary presents to the father.

The number of wives in the Indian country indicates a man's rank and his wealth. A chief must keep open house; to be popular he must entertain. As there are no daily laborers or wage-workers among the Indians, the dignitary must have wives and hand-maidens to perform the duties and the drudgeries of his wigwam. All labor among the tribes is done by the women, who are not only a source of convenience but of wealth. While the Indian is far behind the civilized world in acquisitiveness, he more or less has a passion for wealth and the luxuries of life.

There are other and very rational grounds on which the propriety of such a custom may be urged, one of which is as follows: as all nations of Indians in their natural condition are unceasingly at war with the tribes that are about them, for the adjustment of ancient and never-ending feuds, as well as from a love of glory, to which in Indian life the battle-field is almost the only road, their warriors are killed off to that extent that in many instances two and sometimes three women to a man are found in a tribe. In such instances I have found that the custom of polygamy has kindly helped the community to an evident relief from a cruel and prodigious calamity.

It is a matter of policy among the white men who are traders in this country to ally themselves with one or more of the important families in the tribe. These family connections facilitate their business transactions. Naturally only maidens of the best families can aspire to such marriages, which on their part are considered very desirable; not without reason. Marriage with a white num exempts them from the drudgery of the Indian wigwam. They are generally permitted to live in idleness, to wear mantles of blue and scarlet, decked with beads, trinkets, and ribbons, in which they flounce and flirt about, the envy of all the other maidens of the tribe. In arranging these marriages, if they may be so called, the Indian fathers are very shrewd, and exact the largest price possible from the white men, who, they think, should, and are able to, pay well for such precious wares. The trader, on his part, enters into the arrangement as he would bargain for a horse, and annuls it with just as little ceremony when he wishes to leave the country. The woman is in that case a fair and proper candidate for marriage or speculation if another suitor should come along, and her father equally desirous for another horse or gun. Yet it would be untrue and doing injustice to the Indians to say that they arc in the least behind us in conjugal, in filial, or parental affection.

The girls of this tribe, as those of the other Northwestern tribes, marry at the age of twelve or fourteen, sometimes, indeed, at eleven years. Their beauty, from their youth and the slavish lives they lead, vanishes soon after marriage. Their work is seldom finished, and they go at it, as if from choice and inclination, without a murmur. In this village it consists of getting the wood and water, in cooking, in dressing robes and skins, in drying meat and wild fruit and raising corn. The Mandans are rather good agriculturists. They raise a good deal of corn and some pumpkins and squashes. This is all done by the women, who make their hoes of the shoulder-blade of the buffalo or the elk, and dig the ground over instead of ploughing it, at a great cost of labor. The corn is very small, the ears not being longer than a man's thumb. This, however, is better suited to the climate, which is too cold to allow larger ears to ripen.

The green-corn season is a continual festival, and most of the crop is eaten at this time, and the remainder is gathered and dried on the cob, before it has ripened, and packed away in "caches" (as the French call them), holes dug in the ground, some six or seven feet deep, the insides of which are somewhat in the form of a jug, and tightly closed at the top. The corn, and even dried meat and pemmican, are placed in these caches, being packed tight around the sides, with prairie grass, and effectually preserved through the severest winters.

Corn and dried meat are generally laid in in the fall in sufficient quantities to support them through the winter. These are the principal articles of food during that long and inclement season; and in addition to them they oftentimes have in store great quantities of dried squashes and dried *"pommes blanches,"* a kind of turnip which grows in great abundance in these regions, and of which I have before spoken. These are dried in great quantities, and pounded into a sort of meal, and cooked with the dried meat and corn. Great quantities also of wild fruit of different kinds are dried and laid away in store for the winter season, such as buffalo-berries, service berries, strawberries, and wild plums.

The buffalo meat, however, is the great staple and "staff of life" in this country, and seldom, if ever, fails to afford them an abundant and wholesome means of subsistence. There are, from a fair computation, something like 250,000 Indians in these Western regions, who live almost exclusively on the flesh of these animals through every part of the year. During the summer and fall months they use the meat fresh, and cook it in a great variety of ways – by roasting, broiling, boiling, stewing, smoking, etc. – and by boiling the ribs and joints with the marrow in them make a delicious soup, which is universally used, and in vast quantities. The Mandans, I find, have no regular or stated times for their meals, but generally eat about twice in the twenty-four hours. The pot is always boiling over the fire, and any one who is hungry (either of the household or from any other part of the village) has a right to order it taken off, and to fall to eating as he pleases. Such is an unvarying custom among the North American Indians, and I very much doubt whether the civilized world has in its institutions any system which can properly be called more humane and charitable. Every man, woman, or child in Indian communities is allowed to enter any one's lodge, and even that of the chief of the nation, and eat when they are hungry, provided misfortune or necessity has driven them to it. Even so can the poorest and most worthless drone of the nation; if he is too lazy to hunt or to supply himself, he can walk into any lodge and every one will share with him as long as there is anything to eat. He, however, who thus begs when he is able to hunt pays dear for his meat, for he is stigmatized with the disgraceful epithet of a poltroon and a beggar.

The Mandans, like all other tribes, sit at their meals cross-legged, or rather with their ankles crossed in front of them, and both feet drawn close under their bodies, or, which is very often the case also, take their meals in a reclining posture, with their legs thrown out and the body resting on one elbow and fore-arm, which are under them. The dishes from which they eat are invariably on the ground or floor of the lodge, the group resting on buffalo-robes or mats of various structure and manufacture.

The position in which the women sit at their meals and on other occasions is different from that of the men, and one which they take and rise from again with great ease and much grace. By merely bending the knees both together, inclining the body back and the head and shoulders quite forward, they squat entirely down to the ground, inclining both feet either to the right or the left. In this position they always rest while eating, and it is both modest and graceful, for they seem, with apparent ease, to assume the position and rise out of it without using their hands in any way to assist them.

These women, however, although graceful and civil and ever so beautiful or ever so hungry, are not allowed to sit in the same group with the men while at their meals. So far as I have yet travelled in the Indian country, I never have seen an Indian woman eating with her husband. Men form the first group at the banquet, and women and children and dogs all come together at the next, and these gormandize and glut themselves to an enormous extent, though the men very seldom do.

It is time that an error on this subject, which has generally abroad in the world, was corrected. It is everywhere asserted, and almost universally believed, that the Indians are "enormous eaters," but, comparatively speaking, I assure my readers that this is an error. I venture to say that there are no persons on earth who practise greater prudence and self-denial than the men do (among the wild Indians), who are constantly in war and in the chase, or in their athletic sports and exercises, for all of which they are excited by the highest ideas of pride and honor, and every kind of excess is studiously avoided; and for a very great part of their lives the most painful abstinence is enforced upon themselves for the purpose of preparing their bodies and their limbs for these extravagant exertions.

Their mode of curing and preserving the buffalo meat, which is done by the women, is not only curious but almost incredible, for it is all cured and dried in the sun without the aid of smoke or salt. The choicest parts of the flesh from the buffalo are cut out by the squaws, and carried home on their backs or on horses. It is then cut across the grain, so as to secure alternate layers of lean and fat in strips of about a half inch in thickness. It is then hung up by thousands of pounds on poles resting on crotches, out of the way of dogs or wolves, and exposed to the sun for several days. It is by that time so effectually dried that it can be carried everywhere, even during the hottest months of the year, or in any latitude without damage. I can only account for it by the extraordinary rarity and purity of the air on these great buffalo plains near the base of the Rocky Mountains. Although their country abounds in salt springs, none of the Indian tribes I am familiar with use salt in any manner. The squaws cook their meat longer than we are accustomed to do, and I have found that meat thus cooked can be eaten and relished without salt or any other condiment.

The squaws not only prepare the food, but they make the dishes. The earthen bowls in which the food is served are manufactured by the women of this tribe in a thousand different forms and styles. They are made from a tough black clay and baked in kilns built for the purpose. Although they have not the secret of glazing, the pottery is as hard as that of our part of the country. Seemingly they are as serviceable as our iron pots, for they are hung over the fire and the meat is boiled in them. The pottery found in Indian tombs we regard as a novelty and place in museums. Here on any fine summer day women can be seen modelling bowls and trays by the hundred in many fanciful forms and passing them through the kilns.

When these women have dried the meat, cooked it, and made the dishes in which it is served, there remain the skins to prepare for the robes and dresses. The skindressing of the Indians is unequalled. The first part of the process is called graining. The skin is stretched on the ground or on a frame, the fleshy side up, and covered with a paste made from the brains of the buffalo or elk. Thus covered it lies for several days, when the women, with a chisel made from buffalo bone, scrape it until all the flesh is removed. This is so beautifully done that the skin seems apparently finished. But it remains to be smoked. A hole is dug two or three feet deep and in it a smothered fire is kindled of rotten wood, which produces a peculiar smoke. Over this a tent is made of buffalo-skins to keep the smoke from escaping, and in it the skins are hung for several days, when they are ready for use. As I have said, skins prepared in this manner dry perfectly soft no matter how long exposed to the rain.

While alluding to these women as the slaves of their husbands, since they perform all the acts of drudgery, while the men may be seen lying on the ground smoking at their ease, it is fair to say that the division of labor is more equal than appears. It is the man who mounts his horse and dashes among the wild herds of the prairie to secure the food for his wife and children, enduring many hardships, and frequently at the risk of his life, and it is the man who scours the prairie night and day to protect his wigwam from the assaults of the enemy. The relationship is, after all, one of mutual interest and mutual existence. Indeed, I do not believe that among the poorer classes of any civilized people on earth a better and a more voluntary division of the toils of conjugal life can be found than exists among the American Indians. One thing should be remarked. Every individual within the pale of the domestic relations is considered sacredly protected from the lash or a blow. There does not exist among the Indians one that has beaten his wife or child. Nor is there a pleasanter sight than to see the Indian women in the enjoyment of their domestic happiness, with their little children and dogs around them, and the little cupids taking their first lesson in archery, which is the most important feature of their education.

To the Indian woman's care of her pappoose is due, in my opinion, the handsome, well-proportioned forms of the American Indian, as much as to their constant exercise of their naked limbs in the open air. The child after birth is lashed to a straight board, and secured by bandages which pass around it in front and are laced on the back as tightly as is necessary to hold it in a straight and healthy position. The feet rest on a broad hoop placed around the foot of the cradle. In this manner the child is held on the mother's back by a broad strap that passes across her forehead. The child's position consequently is that of standing erect, a position that it seems to me contributes to a straight back, sound lungs, and a long life. These bandages that serve to hold the child in and keep it in place are frequently beautifully embroidered with porcupine quills and ingenious representations of horses and men. A broad hoop of elastic wood passes around in front of the child's face, to protect it in case of a fall, from the front of which is suspended a little toy of exquisite embroidery for the child to handle and amuse itself with. To this and other little trinkets hanging in front of it there are attached many little tinselled and tinkling things, of the brightest colors, to amuse both the eyes and the ears of the child. While travelling on horseback, the arms of the child are fastened under the bandages, so as not to be endangered if the cradle falls; and when at rest they are generally taken out, allowing the infant to reach and amuse itself with the little toys and trinkets that are placed before it and within its reach.

The child is carried in this manner until it is about seven months old, when it is taken out and carried on the back held within the folds of the robe. If the infant dies during the time that is allotted to it to be carried in this cradle, it is buried, and the disconsolate mother fills the cradle with black quills and feathers, in the parts which the child's body had occupied, and in this way carries it around with her wherever she goes for a year or more, with as much care as if her infant were alive and in it; and she often lays or stands it leaning against the side of the wigwam, where she is all day engaged in her needle-work, and chatting and talking to it as familiarly and affectionately as if it were her loved infant, instead of its shell, that she was talking to. So lasting and so strong is the affection of these women for the lost child, that it matters not how heavy or cruel their load, or how rugged the route they have to pass over, they will faithfully carry this, and carefully from day to day, and even more strictly perform their duties to it than if the child were alive and in it.

CHAPTER XI
MANDAN DANCES AND GAMES

THE Mandans, like all other tribes, lead lives of idleness and leisure, and of course devote a great deal of time to their sports and amusements, of which they have a great variety. Of these, dancing is one of the principal, and may be seen in a variety of forms – such as the buffalo dance, the boasting dance, the begging dance, the scalp dance, and a dozen other kinds of dances, all of which have their peculiar characters and meanings or objects.

These exercises are exceedingly grotesque in their appearance, and to the eye of a traveller who knows not their meaning or importance they are an uncouth and frightful display of starts, and jumps, and yelps, and jarring gutturals, which are sometimes truly terrifying. But when one gives them a little attention, and has been lucky enough to be initiated into their mysterious meaning, they become a subject of the most intense and exciting interest. Every dance has its peculiar step, and every step has its meaning; every dance also has its peculiar song, and that is so intricate and mysterious oftentimes that not one in ten of the young men who are dancing and singing it know the meaning of the song which they are chanting over. None but the medicinemen are allowed to understand them; and even they are generally only initiated into these secret arcana, on the payment of a liberal stipend for their tuition, which requires much application and study. There is evidently a set song and sentiment for every dance, for the songs are perfectly measured, and sung in exact time with the beat of the drum, and always with a uniform and invariable set of sounds and expressions, which clearly indicate certain sentiments, which are expressed by the voice, though sometimes not given in any known language whatever.

They have other dances and songs which are not so mystified, but which are sung and understood by every person in the tribe, being sung in their own language, with much poetry in them, and perfectly metered, but without rhyme.

My ears have been almost continually ringing since I came here, with the din of the yelping and beating of the drums; but I have for several days past been peculiarly engrossed, and my senses almost confounded with the stamping, and grunting, and bellowing of the buffalo dance, which closed a few days since at sunrise, thank Heaven, and which I must needs describe to you.

Buffaloes, it is known, are a sort of roaming creatures, congregating occasionally in huge masses, and strolling away about the country from east to west, or from north to south, or just where their whims or strange fancies may lead them; and the Mandans are sometimes, by this means, most unceremoniously left without anything to eat; and being a small tribe, and unwilling to risk their lives by going far from home in the face of their more powerful enemies, are oftentimes left almost in a state of starvation. In an emergency of this kind every man musters and brings out of his lodge his mask (the skin of the buffalo's head with the horns on), which he is obliged to keep in readiness for this occasion; and then commences the buffalo dance, of which I have above spoken, which is held for the purpose of making "buffalo come" (as they term it), of inducing the buffalo herds to change the direction of their wanderings and bend their course toward the Mandan village, and graze about on the beautiful hills and bluffs in its vicinity, where the Mandans can shoot them down and cook them as they want them for food.

For the most part of the year the young warriors and hunters, by riding out a mile or two from the village, can kill meat in abundance; and sometimes large herds of these animals may be seen grazing in full view of the village. There are other seasons also when the young men have ranged about the country as far as they are willing to risk their lives, on account of their enemies, without finding meat. This sad intelligence is brought back to the chiefs and doctors, who sit in solemn council and consult on the most expedient measures to be taken, until they are sure to decide upon the old and only expedient which "never has failed."

The chief issues his order to his runners or criers, who proclaim it through the village, and in a few minutes the dance begins. The place where this strange operation is carried on is in the public area in the centre of the village, and in front of the great medicine or mystery lodge. About ten or fifteen Mandans at a time join in the dance, each one with the skin of the buffalo's head (or mask), with the horns on, placed over his head, and in his hand his favorite bow or lance with which he used to slay the buffalo.

I mentioned that this dance always had the desired effect, that it never fails, nor can it, for it cannot be stopped (but is going incessantly day and night) until "buffalo come." Drums are beating and rattles are shaken, and songs and yells incessantly are shouted, and lookers-on stand ready, with masks on their heads and weapons in hand, to take the place of each one as he becomes fatigued and jumps out of the ring.

During this excitement spies, or "lookers," are kept on the hills in the neighborhood of the village, who, when they discover buffaloes in sight, give the signal by "throwing their robes." This is seen in the village and understood by the whole tribe. There is an immediate shout of thanks to the Great Spirit, and to the mystery-men and the dancers, who have, of course, combined to bring it about. Then comes the preparation for the chase.

Every man in the Mandan village is required to keep the mask of the buffalo hanging on a post at the head of his bed, which he can put on whenever he is called by the chiefs to dance for the coming of the buffaloes. The mask is put over the head and generally has a strip of skin the length of the animal with the tail attached. When a dancer becomes tired he signifies it by bending forward. Another then draws his bow upon him and hits him with a blunt arrow, when he falls to the ground like a buffalo, and is seized by the by-standers, who drag him out by the heels and go through the motions with their knives of skinning him and cutting him up, while another dancer with his mask on comes into the ring. This scene is kept up night and day until the "buffalo come." It is easy to see why the dance never fails.

The dance which I have just seen had lasted four days when the signal was given from a distant bluff. It was the more grateful from the fact that the chiefs and doctors had been giving out minimum rations from their private caches, and even their meat was almost used up. Instantly all was joy and gladness; the stamping of the horses was heard; the young men threw off their robes and shirts, and, snatching a handful of arrows from their quivers and stringing their sinewy bows, with a glance of their eyes and smiles for their sweethearts, mounted their ponies. While bows were twanging and spears were polished by running their blades into the ground, Louison Frénié, an interpreter of the Fur Company, galloped through the village with his rifle in his hand, his powder-flask at his side, his head and waist tied up with handkerchiefs, and his shirt-sleeves rolled up to his shoulders. The hunter's yell was on his lips and echoed through the village. He flew to the bluffs, and behind him over the graceful swells of the prairie galloped the young Indians.

All the hidden emergency stores were now brought out from the caches, and the village joined in a general carouse of eating; the dishes were half emptied and the bones, half picked, given to the dogs. Nor was I forgotten; generous bowls of pemmican and other food were sent to my painting-room. After this banquet, and after the dogs had licked the dishes, followed the usual games and other amusements, and mirth took possession of every corner of the village. Suddenly piercing screams were heard. Women and children scrambled to the tops of their wigwams, with their eyes and their hands stretched in agonizing earnestness to the prairie, while blackened warriors ran furiously through every winding maze of the village, and issuing their jarring gutturals of vengeance, as they snatched their deadly weapons from their lodges, and struck the reddened post as they furiously passed it by! Two of their hunters were bending their course down the sides of the bluff toward the village, and another broke suddenly out of a deep ravine, and yet another was seen dashing over and down the green hills, and all were goading on their horses at full speed! And then came another, and another, and all entered the village amid shouts and groans of the villagers who crowded around them. The story was told in their looks, for one was bleeding, and the blood that flowed from his naked breast had crimsoned his milk-white steed as it had dripped over him; another grasped in his left hand a scalp that was reeking in blood, and in the other his whip; another grasped nothing save the reins in one hand and the mane of the horse in the other, having thrown his bow and his arrows away and trusted to the fleetness of his horse for his safety. Yet the story was audibly told, and the fatal tragedy recited in irregular and almost suffocating ejaculations; the names of the dead were in turns pronounced, and screams and shrieks burst forth at their recital; murmurs and groans ran through the village, and this happy little community were in a moment smitten with sorrow and distraction.

Their proud band of hunters, who had started full of glee and mirth in the morning, had been surrounded by their enemy, the Sioux, and eight of them killed. The Sioux, who had probably reconnoitred their village during the night, and ascertained that they were dancing for buffaloes, laid a strategem to entrap them in the folowing manner: Some six or eight of them appeared the next morning (on a distant bluff, in sight of their sentinel) under the skins of buffaloes, imitating the movements of those animals while grazing, and being discovered by the sentinel, the intelligence was telegraphed to the village, which brought out their hunters as I have described. The masked buffaloes were seen grazing on the top of the high bluff, and when the hunters had approached within half a mile or so of them they suddenly disappeared over the hill. Louison Frénié, who was leading the little band of hunters, became at that moment suspicious of so strange a movement, and came to a halt.

"Look!" said a Mandan, pointing to a little ravine to the right, and at the foot of the hill, from which suddenly broke some forty or fifty furious Sioux, on fleet horses and under full whip, who were rushing upon them. They wheeled, and in front of them came another band more furious from the other side of the hill! They started for home, poor fellows, and strained every nerve; but the Sioux were too fleet for them. Several miles were run in this desperate race. Frénié got home with several of the Manhans, but eight were killed and scalped by the way. So ended the day and the hunt.

But all the dances of the Mandans are not liable to end so tragically. Of these, one of the most pleasing is the *sham fight* and sham scalp dance of the Mandan boys, which is a part of their regular exercise, and constitutes a material branch of their education. During the pleasant mornings of the summer, the little boys between the ages of seven and fifteen are called out, to the number of several hundred, and being divided into two companies, each of which is headed by some experienced warrior, who leads them on, in the character of a teacher, they are led out into the prairie at sunrise, where this curious discipline is regularly taught them. Their bodies are naked, and each one has a little bow in his hand and a number of arrows made of large spears of grass, which are harmless in their effects. Each one has also a little belt or girdle around his waist, in which he carries a knife made of a piece of wood and equally harmless; on the tops of their heads are slightly attached small tufts of grass, which answer as scalps, and in this plight they follow the dictates of their experienced leaders, who lead them through the judicious evolutions of Indian warfare, of feints, of retreats, of attacks – and at last to a general fight. Many manoeuvres are gone through, and eventually they are brought up face to face, within fifteen or twenty feet of each other, with their leaders at their head stimulating them on. Their bows are bent upon each other and their missiles flying, while they are dodging and fending them off.

If any one is struck with an arrow on any vital part of his body he is obliged to fall, and his adversary rushes up to him, places his foot upon him, and, snatching from his belt his wooden knife, grasps hold of his victim's scalp-lock of grass, and making a feint at it with his wooden knife, twitches it off and puts it into his belt, and enters again into the ranks and front of battle.

This mode of training generally lasts an hour or more in the morning, and is performed on an empty stomach, affording them a rigid and wholesome exercise, while they are instructed in the important science of war. Some five or six miles of ground are run over during these evolutions, giving suppleness to their limbs and strength to their muscles which last and benefit them through life.

After this exciting exhibition is ended, they all return to their village, where the chiefs and braves pay profound attention to their vaunting, and applaud them for their artifice and valor.

Those who have taken scalps then step forward, brandishing them and making their boast as they enter into the scalp dance (in which they are also instructed by their leaders or teachers), jumping and yelling, brandishing their scalps, and reciting their *sanguinary deeds*, to the great astonishment of their tender-aged sweethearts, who are gazing with wonder upon them.

The favorite amusement of the Mandans seems to be unknown to the neighboring tribes. This is called Tchung-kee, an attractive athletic exercise which is played unceasingly. Near the village is a pavement of clay which has been used for this game until it is as hard as a floor. Two champions are named and choose alternately the best players until the sides are made up. The bets are then made, and the stakes held by one of the chiefs or important men. The play then begins by two men, one from each side, starting off abreast at a little trot, one rolling in advance of them a little ring two or three inches in diameter cut out of a stone. Each man holds in his hand his tchung-kee. This is a stick about six feet long with little pieces of leather projecting from its sides an inch or more. Each player throws his tchung- kee before him as he runs by sliding it along the ground. His game is to have it in such position when it stops that the ring may fall on one of the pieces of leather. This counts for game, one, two, three, or four, according to the manner in which the leather catches the ring. The last winner has always the rolling of the ring, and both start and throw their tchung-kees together. If either fails to receive the ring, he gives up his place to another player. It is a game difficult to describe, but of great beauty and a fine physical exercise. These people often gamble away everything they possess, and will even stake their own liberty.

There are days on which I look on at games and plays until I am weary. Sometimes I lend a hand, but in such manner that I only furnish criticism and laughter for the women and children. It would be strange if a people having no office hours to attend to, no professions to study, did not spend the time spared from the chase for food in games and become proficient in them. One of these games among the Mandans they call the "game of the arrow." The young men having paid their entrance fee, a shirt, robe, pipe, or some other article, assemble a short distance away on the prairie, where each in turn sees how many arrows he can have in the air at the same time, shot from the same bow. To do this each archer holds in his bow hand from eight to ten arrows. The first arrow he sends to such height that it will remain in the air while the others follow. These are sent as rapidly as possible, and whoever gets up the greatest number takes the stake. One is surprised not so much at the distance the arrows are sent as at the rapidity with which they are fixed on the string, and their quick succession. One rarely sees Indians shooting at a target. I doubt if their skill would rival that of civilized people in this respect. The most successful use of the bow in the Indian country is on horseback, riding at full speed, with the object of drawing the bow suddenly and with instant effect. In this manner both game and enemies are killed.

The horses which the Indians ride in this country are invariably the wild horses which are found in great numbers on the prairies, and have, unquestionably, strayed from the Mexican borders, into which they were introduced by the Spanish invaders of that country, and now range and subsist themselves, in winter and sum- mer, over the vast plains of prairie that stretch from the Mexican frontiers to Lake Winnipeg on the north, a distance of three thousand miles. These horses are all of small stature, of the pony order, but a very hardy and tough animal, being able to perform for the Indians a continual and essential service. They are taken with the lasso, which is a long halter, or thong, made of rawhide, of some fifteen or twenty yards in length, which the Indians throw with great dexterity. It has a noose at one end of it, which drops over the head of the animal they wish to catch while running at full speed, when the Indian dismounts from his own horse and, holding to the end of the lasso, chokes the animal down, and afterward tames and converts him to his own use.

Scarcely a man in these regions is to be found who is not the owner of one or more of these horses, and in many instances of eight, ten, or even twenty, which he values as his own personal property.

"GAME OF THE ARROW" OR ARCHERY OR THE MANDANS

CHAPTER XII
O-KEE-PA – A RELIGIOUS CEREMONY

BEFORE I arrived at the Mandan village I had heard of its annual religious ceremony called O-kee-pa. While painting one of the chiefs I asked him when this ceremony would take place.

"As soon as the willow-trees are full-grown under the bank of the river," he replied.

I then asked him what the willow had to do with it.

"The twig which the bird brought to the Big Canoe was a willow bough and had full-grown leaves on it."

This from the lips of a wild man in the heart of the Indian country was indeed a surprise. I then asked him what bird he alluded to. Taking me by the arm, he led me through the wandering paths of the village until he discovered two mourning doves pecking at the side of one of the earth-covered wigwams. Pointing to it, he said: "There is the bird. It is great medicine."

I had previously been warned against harming any of the doves, of which there were numbers in the village, as they were held in great veneration.

In the centre of the village is an open space about a hundred and fifty feet in diameter where festivals and public games are held. In the centre of this space stands a hogshead about ten feet high, made of planks and hoops containing some of the choicest mysteries or medicine. Although it has remained there many years it is without a scratch. This hogshead is regarded as the symbol of the Big Canoe. The lodges around this open space have doors looking toward the centre. One of these is the medicine lodge, and in it is held the astounding ceremonies I am about to transcribe.

Thank God they are over, that I have seen them, and am able to tell them to the world, although I shrink from the task. The celebration began by the leading mysteryman presenting himself on the top of a wigwam one morning before sunrise, when he told the people he had discovered something very strange in the western horizon, and he believed that at the rising of the sun a great white man would enter the village from the west and open the medicine lodge. In a few moments the tops of the wigwams were covered with men, women and children on the lookout.

I was sitting at breakfast with the agent, Mr. Kipp, when we were suddenly startled by the shrieking and screaming of the women, the howling of the dogs, all in apparent alarm, preparing their weapons and securing their horses, as if an enemy were at their door. seized my sketch-book and we joined the crowd at the entrance of the picket, where at the distance of a mile or more a solitary human figure was seen descending the prairie hills and approaching the village in a straight line where the warriors were drawn up in battle array. The leader advanced and called out to the stranger to make his errand known and to tell from whence he came.

He replied that he had come from the high mountains in the West and he had come to open the medicine lodge of the Mandans, and that he must not be opposed or certain destruction would be the fate of the tribe.

The head chief and his council assembled in the council-house were sent for, and came in a body with their faces painted black. These recognized the visitor as one they had known before, and called him Nu-mohk-muck-a-nah (the first or only man), and invited him inside the picket.

The body of this strange personage, which was chiefly naked, was painted with white clay, so as to resemble at a little distance a white man; he wore a robe of four white wolfskins falling back over his shoulders; on his head he had a splendid head-dress made of two ravens' skins, and in his left hand he cautiously carried a large pipe, which he seemed to watch and guard as something of great importance. After passing the chiefs and braves as described, he approached the medicine or mystery lodge, which he had the means of opening, and which had been religiously closed during the year except for the performance of these religious rites.

Having opened and entered it, he called in four men whom he appointed to clean it out and put it in readiness for the ceremonies by sweeping it and strewing a profusion of green willow-boughs over its floor, and with them decorating its sides. Wild sage also, and many other aromatic herbs, they gathered from the prairies, and scattered over its floor, and over these were arranged a curious group of buffalo and human skulls and other articles, which were to be used during this strange and unaccountable transaction.

During the whole of this day, and while these prep-parations were making in the medicine lodge, Nu-mohk- muck-a-nah travelled through the village, stopping in front of every man's lodge, and crying until the owner of the lodge came out and asked who he was, and what was the matter, to which he replied by relating the sad catastrophe which had happened on the earth's surface by the overflowing of the waters, saying that "he was the only person saved from the universal calamity; that he landed his Big Canoe on a high mountain in the West, where he now resides; that he had come to open the medicine lodge, which must needs receive a present of some edged tool from the owner of every wigwam. that it may be sacrificed to the water; for, he says, "if this is not done there will be another flood, and no one will be saved, as it was with such tools that the Big Canoe was made."

Having visited every lodge or wigwam in the village, during the day, and having received such a present at each as a hatchet, a knife, etc. (which is undoubtedly always prepared and ready for the occasion), he returned at evening and deposited them in the medicine lodge, where they remained until the afternoon of the last day of the ceremony, when, as the final or closing scene, they were thrown into the river in a deep place, from a bank thirty feet high, and in presence of the whole village, from whence they can never be recovered, and where they were, undoubtedly, *sacrificed* to the Spirit of the Water.

During the first night of this strange character in the village no one could tell where he slept. As soon as he entered the cries of the people instantly ceased, and orders were given by the chiefs that the women and children should go to the wigwams and that the dogs should be muzzled, for the day belonged to the Great Spirit.

The next morning at sunrise Nu-mohk-muck-a-nah came out in front of the medicine lodge and called for all the young men who were candidates for the O-kee-pa honors. In a few moments about fifty young men, who I learned were those who had arrived at maturity during the year, appeared in a beautiful group, their graceful limbs naked but covered with clay from head to foot, some red, some white, yellow, blue, and green, each one carrying his shield of bull's hide on his left arm, his bow in his left hand and his medicine-bag in his right. In this manner they followed Nu-mohk-muck-a-nah, Indian file, into the lodge, where each one hung his bow, quiver, shield, and medicine-bag over him as he reclined on the floor of the wigwam. Nu-mohk-muck-a-nah took his place in the circle, and having lighted and smoked his medicine-pipe for their success, made them a short speech, in which he urged them to trust in the Great Spirit to protect them in the great ordeal they were to go through. He then called into the lodge the principal medicine-man of the tribe, whom he appointed O-kee-pa Ka-se-kah, or conductor of ceremonies by giving him the large pipe he had brought which is the symbol of authority. After this Nu-mohk-muck-a-nah shook hands with him and bade him good-by, saying that he would return to the West, whence he came, and be back in a year's time to open the medicine lodge again.

I was fortunate enough to be permitted to enter the lodge while the young men were being addressed. Although Mr. Kipp had lived in the village eight years he had never been allowed even to glance inside of the medicine lodge. Luckily I had only completed the portrait of the medicine-man in authority the day before, and he had been so pleased with it that he mounted a wigwam holding it up before the villagers, claiming that he must be the greatest man among the Mandans because I had painted his portrait before I painted the great chief. Because I could make so perfect a picture of him, even making his eyes move, I must be the greatest medicine-man of the whites. I was accordingly given this honor by the unanimous voice of the doctors, and pronounced Te-ho-pee-nee-wash-ee-waska-pooska, the white medicine painter.

We were now standing in front of the door of the medicine lodge trying to get a glimpse within, when the master of ceremonies came out and, taking me by the arm, led me within, allowing Mr. Kipp and the two clerks to follow through a vestibule of some length guarded with a double screen and two or three dark and frowning sentinels with spears and war-clubs in their hands. Here we took our seats, where for four days we sat from sunrise to sundown, and where I made many sketches of the scenes we witnessed, the accuracy of which Mr. Kipp and the two men have attested.

We were now in full view of everything that took place in the lodge. The master of ceremonies lay by a small fire in the centre, with his medicine-pipe in his hand, crying to the Great Spirit incessantly, and watching that none of the young men escape or hold any communication whatever with the people outside for four days, during which time they are not allowed to eat, drink, or sleep; for it is by such denial, producing great lassitude and even emaciation, that the young men are prepared for the tortures of the fourth day.

In addition to the preparations and arrangements of the interior of this sanctuary, as above described, there was a curious though a very strict arrangement of buffalo and human skulls placed on the floor of the lodge, and between them (which were divided into two parcels), and in front of the reclining group of young candidates, was a small and very delicate scaffold, elevated about five feet from the ground, made of four posts or crotches, not larger than a gun rod, and placed some four or five feet apart, supporting four equally delicate rods resting in the crotches, thus forming the frame of the scaffold, which was completed by a number of still smaller and more delicate sticks transversely resting upon them. On the centre of this little frame rested some small object, which I could not exactly understand from the distance of twenty or thirty feet which intervened between it and my eye. I started several times from my seat to approach it, but all eyes were instantly upon me, and every mouth in the assembly sent forth a hush-sh! which brought me back to my seat again; and I at length quieted my stifled curiosity as well as I could upon learning the fact that so sacred was that object, and so important its secrets or mysteries, that not *I* alone, but even the young men who were passing the ordeal, and all the village, save the conductor of the mysteries, were stopped from approaching it or knownig what it was.

This little mystery thing, whatever it was, had the appearance, from where I sat, of a small tortoise or frog lying on its back, with its head and legs quite extended, and wound and tasselled off with exceedingly delicate red and blue and yellow ribbons or tassels, and other bright-colored ornaments, and seemed, from the devotions paid to it, to be the very nucleus of their mysteries – the *sanctissimus sanctorum* from which seemed to emanate all the sanctity of their proceedings, and to which all seemed to be paying the highest devotional respect.

This strange yet important *essence of* their mysteries I made every inquiry about; but got no further information of than what I could learn by my eyes, at the distance at which I saw it, and from the silent respect which I saw paid to it. I tried with the doctors, and all of the *fraternity* answered me that that was *"great medicine"* assuring me that it "could not be told."

Immediately under the little frame or scaffold described, and on the floor of the lodge, was placed a knife, and by the side of it a bundle of splints or skewers, which were kept in readiness for the infliction of the cruelties directly to be explained. There were seen also, in this stage of the affair, a number of cords of rawhide hanging down from the top of the lodge, and passing through its roof, with which the young men were to be suspended by the splints passed through their flesh, and drawn up by men placed on the top of the lodge for the purpose, as will be described in a few moments.

There were also four articles of great veneration and importance lying on the floor of the lodge, which were sacks, containing in each some three or four gallons of water. These also were objects of superstitious regard, and made with great labor and much ingenuity; each one of them being constructed of the skin of the buffalo's neck, and most elaborately sewed together in the form of a large tortoise lying on its back, with a bunch of eagle's quills appended to it as a tail; and each of them having a stick, shaped like a drum-stick, lying on them, with which, in a subsequent stage of these ceremonies, as will be seen, they are beaten upon by several of their mystery-men, as a part of their music for the strange dances and mysteries. By the side of these sacks, which they call *Eeh-teeh-ka,* are two other articles of equal importance, which they call *Eeh-na-dee* (rattles), in the form of a gourd-shell made also of dried skins, and used at the same time as the others, in the music (or rather *noise* and *din*) for their dances, etc.

These four sacks of water have the appearance of very great antiquity; and by inquiring of my very ingenious friend and patron, the medicine man, after the ceremonies were over, he very gravely told me that "those four tortoises contained the waters from the four quarters of the world; that these waters had been contained therein ever since the settling down of the waters!" I did not think it best to advance any argument against so ridiculous a theory, and therefore could not even enquire or learn at what period they had been instituted, or how often or on what occasions the water in them had been changed or replenished.

I made several propositions, through my friend Mr. Kipp, the trader and interpreter, to purchase one of these strange things by offering them a very liberal price, to which I received in answer that these, and all the very numerous articles used in the ceremonies, being a *society property*, were sacred and could not be sold. So I abandoned all attempts to obtain anything beyond the exercise of my pencil. Even this they seemed to regard with apprehension as a sort of sacrilege.

Such, then, was the group and such the appearance of the interior of the medicine lodge during the first three and part of the fourth day of the Mandan religious ceremonies. The medicine-man had his young aspirants under his sole control, as was every article and implement to be used, and the sanctity of this gloomy and impressive interior which could not be entered without his permission. Meanwhile many curious and grotesque spectacles in connection with these ceremonies were taking place outside around the Big Canoe.

CHAPTER XIII
DANCES OF THE O-KEE-PA

WHILE the O-kee-pa is regarded by the Man- dans as a religious ceremony and is conducted in some parts with the solemnity of religious worship, there are three other distinct objects for which it is held. The first is the annual celebration of the subsidence of the great flood. The second is the Bel-lohck- na-pic (the bull dance), to which they attribute the coming of the buffalo to supply them with food for the coming year. The third is the testing of the young warriors.

It is the second of these, the bull dance, which was now being celebrated around the Big Canoe. This dance, which is exceedingly amusing and grotesque, is danced four times the first day, eight times the second day, twelve times the third day, and sixteen times the fourth day. There were eight dancers, whose bodies, limbs, and faces were entirely covered with black, red, and white paint. Each joint was marked with two big white rings, even to the joints of the under jaw and of the fingers and toes, and on their abdomens was the representation of a baby's face. Each one of the dancers had a lock of buffalo's hair tied around his ankles, and carried in the right hand a rattle and in the left a slender staff about six feet long. Over their backs they wore buffalo-skins with the horns, hoofs, and tails intact, while they looked out of the eyes as through a mask. Above the buffaloskin on his back each dancer carried a bunch of willow boughs the size of a sheaf of straw.

These eight dancers were divided into pairs, and took their positions on the four sides of the Big Canoe, representing the four points of the compass. Between each pair was another figure, with his back to the hogshead, keeping step with staff and rattles. The bodies of these four men were entirely naked beyond a kilt of eagle quills and ermine and very splendid head-dresses made of the same materials. Two of these figures were painted entirely black with pounded charcoal and grease, whom they called the "firmament or night," and the numerous white spots which were dotted all over their bodies they called "stars." The other two were painted from head to foot as red as vermilion could make them; these they said represented the day, and the white streaks which were painted up and down over their bodies were "ghosts which the morning rays were chasing away."

These twelve are the only persons actually engaged in this strange dance, which is each time repeated in the same form without the slightest variation. There are, however, a great number of characters engaged in giving the whole effect and wildness to this strange and laughable scene, each one acting well his part, and whose offices, strange and inexplicable as they are, I will endeavor to point out and explain as well as I can, from what I saw elucidated by their own descriptions. The bull dance was conducted by the master of ceremonies, O-kee-pa Ka-se-ka, carrying his medicinepipe, his body entirely naked, and covered even to his hair with yellow clay. At a signal for the dancers to assemble this old man danced out of the lodge singing a mournful strain until he reached the Big Canoe against which he leaned, continuing his strain. At this moment four patriarchal men whose bodies were painted red came out of the lodge carrying the four sacks of water, which they placed near the casks, and thumping on them with sticks and brandishing rattles, raised their voices to the highest pitch possible, and the dancing began, continuing for fifteen minutes or more in perfect time and without intermission.

While this was going on two men, whose naked bodies were covered with yellow clay and wearing the skins and masks of the grizzly bears, were growling and threatening to interfere with the ceremony. To appease them the women continued bringing dishes of meat, which, placed before them, were immediately seized by two men whose bodies and limbs were painted black while their heads, feet, and hands were whitened with clay. These men were called bald eagles and carried their prey to the prairie, where they were in turn chased by hundreds of small boys whose bodies were painted yellow, their heads white, and wearing tails of white deer's hair. These represented antelopes and eventually got the food.

Besides these were two men, their bodies naked and painted white, and their noses and feet painted black, representing swans; two men,

BUFFALO DANCE

whose bodies were curiously painted to represent rattlesnakes, each holding a rattle in one hand and a bunch of wild sage in the other; two men covered with buffalo-skins and wearing beaver tails at their belts; two men with their bodies painted brown, their heads and shoulders blue, and their noses red, who were called vultures, and two men wearing wolfskins, who pursued the antelope boys on the prairie to seize their food. All these characters closely copied the habits of the animals they imitated, and all had some peculiar songs, which they constantly sang and chanted during the dances, without perhaps knowing the meaning of them, since they are strictly medicine songs, and are kept as secrets even from the tribe. At the close of each of these bull dances all these animals and birds set up the howl or cry peculiar to their species in a deafening chorus, some dancing, some jumping, some apparently flying, the beavers clapping their tails, the rattlesnakes shaking their rattles, the bears striking with their paws, the wolves howling, the buffaloes rolling in the sand and rearing on their hind feet. Then all danced off together to an adjoining lodge used for painting their bodies and for rest between the dances. A medicine-man was allowed to show me the interior while they were ornamenting their bodies, and the most vivid imagination could scarcely conceive so wild and curious a scene. No man painted himself, but submitted like a statue to other hands. Each painter seemed to have a special department, and worked, ambitious of the effect when he turned out his figure. Of the one hundred and thirty men and boys engaged in this picturesque scene not a single inch of the natural color of their bodies or hair could be seen.

But alas! in the last of these dances, on the fouth day, in the midst of all their mirth and joy, and about noon, and in the height of all these exultations, an instant scream burst forth from the tops of the lodges – men, women, dogs, and all seemed actually to howl and shudder with alarm as they fixed their glaring eyeballs upon the prairie bluff, about a mile in the west, down the side of which a man was seen descending at full speed toward the village! This strange character darted about in a zigzag course in all directions on the prairie, like a boy in pursuit of a butterfly, until he approached the pickets of the village, when it was discovered that his body was entirely naked, and painted as black as a negro, with pounded charcoal and bear's grease. His body was therefore everywhere of a shining black, except occasionally white rings of an inch or more in diameter, which were marked here and there all over him, and frightful indentures of white around his mouth resembling canine teeth. Added to his hideous appearance, he gave the most frightful shrieks and screams as he dashed through the village and entered the terrified group, which was composed (in that quarter) chiefly of females, who had assembled to witness the amusements which were taking place around the Big Canoe.

This unearthly-looking creature carried in his two hands a wand or staff of eight or nine feet in length, with a red ball at the end of it, which he continually slid on the ground ahead of him as he ran. All eyes in the village, save those of the persons engaged in the dance, were centred upon him, and he made a desperate rush toward the women, who screamed for protection as they were endeavoring to retreat, and falling in groups upon each other as they were struggling to get out of his reach. In this moment of general terror and alarm there was an instant check, and all for a few moments were as silent as death.

The old master of ceremonies, who had run from his position at the Big Canoe, had met this monster of fiends, and, having thrust the medicine-pipe before him, held him still and immovable under its charm! This check gave the females an opportunity to get out of his reach, and when they were free from their danger, though all hearts beat yet with the instant excitement, their alarm soon cooled down into the most exorbitant laughter and shouts of applause at his sudden defeat, and the awkward and ridiculous posture in which he was stopped and held. The old man was braced stiff by his side, with his eyeballs glaring him in the face, while the medicine-pipe held in its mystic chains his *Satanic* Majesty, annulling all the powers of his magical wand, and also depriving him of the powers of locomotion! Surely no two human beings ever presented a more striking group than these two individuals did for a few moments, with their eyeballs set in direst mutual hatred upon each other, both struggling for the supremacy, relying on the potency of their medicine or mystery, the one held in check, with his body painted black, representing (or rather assuming to be) his Sable Majesty, O-kee-hee-de (the Evil Spirit) frowning everlasting vengeance on the other, who sternly gazed back at him with a look of exultation and contempt as he held him in check and disarmed under the charm of his sacred mystery-pipe.

In this distressing dilemma, an old woman came slyly up behind him and dashed a handful of yellow clay in his face. His body being covered with grease, after he had received handful after handful from every direction he was in a lamentable plight. One woman seizing his wand broke it in pieces over her knee, and others threw the bits in his face. His power thus gone, he began to cry, and bolting through the crowd ran for the prairie. But here he fell into a band of fresh women and girls, who assailed him with hisses and dirt and beat him with sticks. From these he at length escaped when the women entered the village, and the woman who had deprived him of his wand, supported on each side by two matrons, was lifted by four attendants on to the top of the medicine lodge, where she addressed the crowd. By virtue of her deeds she claimed the power of creation and of life and death; she was the father of all the buffaloes, and could make them come and go as she pleased. In return she demanded the handsomest woman's dress in the village, in which to lead the dance at the Feast of the Buffaloes, which was to take place that night.

After having presented this dress to her, the master of ceremonies said, "Young woman, you have gained great fame this day, and the honor of leading the dance to-night belongs to you."

She then ordered the bull dance to stop and the dancers to retire to their wigwam. The four musicians were then commanded to carry their tortoise drum into the medicine lodge, and the buffalo skulls to be hung on the four posts. This being done, the chiefs were invited to enter the medicine lodge, where the voluntary tortures of the young men were to begin.

CHAPTER XIV
THE MAKING OF BRAVES

THE third and last rite of these ceremonies is almost too revolting to be told were it not a part of the whole of this ancient religious celebration, founded on superstitions and mysteries of which the Mandans know not the origin, but constitute a material part of the code and forms of their belief.

The chiefs having seated themselves in their robes and splendid head-dresses on one side of the lodge, and the band of music placed in another part, the old medicine-man, the O-kee-pa Ka-se-ka, sat down by a little fire in the centre of the lodge and began smoking violently for the success of the young men, whose ordeal was about to take place. Around the room lay the emaciated group who had neither eaten, drunk, nor slept for nearly four days. The two men who were to inflict the tortures now entered and took their positions in the middle of the lodge. These were doubtless medicinemen. But their bodies were painted red and their hands and feet black, and the one who made the incisions wore a mask, that the young men would never know who inflicted their wounds. Moreover, the scars on their own bodies were conspicuously marked with paint, as evidence that they had passed through the same ordeal. The man with the mask carried a large, sharp-pointed knife with two edges that had been notched in order to inflict as much pain as possible. The other had in his hand a bundle of splints to be passed through the wounds as soon as the knife was withdrawn.

Toward these two men the pitiable candidates crawled one by one and submitted themselves. An inch or more of the flesh on each shoulder or each breast was taken up between the thumb and finger by the man who held the knife in his right hand, and the knife, which had been ground sharp on both edges, and then hacked and notched with the blade of another, to make it produce as much pain as possible, was forced through the flesh below the fingers, and, being withdrawn, was followed with a splint or skewer from the other, who held a bunch of such in his left hand and was ready to force them through the wound.

There were then two cords lowered down from the top of the lodge (by men who were placed on the lodge outside, for the purpose), which were fastened to these splints or skewers, and they instantly began to haul him up. He was thus raised until his body was suspended from the ground where he rested, until the knife and a splint were passed through the flesh or integuments in a similar manner on each arm below the shoulder (over the *brachialis externus*), below the elbow (over the *extensor carpi radialis*), on the thighs (over the *vastus externus*), and below the knees (over the *peroneus*).

In some instances they remained in a reclining position on the ground until this painful operation was finished, which was performed, in all instances, exactly on the same parts of the body and limbs, and which, in its progress, occupied some five or six minutes.

Each one was then instantly raised with the cords, until the weight of his body was suspended by them, and then, while the blood was streaming down their limbs, the by-standers hung upon the splints each man's appropriate shield, bow, and quiver, etc.; and in many instances the skull of a buffalo, with the horns on it, was attached to each lower arm and each lower leg, for the purpose, probably, of preventing, by their great weight, the struggling which might otherwise have taken place to their disadvantage while they were hung up.

When these things were all adjusted, each one was raised higher by the cords, until these weights all swung clear from the ground, leaving his feet, in most cases, some six or eight feet above the ground. In this plight they at once became appalling and frightful to look at – the flesh, to support the weight of their bodies, with the additional weights which were attached to them, was raised six or eight inches by the skewers, and their heads sunk forward on the breasts, or thrown backward, in a much more frightful condition, according to the way in which they were hung up.

The unflinching fortitude with which every one of them bore this part of the torture surpassed credulity; each one, as the knife was passed through his flesh, sustained an unchangeable countenance; and several of them, seeing me making sketches, beckoned me to look at their faces, which I watched through all this horrid operation, without being able to detect anything but the pleasantest smiles as they looked me in the eye, while I could hear the knife rip through the flesh, and feel enough of it myself to start involuntary and uncontrollable tears over my cheeks.

When the victim was suspended as above described, another candidate promptly gave himself into the bloody hands of the two executioners. Each then in his turn passed into the charge of others, who instantly introduced him to a new and improved stage of their refinements in cruelty.

Surrounded by imps and demons as they appear, a dozen or more, who seem to be concerting and devising means for his exquisite agony, gather around him, when one of the number advances toward him in a sneering manner, and commences turning him around with a pole which he brings in his hand for the purpose. This is done in a gentle manner at first, but gradually increased, when the brave fellow, whose proud spirit can control its agony no longer, bursts out in the most lamentable and heartrending cries that the human voice is capable of producing, crying forth a prayer to the Great Spirit to support and protect him in this dreadful trial, and continually repeating his confidence in his protection. In this condition he is continued to be turned, faster and faster – and there is no hope of escape from it nor chance for the slightest relief, until, by fainting, his voice falters and his struggling ceases, and he hangs, apparently, a still and lifeless corpse! When he is, by turning, gradually brought to this condition, which is generally done within ten or fifteen minutes, there is a close scrutiny passed upon him among his tormentors, who are checking and holding each other back as long as the least struggling or tremor can be discovered, lest he should be removed before he is, as they term it, "entirely dead."

When brought to this alarming and most frightful condition, and the turning has gradually ceased, as his voice and his strength have given out, leaving him to hang entirely still and apparently lifeless; when his tongue is distended from his mouth and his medicinebag, which he has affectionately and superstitiously clung to with his left hand, has dropped to the ground, the signal is given to the men on top of the lodge, by gently striking the cord with the pole below, when they very gradually and carefully lower him to the ground.

In this helpless condition he lies, like a loathsome corpse to look at, though in the keeping, as they call it, of the Great Spirit, whom he trusts will protect him, and enable him to get up and walk away. As soon as he is lowered to the ground thus, one of the by-standers advances and pulls out the two splints or pins from the breasts and shoulders, thereby disengaging him from the cords which hung him up, but leaving all the weights hanging to his flesh.

The excessive pain caused by this turning, and the sickening distress of the rotary motion, probably no human being but a Mandan ever knew. There were usually two or three bodies hanging at the same time.

When lowered they lay on the ground for several minutes like the dead, for no one is allowed to assist them. Each victim as he got strength dragged his body with all the weights to another part of the lodge, where sat an Indian with a hatchet and a dried buffalo skull before him, his body painted red and his feet and hands black, and over his face a mask. To him each held up the little finger of his left hand as a sacrifice to the Great Spirit, then, laying it on the buffalo skull, the executioner struck it off with one blow of the hatchet. In several instances I saw them also give the forefinger of the same hand, leaving only two to hold the bow. The young men seemed to take no notice of their wounds, and neither bleeding nor inflammation ensued, although arteries were severed. This was probably owing to the low circulation caused by their previous fasting.

During the whole of the time of this cruel part of these most extraordinary inflictions the chiefs and dignitaries of the tribe are looking on, to decide who are the hardiest and "stoutest-hearted" – who can hang the longest by his flesh before he faints, and who will be soonest up after he has been down – that they may know whom to appoint to lead a war-party or place at the most honorable and desperate post. The four old men are incessantly beating upon the sacks of water and singing the whole time, with their voices strained to the highest key, vaunting forth, for the encouragement of the young men, the power and efficacy of the medicinepipe, which has disarmed the monster O-kee-hee-de (the Evil Spirit) and driven him from the village, and will be sure to protect them and watch over them through their present severe trial.

As soon as six or eight had passed the ordeal as above described, they were led out of the lodge, with their weights hanging to their flesh and dragging on the ground, to undergo another, and a still more appalling mode of suffering in the centre of the village, and in presence of the whole nation, in the manner as follows:

The signal of the commencement of this part of the cruelties was given by the old master of ceremonies, who again ran out as in the buffalo dance, and leaning against the Big Canoe, with his medicine-pipe in his hand, began to cry. This was done several times in the afternoon, as often as there were six or eight who had passed the ordeal just described within the lodge, who were then taken out in the open area, in the presence of the whole village, with the buffalo skulls and other weights attached to their flesh and dragging on the ground! There were then in readiness, and prepared for the purpose, about twenty young men, selected of equal height and equal age, with their bodies chiefly naked, with beautiful (and similar) head-dresses of war-eagles' quills on their heads, and a wreath made of willow boughs held in the hands between them, connecting them in a chain or circle in which they ran around the Big Canoe, with all possible speed raising their voices in screams and yelps to the highest pitch that was possible, and keeping the curb or Big Canoe in the centre as their nucleus.

Then were led forward the young men who were further to suffer, and being placed at equal distances apart, and outside of the ring just described, each one was taken in charge by two athletic young men, fresh and strong, who stepped up to him, one on each side, and by wrapping a broad leather strap around his wrists, without tying it, grasped it firm underneath the hand, and stood prepared for what they call Eh-ke-nah-ka-nah-pick (the last race). This the spectator looking on would suppose was most correctly named, for he would think it was the last race they could possibly run in this world.

In this condition they stand, pale and ghastly from abstinence and loss of blood, until all are prepared and the word is given, when all start and run around, outside of the other ring; and each poor fellow, with his weights dragging on the ground, and his two conductors ran around the Big Canoe amid the deafening shouts of the spectators, who thus endeavored to drown the cries of the poor sufferers.

The ambition of these young warriors is to see who can run the longest without fainting, and who can soonest get his feet after fainting. However, so exhausted were they that the greater number fainted before they had run half the circle. They were then dragged with their faces on the ground until every weight attached to their flesh was left behind. This must be done to produce honorable scars, which could not be made by drawing out the splints. The flesh must be broken through, and to do this there were several instances in which the buffalo skulls adhered so long they were jumped upon by the by-standers as the victims were being dragged at full speed. In this pitiable condition each' sufferer was left praying to the Great Spirit for his recovery, while his two torturers, having dropped their willow boughs, ran for the prairie as if to escape punishment for their crime. This reliance on the Great Spirit for recovery is so implicit that no chief or relation would dare step forward to aid the victim. When at last he is able to rise he staggers like a drunken man to the wigwam, where his wounds are doubtless dressed and he is permitted to eat and sleep.

In this frightful scene, as in the buffalo dance, the whole nation was assembled as spectators, and all raised the most piercing and violent yells and screams they could possibly produce, to drown the cries of the suffering ones that no heart could even be touched with sympathy for them. I have mentioned before that six or eight of the young men were brought from the medicine lodge at a time, and when they were thus passed through this shocking ordeal, the medicine-men and the chiefs returned to the interior, where as many more were soon prepared and underwent a similar treatment; and after that another batch, and another, and so on, until the whole number, some forty-five or fifty, had run in this sickening circle, and, by leaving their weights, had opened the flesh for honorable scars. I say *all*, but there was one poor fellow, though (and I shudder to tell it), who was dragged around and around the circle, with the skull of an elk hanging to the flesh on one of his legs – several had jumped upon it, but to no effect, for the splint was under the sinew, which could not be broken. The dragging became every instant more and more furious, and the apprehensions for the poor fellow's life, apparent by the piteous howl which was set up for him by the multitude around; and at last the medicine-man ran, with his medicine-pipe in his hand, and held them in check, when the body was dropped and left upon the ground with the skull yet hanging to it. The boy, who was an extremely interesting and fine-looking youth, soon recovered his senses and his strength, looking deliberately at his torn and bleeding limbs, and also with the most pleasant smile of defiance, upon the misfortune which had now fallen to his peculiar lot, crawled through the crowd (instead of walking, which they are never again at liberty to do until the flesh is torn out and the article left) to the prairie, and over which, for the distance of half a mile, to a sequestered spot, without any attendant, where he laid three days and three nights yet longer, without food, and praying to the Great Spirit until suppuration took place in the wound, and by the decaying of the flesh the weight was dropped, and the splint also, which he dare not extricate in another way. At the end of this he crawled back to the village on his hands and knees, being too much emaciated to walk, and begged for something to eat, which was at once given him, and he was soon restored to health.

These extreme and difficult cases often occur, and I learn that in such instances the youth has it at his option to get rid of the weight that is thus left upon him in such way as he may choose, and some of those modes are almost more terrible than the affliction itself.

As soon as six or eight were thus treated as many more were led out of the medicine-lodge and went through the same or kindred ordeals until the entire fifty had suffered in succession. The number of wounds inflicted were required to be the same on each, and the number of weights the same, but the candidates had the choice of being suspended by the shoulders or the breast, and in the last race of being dragged, or of wandering in the prairies without food, until their weights were released by the decay of the flesh.

I inquired if any of the young men had lost their lives in this ceremony. In their recollection I was told there was once a young man who lay for three days on the ground before they were quite certain the Great Spirit did not intend to help him. They all spoke of his death, however, as a rather enviable fate. After the medicinelodge had been thus cleared of its victims, the master of ceremonies returned to it alone, and gathering up the edged tools that had been collected at the door of every man's wigwam, accompanied by all the tribe he went to the bank of the river, and sacrificed them to the water by throwing them into the deepest part that they might never be recovered. This part of the rites took place exactly at sundown and closed the scene, being the end of the Mandan religious ceremony.

The Feast of the Buffaloes, which follows the religious ceremonies, I did not see, but this has been described to me by another white man who had visited the Mandans. This is not to be confounded with the buffalo feast, which is another ceremony. In this case the buffaloes are the eight dancers described in the bull dance, with the medicine-men, the musicians, and the old chiefs, who are invited to participate by the young woman who disarmed the Evil Spirit and is for the time in temporary control of her tribe. Assisting her are eight or ten of the young married women, who serve the wooden bowls of food, pass the pipe, and dance. This feast partakes of the nature of a debauch, while all the rest of the village are required to keep within their wigwams.

CHAPTER XV
MANDAN LEGEND OF THE DELUGE

THAT THESE people should have a tradition of the Flood is by no means surprising, as I have learned from every tribe I have visited that they all have some high mountain in their vicinity where they insist upon it that the Big Canoe landed; but that these people should hold an annual celebration of the event, and the season of that decided by such circumstances as the full leaf of the willow, and the medicine-lodge opened by such a man as Nu-mohk-muck-a-na (who appears to be a white man), and making his appearance "from the high mountains of the West," and some other circumstances, is surely a very remarkable thing and requires some extraordinary attention.

This Nu-mohk-muck-a-na (first or only man) is undoubtedly some mystery or medicine-man of the tribe, who has gone out on the prairie on the evening previous, and having dressed and painted himself for the occasion, comes into the village in the morning, endeavoring to keep up the semblance of reality; for their tradition says that at a very ancient period such a man did actually come from the West ; that his body was of the white color, as this man's body is represented; that he wore a robe of four white wolfskins; his head-dress was made of two ravens' skins; and in his left hand was a huge pipe. He said he was at one time the only man – he told them of the destruction of everything on the earth's surface by the water; that he stopped in his Big Canoe on a high mountain in the West, where he landed and was saved; that the Mandans and all other people were bound to make yearly sacrifices of some edged tools to the water, for of such things the big canoe was made; that he instructed the Mandans how to build their medicinelodge, and taught them also the forms of these annual ceremonies, and told them that as long as they made these sacrifices, and performed their rites to the full letter, they might be assured of the fact that they would be the favorite people of the Almighty, and would always have enough to eat and drink; and that so soon as they should depart in one tittle from these forms they might be assured that their race would decrease and finally run out; and that they might date their nation's calamity to that omission or neglect.

It seems from their tradition of the willow branch and the dove that these people must have at some time come into contact with the civilized world, since these two emblems are peculiar to this tribe, although the tradition of the Deluge is held by every tribe. Two legends as related to me by old chiefs enforce this theory by seeming to relate to the transgression of Eve and the birth of Jesus. I will give you two curious stories I heard from several of the old chiefs that are evidently accredited traditions with their tribe:

"The Mandans, or People of the Pheasants, were the first people created in the world. Originally they lived inside the earth, where they raised many vines. One of these vines pushed its way through a hole in the earth overhead, and one of our young men climbed up it until he came out on top of the ground. Here he found himself on the banks of a river. He looked around and admired the prairies and the beautiful country about him. He also saw many buffaloes, and killed one with his bow and arrow and found the meat good to eat.

"He then came back and told what he had seen. Then a number of others climbed up the vine with him and saw the same things. Among those who went were two pretty girls, who were great favorites and permitted to go. There was also among those trying to climb up a large, fat woman, who was forbidden to go by the chiefs. But her curiosity was too great, and as soon as she got an opportunity, when no one was by, she began to climb the vine, and when she got partly up the vine broke under the great weight of her body and she fell down. She was very much hurt by the fall, but she did not die.

"The Mandans were very sorry about this, and she was forever disgraced for the calamity she had brought upon them, for no more Mandans could ever climb out, and those outside could never get back. These built the Mandan village, where it formerly stood far down the river, but the remainder of the Mandan people live under the ground to this day."

This story is told with great gravity by the chiefs and mystery-men, and the latter profess to talk with their friends under the earth and to frequently get their advice.

The next tradition runs thus:

"At a very ancient period, O-kee-hee-de (the Evil Spirit, the black fellow mentioned in the religious ceremonies) came to the Mandan village with Nu-mohk- muck-a-na (the first or only man) from the West, and sat down by a woman who had but one eye and was hoeing corn. Her daughter, who was very pretty, came up to her, and the Evil Spirit desired her to go and bring some water, but wished that, before she started, she would come to him and eat some buffalo meat. He told her to take a piece out of his side, which she did, and ate it, which proved to be buffalo fat. She then went for the water, which she brought, and met them in the village where they had walked, and they both drank of it.

"The girl then went off to the upper Mandan village without telling any one. There was great excitement in the tribe, for she could not be found. When she was discovered a child had been born to her. Owing to these strange circumstances they believed that this child would be 'great medicine' and important to the welfare of the tribe. This soon became true in the wonderful things he did at a very early age. Among other miracles he performed, when the Mandans were like to starve, he gave them four buffalo bulls, which filled the whole village, leaving as much meat as there was before they had eaten, and saying that these four bulls would supply them forever. Nu-mohk-muck-a-na was bent on the destruction of the child, and, after making many fruitless searches for it, found it hidden in a dark place, and put it to death by throwing it into the river.

"When O-kee-hee-de heard of the death of this child he sought for Nu-mohk-muck-a-na with intent to kill him. He traced him a long distance, and at length found him at Heart River, about seventy miles below the village, with the big medicine-pipe in his hand, the charm or mystery of which protects him from all of his enemies. They soon agreed, however, to become friends, smoked the big pipe together, and returned to the Mandan village. The Evil Spirit was satisfied, and Nuh-mohk-muck-a-na told the Mandans never to pass Heart River to live, for it was the centre of the world, and to live beyond it would be destruction to them; and he named it Nat-com-pa-sa-hah (heart or centre of the world)."

I am travelling in this country not to prove theories, but to see all that I am able to see and to tell it in the simplest manner. But I find so many peculiarities in this decaying tribe that I am led to believe that it is an amalgam of some foreign and some aboriginal stock. I should like, for example, to revive inquiry concerning the ten ships that sailed from north Wales, under Prince Madoc, in the early part of the fourteenth century, for this country. It has been pretty clearly shown that it landed somewhere on the coast of the Gulf of Mexico, and the legends and poetry of Wales relate that it settled somewhere in the interior of America, where it remained mingled with the Indian tribes.

In no other tribe have I met anything that might seem to account for the existence of this colony. Among the Mandans there is much. The Mandan method of constructing their houses is much like that of the rude peasant huts of north Wales. The pottery made by the Mandans is very similar to that made in Wales at the present time, and is exactly like that found in the tumuli on the banks of the Ohio and Muskingham Rivers. This seems to suggest that the Mandans formerly lived by those rivers. A peculiar and beautiful sort of blue beads is made by the Mandans, the secret of which they carefully guard. These beads command a high price among the neighboring tribes, and the Fur Company has vainly made liberal offers to buy from them the secret of their composition. Beads like these and those found in the tumuli are now manufactured in Wales.

Moreover, the canoes or boats of the Mandans differ from those of all other tribes. These are precisely like the Welsh coracle. They are made by stretching a bull's hide over a frame of willow rods bent and interlocked, and are pulled over the water by the paddle in the same manner as the coracle is pulled, by reaching forward with the paddle instead of passing it by the side of the boat, which is nearly round, with the paddler seated or kneeling in front. From the translation of their name, Nu-mah-ka-kee (pheasants), the inference is that at one time they lived much farther south, since the pheasant is not found on the prairies of the upper Missouri, but exists in numbers in the forests of Ohio and Indiana. Their familiar name – Mandan – is not an Indian word. They themselves know nothing of the name or how they got it.

But the word Mandan, in the Welsh language, means red dye. Now the Man-dans are celebrated among the tribes for their beautiful dyes. It seems a reasonable conjecture that the half-castes, who were the result of intermarriage with the Indians, formed, as is the custom, a separate but adjacent village, supporting themselves by embroidery with porcupine quills, to which they gave the dyes for which the Mandans are famous, and were called by their Welsh neighbors, in the Welsh language, Man-dans, or red dyers.

At the time of the extermination of the colony by the savages, those who intermarried with the Indians doubtless escaped. Forming a separate community and living on the hunting lands of the powerful tribe, they were repeatedly obliged to move. This fact the numerous remains of their old lodges, which cannot be mistaken for those of other tribes on the Missouri River, clearly show.

When an Indian story is told it is, like all other gifts, "to be taken for what it is worth," and for any seeming inconsistency in their traditions there is no remedy; for, as far as I have tried to reconcile them by reasoning with or questioning them, I have been entirely defeated, and, more than that, have generally incurred their distrust and ill-will. One of the Mandan doctors told me very gravely a few days since that the earth was a large tortoise, that it carried the dirt on its back; that a tribe of people, who are now dead and whose faces were white, used to dig down very deep in this ground to catch *badgers;* and that one day they stuck a knife through the tortoise-shell and it sunk down so that the water ran over its back and drowned all but one man. And on the next day, while I was painting his portrait, he told me there were *four tortoises* – one in the north, one in the east, one in the south, and one in the west; that each one of these rained ten days, and the water covered over the earth.

I have dwelt longer on the appearance, customs, and peculiarities of this tribe because I believe them to be a people of different origin from the other tribes. This seems the more important because the powerful Sioux are continually waging war against them, and they are not likely to hold out long in their struggle for existence.[1]

---

[1] The Mandans were entirely destroyed as a tribe by an epidemic of small pox in 1837. — Ed.

From the ignorant and barbarous and disgusting customs just recited the world would naturally infer that these people must be the most cruel and inhuman beings in the world; yet such is not the case, and it becomes my duty to say it – a better, more honest, hospitable, and kind people, as a community, are not to be found in the world. No set *of* men that ever I associated with have better hearts than the Mandans, and none are quicker to embrace and welcome a white man than they are; none will press him closer to his bosom, that the pulsation of his heart may be felt, than a Mandan; and no man in any country will keep his word and guard his honor more closely.

CHAPTER XVI
CORN DANCE OF THE MINATAREES

THE MINATAREES, or people of the willows, is a small tribe occupying three villages on the river Knife, which meanders through a lovely prairie into the Missouri. The Minatarees are undoubtedly a part of the Crow tribe, which they resemble in appearance and stature, and from which they were doubtless run off by a war party. At present they are part of the Mandan confederacy, whose wigwams and many of whose customs they have adopted. Although scarcely a man in the tribe can speak Mandan, the Mandans can speak the tongue of the Minatarees, who, by the way, are called by the French traders Gros Ventres.

Their chief sachem, whose guest I am, is a patriarchal man named Eeh-tohk-pah-shee-pee-shah (the black moccasin), who claims more than a "hundred snows." His voice and sight are nearly gone, but his gestures are still energetic and youthful. I have been treated in the kindest manner by this old chief, and have painted his portrait seated on the floor of his wigwam smoking his pipe, a beautiful Crow robe thrown around him, and his hair wound in the form of a cone on the top of his head and fastened by a wooden pin.

As I painted he related to me some of the extraordinary events of his life. He distinctly recalls Lewis and Clarke, who have told how kindly they were treated by this chief. He inquired earnestly for Red Hair and Long Knife, as he called them. I told him that Long Knife had long been dead, but that Red Hair lived in St. Louis and would be glad to hear of him. This pleased him greatly.

I have also painted his son, the Red Thunder, who is one of the most desperate of the Minatarees, who are a warlike people, unlike their neighbors the Mandans. He was painted in his war-dress; that is, he was almost naked, and his body so profusely daubed with red and black paint that it was almost disguised. This is the custom of all Indian warriors, the chief only pluming himself to lead his band and form a conspicuous target for the enemy.

The women of this tribe are unusually good-looking, voluptuous, and free with their bewitching smiles. But I have only been able to get one to consent to be painted, and she was compelled to stand for her portrait by her relatives, who were of the family of the old chief. All the while she modestly urged that "she was not pretty enough to be painted and her picture would be laughed at." She wore a beautiful costume of the skin of the mountain-sheep, handsomely embroidered with quills and beads, and even if she were not comely, the beauty of her name, Seet-se-be-a (the mid-day sun), •would make up for it.

The only places where I find I can write is under the shade of some remote tree, or in my bed, where I now am, lying on sacking of buffalo hide, and surrounded by curtains made from the skins of the elk or buffalo. Meanwhile the roar and unintelligible din of savage conviviality is going on under the same roof. There are other distinguished guests here besides myself. Two Crow chiefs are visiting Black Moccasin in return for a visit made the Crows by several Minatarees. I have already said that no people present a more picturesque and thrilling appearance than the Crows in all their plumes and trappings in a war parade or sham fight.

From among these showy fellows, who have been entertaining us and pleasing themselves with their extraordinary feats of horsemanship, I have selected one of the most conspicuous, and transferred him and his horse, with arms and trappings, as faithfully as I could, to the canvas, for the information of the world, who will learn vastly more from lines and colors than they could from oral or written delineations.

I have painted him as he sat for me, balanced on his leaping wild horse, with his shield and quiver slung on his back and his long lance decorated with the eagle's quills trailed in his right hand. His shirt and his leggings and moccasins were of the mountain-goat skins, beautifully dressed, and their seams everywhere fringed with a profusion of scalp-locks taken from the heads of his enemies slain in battle. His long hair, which reached almost to the ground while he was standing on his feet, was now lifted in the air and floating in black waves over the hips of his leaping charger. On his head and over his shining black locks he wore a magnificent crest or head-dress made of the quills of the war-eagle and ermine-skins. On his horse's head also was another of equal beauty and precisely the same in pattern and material. Added to these ornaments there were yet many others which contributed to his picturesque appearance, and among them a beautiful netting of various colors that completely covered and almost obscured the horse's head and neck, and extended over its back and its hips, where it terminated in a most extravagant and magnificent crupper, embossed and fringed with rows of beautiful shells and porcupine quills of various colors.

With all these pictuesque trappings about him, with a noble figure and the stamp of a wild gentleman on his face, he leaned gracefully forward, his long locks and fringes floating in the wind, sending forth startling though smothered yelps in unison with the leaps of his wild horse. He was clearly pleased at displaying in this manner the extraordinary skill in the managment of his horse, as well as the graceful motion of his weapons as he brandished them in the air, and of his ornaments as they floated in the wind.

These people raise an abundance of corn or maize, and it is my good fortune to visit them in the season of their festivities, which annually take place when the ears of corn are of the proper size for eating. The green corn is considered a great luxury by all those tribes who cultivate it, and is ready for eating as soon as the ear is of full size and the kernels are expanded to their full growth but are yet soft and pulpy. In this green state of the corn it is boiled and dealt out in great profusion to the whole tribe, who feast and surfeit upon it while it lasts, rendering thanks to the Great Spirit for the return of this joyful season, which they do by making sacrifices, by dancing, and singing songs of thanksgiving. This joyful occasion is one valued alike, and conducted in a similar manner, by most of the tribes who raise the corn, however remote they may be from each other. It lasts but for a week or ten days, being limited to the longest term that the corn remains in this tender and palatable state, during which time all hunting and all war excursions and all other avocations are positively dispensed with, and all join in the most excessive indulgence of gluttony and conviviality that can possibly be conceived. The fields of corn are generally pretty well stripped during this excess, and the poor improvident Indian thanks the Great Spirit for the indulgence he has had, and is satisfied to ripen merely the few ears that are necessary for his next year's planting, without reproaching himself for his wanton lavishness, which has laid waste his fine fields and robbed him of the golden harvest which might have gladdened his heart, with those of his wife and little children, through the cold and dreariness of winter.

The most remarkable feature of these joyous occasions is the *green-corn dance*, which is always given as preparatory to the feast and by most of the tribes in the following manner:

At the usual season, and the time when from the outward appearance of the stalks and ears of the corn it is supposed to be nearly ready for use, several of the old women, who are the owners of fields or patches of corn (for such are the proprietors and cultivators of all crops in Indian countries, the men never turning their hands to such degrading occupations), are delegated by the medicine-men to look at the corn fields every morning at sunrise, and bring into the council-house, where the kettle is ready, several ears of corn, the husks of which the women are not allowed to break open or even to peep through. The women then are from day to day discharged and the doctors left to decide, until, from repeated examinations, they come to the decision that it will do, when they despatch *runners* or *criers*, announcing to every part of the village or tribe that the Great Spirit has been kind to them, and that they must all meet on the next day to return thanks for his goodness; that all must empty their stomachs and prepare for the feast that is approaching.

On the day appointed by the doctors the villagers are all assembled, and in the midst of the group a kettle is hung over a fire and filled with the green corn, which is well boiled, to be given to the Great Spirit as a sacrifice necessary to be made before any one can indulge the cravings of his appetite. While this first kettleful is boiling, four medicine-men, with a stalk of the corn in one hand and a rattle (she-she-quoi) in the other, and with their bodies painted with white clay, dance around the kettle, chanting a song of thanksgiving to the Great Spirit to whom the offering is to be made. At the same time a number of warriors are dancing around in a more extended circle, with stalks of the corn in their hands, and joining also in the song of thanksgiving, while the villagers are all assembled and looking on. During this scene there is an arrangement of wooden bowls laid upon the ground, in which the feast is to be dealt out, each one using a spoon made of the buffalo or mountainsheep's horn.

In this wise the dance continues until the doctors decide that the corn is sufficiently boiled; it then stops for a few moments, and again assumes a different form and a different song while the doctors are placing the ears on a little scaffold of sticks, which they erect immediately over the fire, where it is entirely consumed as they join again in the dance around it.

The fire is then removed, and with it the ashes, which together are buried in the ground, and *new fire* is originated, on the same spot where the old one was, by friction. This is done with desperate and painful exertion by three men seated on the ground, facing each other and violently drilling the end of a stick into a hard block of wood by rolling it between the hands, each one catching it in turn from the others without allowing the motion to stop until smoke, and at last a spark of fire, is seen and caught in a piece of spunk, when there is great rejoicing in the crowd. With this a fire is kindled and the kettle of corn again boiled for the feast at which the chiefs, doctors, and warriors are seated. After this permission is given to the whole tribe to indulge, which they do to excess and until the corn is too hard for mastication.

Having heard that I was "great medicine," a party of young men, accompanied by some of the chiefs and doctors, came in a formal body to present a grievance which it was hoped I might remedy. After several profound speeches, it appeared that a few years ago an unknown small animal was seen stealing slyly among the pots and kettles of one of the chief's wigwams. It was described as having the size of a ground-squirrel, but with a long, round tail, and was regarded as such "great medicine" that hundreds came to see it. On one occasion this little animal was seen devouring a deer-mouse, which is very destructive to the wearing apparel of the Indians. It was at once decided that the little creature had been sent by the Great Spirit to protect their clothing, and a council issued a solemn decree for its preservation. Having been thus preserved, the numbers of these little animals, which my man Batiste calls Monsieur Ratipon, had so increased that the wigwams were now infested by rats, the caches that contained the corn and other food were robbed, and the very pavements of their wigwams were so vaulted and sapped that they were falling in. The object of this meeting was to see if I could not relieve them of this public calamity. I could only assure them of my deep regret, but there was too much medicine in the thing for me to undertake it.

As I wished to visit another Minataree village on the other side of the river Knife, the old chief gave directions to one of the numerous women of his household, who took upon her head a skin canoe, called in this country a bull boat, made in the form of a tub, of buffalo's hide, and, carrying it to the water's edge, made signs for the three of us to get in. When we were seated flat in the bottom, with scarcely room to adjust our legs and our feet (as we sat necessarily facing each other), she stepped before the boat, and, pulling it along, waded toward the deeper water, with her back toward us, carefully with the other hand attending to her dress. This seemed to be but a light slip, floating upon the surface until the water was above her waist, when it was instantly turned off, over her head, and thrown ashore, and she boldly plunged forward, swimming and drawing the boat with one hand, which she did with apparent ease. In this manner we were conveyed to the middle of the stream, where we were soon surrounded by a dozen or more beautiful girls, from twelve to fifteen and eighteen years of age, who were at that time bathing on the opposite shore.

They all swam in a bold and graceful manner, and as confidently as so many otters or beavers, as they gathered around us, with their long black hair floating about on the water, while their faces were glowing with jokes and fun, which they were cracking about us, and which we could not understand.

In the midst of this delightful little aquatic group we three sat in our little skin-bound tub (like the "three wise men of Gotham who went to sea in a bowl," etc.), floating along down the current, losing sight and all thoughts of the shore, which was equidistant from us on either side, whilst we were amusing ourselves with the playfulness of these dear little creatures who were floating about under the clear blue water, catching their hands onto the sides of our boat, occasionally raising one-half of their bodies out of the water, and sinking again, like so many mermaids.

In the midst of this bewildering and tantalizing entertainment, in which poor Batiste and Bogard, as well as myself, were all taking infinite pleasure, and which we supposed was all intended for our especial amusement, we found ourselves suddenly in the delightful dilemma of floating down the current in the middle of the river, and of being turned round and round, to the excessive amusement of the villagers, who were laughing at us from the shore, as well as these little tyros, whose delicate hands were besetting our tub on all sides, and for an escape from whom, or for fending off, we had neither an oar nor anything else that we could wield in self-defence or for self-preservation. In this awkward predicament our feelings of excessive admiration were immediately changed to those of exceeding vexation as we now learned that they had peremptorily discharged from her occupation our fair conductress, who had undertaken to ferry us safely across the river, and had also very ingeniously laid their plans, of which we had been ignorant until the present moment, to extort from us in this way some little evidences of our liberality, which, in fact, it was impossible to refuse them, after so liberal and bewitching an exhibition on their part, as well as from the imperative obligation which the awkwardness of our situation had laid us under. I had some awls in my pockets, which I presented to them, and also a few strings of beautiful beads, which I placed over their delicate necks as they raised them out of the water by the side of our boat. They all then joined in conducting our craft to the shore, by swimming by the sides of and behind it, pushing it along in the direction where they designed to land it, until the water became so shallow that their feet were upon the bottom, when they waded along with great coyness, dragging us toward the shore so long as their bodies, in a crouching position, could possibly be half concealed under the water. They then gave our boat the last push for the shore, and, raising a loud and exulting laugh, plunged back again into the river, leaving us the only alternative of sitting still where we were or of stepping out into the water at half-leg deep and of wading to the shore, which we at once did, and soon escaped from the view of our little tormentors, and the numerous lookers-on, on our way to the upper village which I have before mentioned.

Here I was very politely treated by Yellow Moccasin, quite an old man, and who seemed to be chief of this band or family, constituting their little community of thirty or forty lodges, averaging perhaps twenty persons to each. I was feasted in this man's lodge, and afterward invited to accompany him and several others to a beautiful prairie, a mile or so above the village, where the young men and young women of this town, and many from the village below, had assembled for their amusements, the chief of which seemed to be that of racing their horses. In the midst of these scenes, after I had been for some time a looker-on, and had felt some considerable degree of sympathy for a fine- looking young fellow, whose horse had been twice beaten on the course, and whose losses had been considerable – for which his sister, a very modest and pretty girl, was most piteously howling and crying – I selected and brought forward an ordinary-looking pony, that was evidently too fat and too sleek to run against his fine-limbed little horse that had disappointed his high hopes; and I began to comment extravagantly upon its muscle, etc., when I discovered him evidently cheering up with the hope of getting me and my pony onto the turf with him, for which he soon made me a proposition. I, having lauded the limbs of my little nag too much to "back out," agreed to run a short race with him of half a mile, for three yards of scarlet cloth, a knife, and half a dozen strings of beads, which I was willing to stake against a handsome pair of leggings, which he was wearing at the time. The greatest imaginable excitement was now raised among the crowd by this arrangement, to see a white man preparing to run with an Indian jockey, and that with a scrub of a pony in whose powers of running no Indian had the least confidence. Yet there was no one in the crowd who dared to take up the several other little bets I was willing to tender (merely for their amusement and for their final exultation), owing, undoubtedly, to the bold and confident manner in which I had ventured on the merits of this little horse, which the tribe had all overlooked and needs must have some *medicine* about it.

So far was this panic carried that even my champion was ready to withdraw, but his friends encouraged him, and at length we galloped our horses to the other end of the course, accompanied by a number of horsemen to see the "set-off." Here a condition was named to me that I had not anticipated. In all the races of this day the riders were to be naked and to ride a naked horse. I found that remonstrance availed little, and as I had volunteered to ride to gratify them it seemed wise to comply. Accordingly I took off my clothes, straddled the naked back of my round and glossy little pony, by the side of my competitor, who was also mounted and stripped to the skin eager for the start.

Can any one imagine that a man in middle life could be so suddenly transported back to infancy and breathe the air of naked, untasted liberty. If not, disrobe, and fancy yourself, as I was, naked, with my trembling little steed under me, and the cool breeze ready to close and embrace me, as it did the next moment when we "were off." Though my little Pegasus seemed to dart through the clouds, and I to be wafted on the wings of Mercury, yet my red adversary soon left me far behind. No longer a competitor, I wheeled to the left and made the circuit of the prairie back to the starting-point, much to the satisfaction of the jockeys, but greatly to the disappointment of the women and children, who had come out in throngs to witness the "coming out" of the white medicine-man.

I clothed myself rapidly and came back acknowledging my defeat and the superior skill of my competitor, as well as the wonderful muscle of his little charger, which pleased him greatly. His sister's disappointment I soon turned to joy by giving her a fine scarlet robe and a profusion of varicolored beads, which she was soon parading on her copper-colored neck.

The Minatarees as well as the Mandans had suffered for some months for want of meat. It was feared that the buffalo herds were emigrating and actual starvation might ensue. Suddenly one morning a herd was sighted, and a hundred or more young men jumped on their horses, with their weapons, and made for the prairie. The chief offered me one of his horses and said I had better go and see an interesting sight. I took my pencil and sketch-book and took my position in the rear, where I could witness every manoeuvre. The plan of attack in this country is called a "surround." The hunters were all mounted on their "buffalo horses," and armed with bows, arrows, and long lances.

Dividing into two columns and taking opposite directions, they drew themselves gradually around the herd a mile or more distant from it, forming a circle of horsemen at equal distances apart, who gradually closed in upon them with a moderate pace, at a signal given. The unsuspecting herd at length "got the wind" of the approaching enemy, and fled in a mass in the greatest confusion. To the point where they were aiming to cross the line the horsemen were seen at full speed, gathering and forming in a column, brandishing their weapons, and yelling in the most frightful manner, by which means they turned the black and rushing mass, which moved off in an opposite direction, where they were again met and foiled in a similar manner and wheeled back in utter confusion. By this time the horsemen had closed in from all directions, forming a continuous line around them, while the poor affrighted animals were eddying about in a crowded and confused mass, hooking and climbing upon each other, when the work of death commenced. I had ridden up in the rear and occupied an elevated position at a few rods' distance, from which I could (like the general of a battlefield) survey from my horse's back the nature and the progress of the grand mêlée, but (unlike him) without the power of issuing a command or in any way directing its issue.

In this grand turmoil a cloud of dust was soon raised, obscuring the throng where the hunters were galloping their horses around and driving the whizzing arrows or their long lances to the hearts of these noble animals. These, in many instances becoming infuriated with deadly wounds in their sides, plunged forward at the sides of their assailants' horses, sometimes goring them to death at a lunge and putting their dismounted riders to flight for their lives. Sometimes their dense crowd was opened, and the blinded horsemen, too intent on their prey amid the cloud of dust, were hemmed and wedged in amid the crowding beasts, over whose backs they were obliged to leap for security, leaving their horses to the fate that might await them in the results of this wild and desperate war. Many were the bulls that turned upon their assailants and met them with desperate resistance, and many were the warriors who were dismounted and saved themselves by the superior muscles of their legs; some, who were closely pursued by the bulls, wheeled suddenly around, and, snatching the part of a buffalo-robe from around their waists, threw it over the horns and the eyes of the infuriated beast, and darting by its side drove the arrow or the lance to its heart. Others suddenly dashed off upon the prairies by the side of the affrighted animals which had escaped from the throng, and, closely escorting them for a few rods, brought down their hearts' blood in streams and their huge carcasses upon the green and enamelled turf.

I had sat in trembling silence upon my horse and witnessed this extraordinary scene, which allowed not one of these animals to escape out of my sight. Many plunged off upon the prairie for a distance, but were overtaken and killed; and although I could not distinctly estimate the number that were slain, yet I am sure that some hundreds of these noble animals fell in this grand mêlée,

The scene after the battle was over was novel and curious in the extreme; the hunters were moving about among the dead and dying animals, leading their horses by their halters, and claiming their victims by the private marks upon the arrows, which they were drawing from the wounds in the animals' sides.

The poor affrighted creatures that had occasionally dashed through the ranks of their enemy and sought safety in flight upon the prairie (and in some instances had undoubtedly gained it), I saw stand awhile, looking back when they turned, and, as if bent on their own destruction, retrace their steps and mingle themselves and their deaths with those of the dying throng. Others had fled to a distance on the prairies, and for want of company, of friends or of foes, had stood and gazed on till the battle-scene was over, seemingly taking pains to stay and hold their lives in readiness for their destroyers until the general destruction was over, to whose weapons they fell easy victims – making the slaughter complete.

After this scene, and after arrows had been claimed and recovered, a general council was held, when all hands were seated on the ground and a few pipes smoked, after which all mounted their horses and rode back to the village.

Several of the warriors were sent to the chief, to inform him of their success; and the same intelligence was soon communicated by little squads to every family in the village, and preparations were at once made for securing the meat. For this purpose some hundreds of women and children, to whose lot fall all the drudgeries of Indian life, started out upon the trail which led them to the battle-field, where they spent the day in skinning the animals and cutting up the meat, which was mostly brought into the villages on their backs, as they tugged and sweated under their enormous and cruel loads.

I rode out to see this curious scene, and I regret ex- exceedgly that I kept no memorandum of it in my sketch-book. Amid the throng of women and children that had been assembled, and all of whom seemed busily at work, were many superannuated and disabled nags, which they had brought out to assist in carrying in the meat, and at least one thousand semi-loup dogs and whelps, whose keen appetites and sagacity had brought them out to claim their share of this abundant and sumptuous supply.

I stayed and inspected this curious group for an hour or more, during which time I was almost continually amused by the clamorous contentions that arose and generally ended in desperate combats, both among dogs and women, who seemed alike tenacious of their rights and disposed to settle their claims tooth and nail.

When I had seen enough of this I withdrew to the top of a beautiful prairie bluff a mile or two from the scene, and overlooking the route through the undulating green fields, watched the continuous passing of women, dogs, and horses carrying home their heavy burdens to the village, resembling from afar nothing so much as a busy community of ants sacking and carrying away the treasures of a cupboard or the sweets of a sugar-bowl.

CHAPTER XVII
THE ATTACK ON THE CANOE

BEFORE leaving that part of the country I visited the lower Mandan village of about eighty lodges, which appears to be a summer resort for some of the most noted families and in winter is untenanted. Here I experienced again the unbounded hospitality of these people and something more.

Suffering from influenza, I left my bed by the side of the lodge and, wrapped in my blanket of buffalo-hide, lay on the floor, with my feet to the fire in the centre, Indian fashion. Here a young man, whom I had observed reverently watching the movements of my brush, insisted on the honor of offering his body as a pillow for my head. It was impossible to resist his importunities, and for several nights I lay pillowed on his bear-greased, bedaubed body. I took some pains to inquire concerning him, and learned that he was a Riccaree brave named Pah-too-ca-ra (he who strikes), who, with several others of his tribe, are on a friendly visit to this hostile village. I think he hoped in this manner to gain my protection, and I in return have tried to give him immortality by painting his portrait. By his side I have painted a beautiful little girl of the same tribe named Pshan-shaw (the sweet-scented grass), giving a very pretty specimen of the dress and fashion of the women of this tribe. The inner garment, which is like a slip or frock, is in one piece, lavishly ornamented with embroidery and, beads, and for a necklace, elks' teeth passing across her breast. A young buffalo's skin, tastefully and elaborately embroidered, was gracefully thrown over her shoulders and hung down to the ground in the back.

The Riccaree village is about two hundred miles down the river. Coming up on the steamer I made a sketch of it on the open prairie, with the graceful and verdant undulating prairie for a background, and not a bush to be seen. It is impossible to visit them, for at present they have sworn death to every white man who comes in their way. When Lewis and Clarke first visited these people, as they have stated in their writings, the Riccarees received them with great kindness and hospitality. Since that time the system of trade, as it is conducted in this country, has inflicted on them wrongs, real or imaginary – they and the fur traders are the best judges of which – so, having no desire to have my "scalp danced," I passed them by.

The last I saw of my friends the Mandans was at the shore of the river in front of their village. My canoe and all my packs were brought down to the water's edge, with the whole tribe on the beach. My friends Mah-to- toh-pa, the Wolf Chief, and the Great Medicine each embraced me, warriors and braves shook hands with me, and the women and children saluted me with shouts of farewell; then Batiste, Bogard, and I were again afloat. When we were well under way a gallant young warrior I recognized followed us, and at the water's edge leaned over and safely tossed a bundle he took out from under his robe into the canoe. I attempted to unfold it, when he waved his hand, shook his head, and made a sign for me to lay it down in the canoe, which I did. After we had paddled a mile away from the village, by untying many thongs I opened the package, and found the most beautiful pair of leggings I had ever seen, fringed with a profusion of scalp-locks and ornamented with porcupine quills. These I instantly recognized as belonging to the son of a famous chief, the Four Men, and I had been for some time trying to buy them. I had offered the young man a horse, but his only reply was that he could not sell them, as the scalp-locks were precious as trophies and his fellow-warriors would laugh at him if he sold them.

Having parted from me without the least prospect of ever seeing me again, and enveloped with an intricacy of thongs that I could not possibly untie before the current had carried me beyond the power of making any compensation, he had compelled me to accept as a present what he could not sell to me the day before for the price of a horse.

On and on glided our little boat, every turn presenting a new and cheerful landscape. We indeed seemed to be passing through an old and beautifully cultivated country, whose ploughed fields had become greensward and whose houses and hedges were only removed. Such is the American prairie. Night after night, and for weeks of nights, our little craft was hauled ashore and our robes spread upon the grass or sand-bars, while the silvery but discordant notes of the bands of howling wolves serenaded us. When our larder was low and a lazy little herd sleeping or quietly grazing tempted us, we would silently land the canoe and secure two or three tongues and humps without the slightest trouble. When we had enough to eat and our paddles were at work, we would sing, whistle, and tell stories for our entertainment.

Once while Batiste and Bogard were relating some amusing and exciting stories about the Crows and Blackfeet, bang! went a gun, and a bullet skipped before us on the water. An Indian was seen standing alone at the water's edge. A shot fired ahead is the usual friendly mode of inviting parties ashore on this river, but it is the second invitation; the first is by signalling or calling. Bogard was anxious to go ashore, but I did not exactly like the position of things. The man had placed himself on the shore just above a sudden bend in the river, where the current would carry us inshore if we drifted, and here his companions could easily await us if they had any unfriendly design; and there were many unsettled feuds between the Indians and the fur traders for which I or any other traveller might suffer.

The river was very wide where we were and I steered for the opposite shore. Bogard, who thought this might be an opportunity for a drink, said in rather an authoritative tone, "We will go ashore." Batiste echoed him, "Oui, oui." "No," I said, "the canoe is mine, and I won't go ashore. I don't like the look of things." Both men threw their paddles in the bottom of the canoe and looked over their shoulders for their rifles, which were lying under a buffalo-robe between us. I instantly seized my double-barrelled gun and, cocking it, laid it across my knee. They understood this movement and what would be the consequence if either reached for his gun. I then commenced paddling the canoe myself, forcing it toward the opposite side.

Just at this moment, when the two men were growling at me for "being afraid of one poor solitary Indian," some twenty or thirty naked warriors rose from behind the rocks and, raising the war-whoop, ran down the shore to meet us behind the bend.

"Sacré, diable, il faut combattre!" exclaimed Batiste as he seized his rifle. "No," said I. "On ne combat pas. Il faut ramer, ramer." "On rame," answered Batiste, laying down his gun and taking up his paddle, and all three paddled with all our might. In order to take advantage of the strongest current, I kept the canoe amid-stream, while the

Indians, sounding the war-whoop, ran along the beach. Notwithstanding our exertions they were soon a little ahead of us, when eight or ten sprang into the water and came swimming toward us, holding their bows and arrows in their left hands above the water.

Seeing them nearing the boat, I said, "Now take up your rifles, but don't fire until I give the word."

I signalled the Indians to go back, but, advancing to within a few rods of the boat, I raised my rifle as if to fire, when they sank almost under the water and turned toward the shore. Meanwhile those on shore were still running, yelling, and setting them on us again. As they were armed only with bows and arrows I felt no further alarm, for, if obliged to fire, we could easily have killed them all. Whether they were Sioux or Riccarees we were never able to learn.

A few days' more paddling brought us to the country of the Sioux, as they are called by the French traders, or the Dacotahs, as they are known in their own language. This tribe is one of the most numerous as it is one of the most vigorous and warlike on the plains. It could undoubtedly send forth eight or ten thousand well-mounted, well-armed warriors, which estimate allows for forty or fifty thousand Indians in the lodges. The greater number are armed with bows and arrows, although many are supplied with guns. The personal appearance of these people is most prepossessing. They are tall; at least one-half of the warriors are over six feet, and their movements are elastic and graceful. No tribe is better clad or better supplied with the necessaries of life. This part of the great plain is finely stocked with buffaloes and wild horses, and no people are more bold in destroying the one for food or appropriating the other.

I am living here with a Scotchman named Laidlaw, who, with Mr. McKenzie and Lamont, has the whole agency of the Fur Company in the upper Missouri and the Rocky Mountains. This gentleman has a finely equipped fort two or three hundred feet square, enclosing eight or ten of their factories, houses, and stores, in the centre of which he occupies comfortable and spacious apartments, well supplied with the luxuries of life, and neatly and respectably conducted by a fine-looking, modest, and dignified Sioux woman, the kind and affectionate mother of his little flock of pretty and interesting children. The fort is called Fort Pierre, after Mr. Pierre Chouteau, one of the members of the company, whose hospitality I enjoyed on the steamer "Yellowstone."

This was not my first visit to the Sioux. Coming up the river the "Yellowstone" ran aground on a sand-bar. After a week's delay, Mr. Chouteau determined to send twenty men across the prairie, two hundred miles to the fort. Having heard there was an encampment of Sioux at the fort, I decided to accompany them. We were a week making the march over the continuous prairie, in which the grass, half a foot high, was enamelled with flowers and abounding in strawberries. This discouraging sea of green soon became monotonous, and the halfbreeds and Frenchmen, whose lives are spent on the prairie, set us a killing pace. I got on for a couple of days finely, but at length, with several others, fell behind, and finally felt like throwing myself on the ground in helpless despair.

Our delay at length brought the leaders back to us, and I explained that the pain in my legs was too great to go further. One of the halfbreeds then told me in French that if I would turn my toes in like the Indians I could go on very well. We halted half an hour while he gave me a lesson, and I found that by turning my toes in my feet not only went more easily through the grass but the weight of my body was more equally distributed on each toe, instead of throwing it all on the joints of the great toe, as one does in walking with the toes turned out. I soon got relief, and on the third and fourth days I took the lead of the whole party and kept it until the end of the journey.

At last we found a landmark in a distant range of blue hills, called the Bijou Hills by a French fur trader, who was finally killed by the Sioux. Some miles back of these we came suddenly upon a singular scene. This was a depression of some hundreds of acres, so incrusted with salt that the ground seemed to be covered with snow, in vivid contrast to the green fields that hemmed them in. Through these salt meadows meanders a small stream of water fed by salt springs. On nearing the banks we were amazed at the buffaloes in incredible numbers stretching down to lick up the salt, a vast mass of black contrasting with the snow white and vivid green. This salt meadow required us to make a long détour, and at last we arrived, pretty well jaded, at Fort Pierre, where six hundred lodges of Sioux were encamped waiting for the steamer of which they had heard and were eager to see.

CHAPTER XVIII
THE DEATH OF LITTLE BEAR:
A SIOUX TRAGEDY

AFTER resting a few days and making the acquaintance of the village, I made known my desire to the chiefs and white men, to paint some portraits. A tent was prepared as a studio, and my first sitter was the head civil chief, Ha-won-je-tah (The One Horn), a man of middle age, medium stature, a noble countenance, and the figure of an Apollo. He told me that he took his name from a small shell that hung around his neck rather than from any of his own deeds. This shell had descended to him from his father, and he valued it more than anything else in life. This was a striking instance of the affection of these people for their dead, for he owed his position as chief to his athletic achievements. He was the fleetest of his tribe, and could run down a buffalo on his own legs and pierce it to the heart.

His costume was of elk-skins, beautifully dressed and hung with scalp-locks and porcupine quills. But the most significant feature was his hair. This was divided into two locks and wound around his head like a Turkish turban.

This portrait was finished before any one of the tribe knew about it. A few of the big men were allowed in to see it, and at last it became a matter of gossip and numbers of the people gathered about the tent. The chief and the big medicine then carried the painting out and held it up before them, while the big medicine addressed the crowd.

"Look, my friends. We have now got two chiefs. When one is dead the other will be alive. Look at him and be ashamed. He smiles upon you and is alive. Tomorrow you will see me. Be patient, my friends. I am but a little boy." I had made a dead coloring of the old man and had put it aside to dry. "Mine is put in a box to grow overnight. To-morrow my face will shine upon you. This is the wonderful work of a great white medicine-man. He is now sitting and smoking with the chief. You cannot see him; but perhaps he will sometimes walk through the village, and then you can look at him. The Great Spirit has shown him how to do these things, and you must make but little noise. He says that I can do the same thing, and I think so, too, my friends."

The doctor's address was long and very curious. Looking through the crevices in my tent I beheld an interminable mass of red and painted heads, of eagles' quills or ermine-skins, of beads and brooches, of shields, spears, lances, and quivers. Some were mounted, others were raised on shoulders, and all gazing in astonishment on the chief that had life, the corners of whose mouth many said they could see move, and the eyes of which turned as they changed their positions.

After the exhibition of the portrait the village was in great excitement. The other medicine-men took a decided stand against me, predicting bad luck and premature death to all who subjected themselves to so mysterious an operation. The women and children were crying with their hands over their mouths, making the most pitiful and doleful sounds, and the result was I could get no sitters. In this perplexing dilemma the old chief addressed them, assuring them there was no harm in what I did, since he had gone through it. His speech had the desired effect, and some of the chiefs went immediately away to dress for their portraits.

I now had all I could do. One of the first to present himself was Black Rock, of the Nee-caw-wee-gee band, a man of six feet or more, in a splendid dress, lance in hand, with his pictured robe thrown over his shoulders, his head-dress of war-eagle quills and ermineskins falling quite down to his feet, and surmounted with a pair of horns, which, as I have said, denoted that he was the leader of his band. Another chief was The Stone with Horns, chief of the Yanckton band, who was so curiously tattooed with gunpowder and vermilion that at a little distance it appeared like a finely embroidered dress. Around his body was a robe of the grizzly bear and on his neck several strings of wampum. This is very unusual. Wampum is rarely seen in this country, having been so cheapened by the imitations manufactured by the fur traders that the Indians no longer use it in barter. I was much amused by the vanity of this man, who, as he sat, kept the inter- preter engaged telling me of the wonderful effects his oratory produced on the tribes. It was an easy thing, he said, to set all the women crying, and that the chiefs listened seriously to his voice before they went to war. My wigwam was full of the chiefs waiting their turn, smoking and talking gayly, generally at the expense of the sitter, whose mouth was shut and unable to reply, while they related anecdotes, creditable and otherwise, of his life, and were unsparing in criticisms about his looks.

The necessity of observing their rank gave rise to various difficulties. As there are forty bands among the Sioux, each with its chief, and ten times that number of big men, jealousies were rife. I now desired to paint some of the younger men for their looks. At this juncture Mr. Laidlaw brought to me a fine young man, in his war-dress, Mah-to-chee-ga (the little bear), telling me that he was a warrior of such distinction that he was sure the chiefs would be willing to have him painted. To this the chiefs agreed, and I began immediately. The first attitude of the young man was so beautiful that I did not change it. He was looking off toward the sides of the wigwam, as if gazing over the boundless prairie. The face was therefore what we painters call a three-quarter face, one half in shadow.

While I was painting and had the portrait pretty well along, one of the secondary chiefs, Shonka (the dog), a surly fellow I had painted a few days before, crept round behind me, and, watching my brush for a time, said, "I see you are but half a man."

"Who says that ?" said Mah-to-chee-ga in a low tone, and without the change of a muscle or the direction of his eye. "Shonka says it," replied The Dog. "Let Shonka prove it," answered Mah-to-chee-ga. "Shonka proves it this way. The white medicine-man knows that one half your face is good for nothing, as he has left it out in the picture." Mah-to-chee-ga, still with his eyes as if gazing over a distant prairie, said, "If I am but half a man, I am man enough for Shonka in any way he pleases to try it." This repartee kept up for some minutes, to the amusement of the chiefs, as Mah-to- chee-ga seemed to have the advantage, Shonka sprang upon his feet, and, wrapping his robe around him, darted out of the wigwam in a rage.

The chiefs, from their manner, seemed somewhat disturbed, but my subject, still without change or apparent emotion, stood until the portrait was finished, when he took off of his legs a beautiful pair of leggings fringed with scalp-locks, and asked me to accept them. After smoking a pipe with the chiefs and hearing their comments on his portrait, with which they were all pleased, he got up, shook hands with me, and went to his own wigwam, which was but a few paces from mine. There, fearing what The Dog might do, he took down his gun and loaded it, and, according to their custom when danger is near, he prostrated himself before the Great Spirit. While doing this his wife, to prevent mischief, took the ball from his rifle unknown to him.

Just then the voice of Shonka was heard without. "If Mah-to-chee-ga is man enough for Shonka, let him come and prove it." Like a flash the young man rushed out, and the two guns, overlapping each other, were fired. Mah-to-chee-ga fell, that side of his face blown away which had been "left out" in the painting. The Dog fled to the outer part of the village and called on his warriors to protect him. At the firing of the guns the chiefs all rushed out of my wigwam. I was left alone and heard nothing for some time. Peeping through the cracks in my wigwam, I saw women and children running; the horses were brought in at full gallop, and the dogs were all howling. As I was slipping my pistols in my belt Laidlaw dashed into my wigwam.

"Now we shall have it. That splendid fellow, The Little Bear, is dead. All that side of the face you left out in the portrait has been shot away. The devil take the pictures! I have been afraid of them. They say you are the cause of Little Bear's death, and if they can't kill The Dog they will look to you for satisfaction." At this moment guns were heard on the outskirts of the village, and we fled to the Fort. Here we took possession of one of the unarmed bastions, barricaded the doors and windows as well as we could, and with several dozen of the company's muskets awaited results. We kept our quarters dark through the night, and from the sound of the guns on the prairie concluded that The Dog and his warriors were retreating, pursued by the friends of The Little Bear.

In the morning the village was silent but sullen. Several young men were reported dead. I found my wigwam just as I left it, my paintings untouched. We joined in burying the fallen warrior and raising an honorable monument over his grave. I made liberal presents to his wife and relations, which doubtless saved us from violence. Fortunately, the steamer "Yellowstone" being released, I was able to continue my journey. But this was not the first time I got myself into serious perplexity during this visit to the Sioux.

Having painted the chiefs and braves I proposed to paint some of the women. This unaccountable condescension on my part brought on me the laughter of the whole tribe. Those who had been painted were now jeered at by those who had not been painted for assuming as a special honor that now to be given to squaws. These immediately came to me and asked to have their portraits destroyed. I had told them I wished their portraits to show to great white chiefs because they were distinguished men. The women had never taken any scalps. They only built fires and dressed skins.

This was very awkward for me, but I explained that I wanted the portraits of the women to hang *under* those of their husbands, merely to show how their women *looked* and how they *dressed,* without saying any more of them. After some considerable delay in my operations, and much deliberation on the subject through the village, I succeeded in getting a number of women's portraits. One was the daughter of Black Rock, an unmarried girl and much admired in the tribe for her modesty and beauty. She was beautifully dressed in skins ornamented with brass buttons and beads, with her hair plaited and over her ears a profusion of beads. Another of these women had the upper part of her garment covered with brass buttons, and her hair, left free, fell over her shoulders in soft, glossy waves, produced by braiding it, for their hair is naturally straight and graceless.

The vanity of these men, after they had agreed to be painted, was beyond all description, and far surpassing that which is oftentimes immodest enough in civilized society, where the sitter generally leaves the picture, when it is done, to speak for and to take care of itself; while an Indian often lies down from morning till night in front of his portrait, admiring his own beautiful face, and faithfully guarding it from day to day to save it from accident or harm.

This guardianship was of great service to me, since I frequently was anxious lest my paintings be injured by the great crowds.

CHAPTER XIX
THE DANCES AND MUSIC OF THE SIOUX

DURING THE time that I was engaged in painting my portraits I was occasionally inducing the young men to give me their dances, a great variety of which they gave me by being slightly paid, and I was glad to say in order to enable me to study their character and expression thoroughly, which I am sure I have done. The dancing is generally done by the young men, and it is considered undignified for the chiefs or doctors to join in. Yet so great was my medicine that chiefs and medicine-men turned out and agreed to compliment me with a dance. I looked on with great satisfaction, having been assured by the interpreters and traders that this was the highest honor they had ever known them to pay to any stranger among them.

This dance, which I have called "the dance of the chiefs," for want of a more significant title, was given by fifteen or twenty chiefs and doctors, many of whom were very old and venerable men. All of them came out in their head-dresses of war-eagle quills, with a spear or staff in the left hand and a rattle in the right. It was given in the midst of the Sioux village, in front of the head chief's lodge; and, besides the medicine-man who beat on the drum and sang for the dance, there were four young women standing in a row and chanting a sort of chorus for the dancers, forming one of the very few instances that I have ever known where the women are allowed to take any part in the dancing or other game or amusement with the men.

This dance was a very spirited thing, and pleased me much, as well as all the village, who were assembled around to witness what most of them never before had seen – their aged and venerable chiefs united in giving a dance.

Dancing is one of the principal and most frequent amusements among all the tribes. In their dances both vocal and instrumental music are introduced. These dances are made up of not more than four different steps, but the figures are numerous. These are produced by violent jumps and contortions, accompanied by songs and beats of the drum, given in exact time with the movements of the dancers. It has been said that the Indian has neither harmony nor melody in his music. I grant that in their vocal exercises what the musical world calls melody is absent. Their songs are made up, for the most part, of a sort of violent chant of harsh and jarring gutturals, of yelps and barks and screams. But these are given out in perfect time and with at least harmony in their madness. There are times, as every traveller in the Indian country will attest, when the Indian lies by his fireside, his drum in his hand, lightly touching it as he murmurs dulcet sounds that might come from the most tender and delicate woman. These quiet and tender songs are very different from those which are sung at their dances in full chorus and with wild gesticulation. Many of them seem to be quite rich in plaintive expression and melody although barren of change and variety.

I saw so many of their different varieties of dances among the Sioux that I should almost be disposed to denominate them the "dancing Indians." It would actually seem as if they had dances for everything. And in so large a village there was scarcely an hour in any day or night but the beat of the drum could somewhere be heard. These dances are almost as various and different in their character as they are numerous. Some of them are so exceedingly grotesque and laughable as to keep the by-standers in an irresistible roar of laughter. Others are calculated to excite his pity and forcibly appeal to his sympathies; while others disgust and yet others terrify and alarm him with their frightful threats and contortions.

All the world has heard of the bear dance, though I doubt whether more than a very small proportion of persons have ever seen it. The Sioux, like all the others of these Western tribes, are fond of bear's meat, and must have good stores of the "bear's grease" laid in, to oil their long and glossy locks as well as the surface of their bodies. And they all like the fine pleasure of a bear hunt, and also a participation in the bear dance, which is given several days in succession previous to their starting out, and in which they all join in a song to the Bear Spirit, which they think holds somewhere an invisible existence, and must be consulted and conciliated before they can enter upon their excursion with any prospect of success. For this grotesque and amusing scene one of the chief medicine-men placed over his body the entire skin of a bear, with a war-eagle's quill on his head, taking the lead in the dance, and looking through the skin which formed a mask that hung over his face. Many others in the dance wore masks on their faces made of the skin from the bear's head; and all, with the motions of their hands, closely imitated the movements of that animal; some representing its motion in running, and others the peculiar attitude and hanging of the paws when it is sitting up on its hind feet and looking out for the approach of an enemy. This grotesque and amusing masquerade oftentimes is continued at intervals for several days previous to the starting of a party on the bear hunt, who would scarcely count upon a tolerable prospect of success without a strict adherence to this most important and indispensable form.

Dancing is done here, too, as it is oftentimes done in the enlightened world, to get favors – to buy the world's goods – and in both countries danced with about equal merit, except that the Indian has surpassed us in honesty by christening it in his own country the "beggar's dance." This spirited dance was given, not by a set of *beggars* though, literally speaking, but by the first and most independent young men in the tribe, beautifully dressed (*i. e.*, not dressed at all, except with their breech clouts, or *kelts*, made of eagles' and ravens' quills), with their lances and pipes and rattles in their hands, and a medicine-man beating the drum and joining in the song at the highest key of his voice. In this dance every one sings as loud as he can halloo, uniting his voice with the others in an appeal to the Great Spirit to open the hearts of the by-standers to give to the poor and not to themselves, assuring them that the Great Spirit will be kind to those who are kind to the helpless and poor.

There are two dances among the Sioux for the purpose of teaching courage and endurance. One is the war dance, in which each warrior must dance through a fire in order to touch a red post, at the same time vaunting his prowess and taking an oath. The other is the straw dance. In this the children are made to dance with burning straws tied to their bodies to make them tough and brave. The scalp dance is

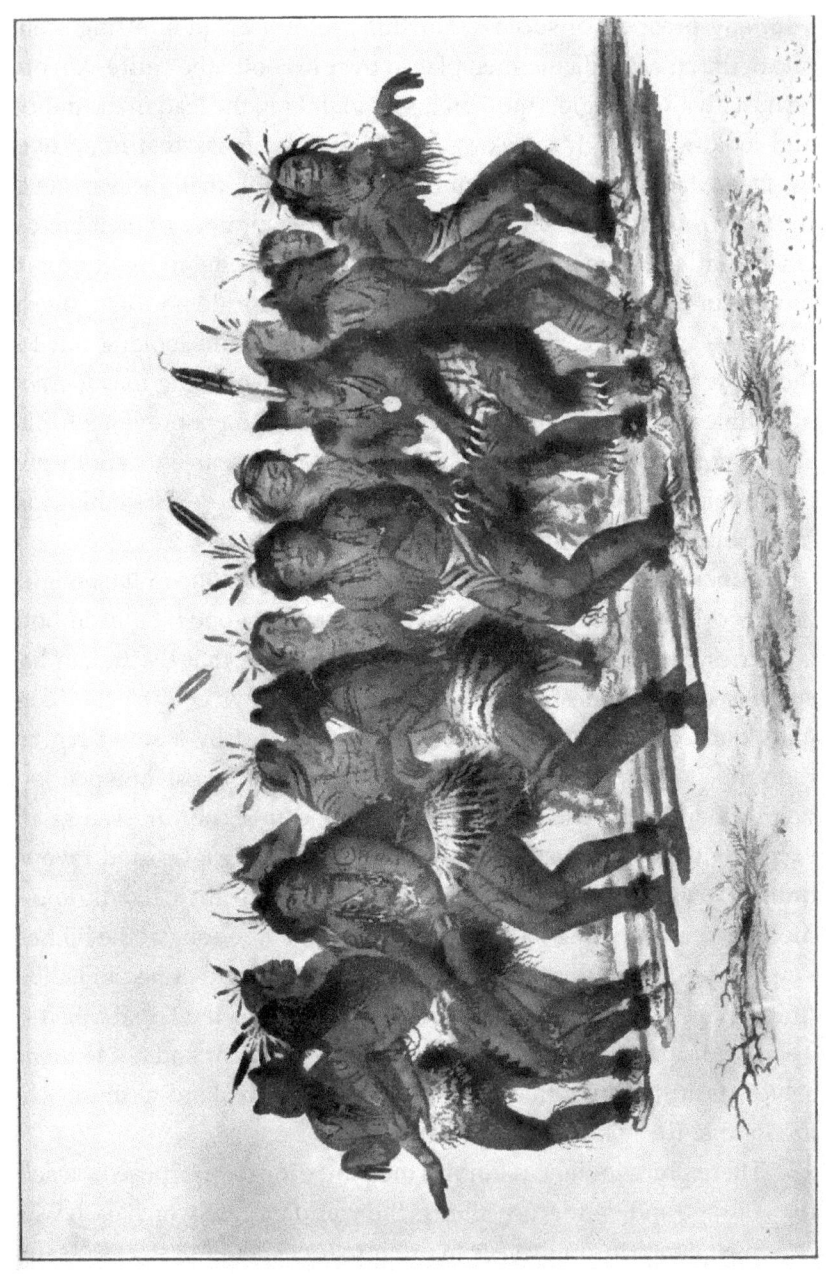

THE BEAR DANCE

given as a celebration of a victory, and among this tribe, as I learned while residing with them, danced in the night by the light of their torches and just before retiring to bed. When a war party returns from a war excursion, bringing home with them the scalps of their enemies, they generally "dance them" for fifteen nights in succession, vaunting the most extravagant boasts of their wonderful prowess in war, while they brandish their war weapons in their hands. A number of young women are selected to aid, although they do not actually join in the dance, by stepping into the centre of the ring and holding up the scalps that have been recently taken, while the warriors dance, or rather jump, around in a circle, barking and yelping in a frightful manner, using both feet at a time as they threaten with their weapons, as if they were actually cutting one another to pieces.

During these frantic leaps and thrusts every man distorts his face to the utmost of his muscles, darting his glaring eyeballs, snapping his teeth, and breathing through his inflated nostrils the very hissing death of battle. No description could be written that would do more than feebly convey the frightful effect of these scenes enacted in the darkness of night under the glaring light of their flaring flambeaux.

Something should be said of the custom of scalping as it is practised by all of the North American Indians. A genuine scalp must contain and show the crown of the head, that part directly over what the phrenologists call "self-esteem," or where the hair divides and radiates from the centre. This is a precaution lest two scalps be taken from the same head. Scalping is done by passing the knife under the skin and removing a piece as large as the palm of a man's hand. It is not an operation that destroys life, since it must be done without injury to the bone. Besides the scalp, the Indian usually cuts off as much of the hair of his enemy as he can. This hair his wife uses in fringing the seams of his leggings and shirt with what are called "scalplocks."

In his native state the Indian makes his scalping-knife of a sharpened bone or the edge of a piece of silex, while his war-club is carved from wood. and often with considerable grace. The Indian does not work in metals. His scalping-knives are now made expressly for Indian use and shipped into the Indian country by the tens of thousands.

The knife resembles a common butcher knife with one edge, and is made at Sheffield for perhaps a sixpence, and is sold to the Indian for the price of a horse. Every scalping-knife I have found bears on its blade the impress of "G. R.," which English people will understand. His war-club is also another civilized refinement. It is a blade of steel about ten inches long set in a club studded around with hundreds of brass nails. The scabbards of these weapons the Indian makes for himself and often ornaments handsomely.

The scalp itself is preserved as a trophy. The most usual way of preparing and dressing the scalp is that of stretching it on a little hoop at the end of a stick two or three feet long, for the purpose of "dancing it," as they term it, which will be described in the scalp dance in a few moments. There are many, again, which are small and not "dressed," sometimes not larger than a crown piece, and hung to different parts of the dress. In public shows and parades they are often suspended from the bridle-bits or halter when they are paraded and carried as trophies. Sometimes they are cut out, as it were, into a string, the hair forming a fringe to line the handle of a war-club. Sometimes they are hung at the end of the club, and at other times, by the order of the chief, they are hung over the wigwams suspended from a pole called the "scalp pole."

"Scalp day" is a national holiday. The Sioux have several days for scalp counting. The pole is stuck out of the side of the wigwams like a flagpole. When the chief has his pole ready it is the signal for the rest of the tribe to make ready, so that all the village can count each warrior's scalps and claims to promotion.

As the scalp is an evidence of the death of an enemy, an Indian has neither business nor inclination to take it from the living. It of course, sometimes happens on the frontier, when a man is stunned by a war-club or receives a gun-shot and falls, that an Indian rushing over his body snatches his scalp supposing him dead. But a scalp is supposed to be from the head of a dead enemy or it subjects its owner to disgrace.

There is no custom practised by the Indians held in greater horror than that of scalping. At the same time there is some excuse for them, I think, since they have no other means of keeping what from ancient times they have held to be a glorious record of service to their tribe.

Among the Indians there is no historian to preserve the heroic deeds of those who have gained their laurels in battle as there is in Christian countries. The poor Indian is bound to do this for himself or he loses such laurels. The motives for the scalp dance, which is a strict ceremony among all tribes, is certainly public exultation. But there seems to be in it something more. Among some of the tribes it is the custom, after thus publicly displaying the scalps and formally receiving credit for them, to require their burial. The great respect which seems to be paid the scalps while they retain them, and the pitying and mournful song which they howl to the manes of their unfortunate victims, as well as the precise care and solemnity with which they bury them, convinces me that they have a superstitious dread of the spirits of their slain enemies and perform these conciliatory offices to appease them.

If the reader thinks that I am taking too much pains to defend the Indians for this and others of their seemingly abominable customs, he will bear it in mind that I have lived with these people until I have learned the necessities of Indian life in which these customs are founded; and also, that I have met with so many acts of kindness and hospitality at the hands of the poor Indian that I feel bound, when I can do it, to render what excuse I can for a people who are dying with broken hearts and never can speak in the civilized world in their own defence.

The musical instruments used among these people are few, and these are rude and imperfect, consisting chiefly of rattles, drums, whistles, and flutes.

The *rattles* (or she-she-quois) most generally used are made of rawhide, which becomes very hard when dry, and charged with pebbles or something of the kind, which produce a shrill noise to mark the time in their dances and songs. Their drums are made in a very rude manner, oftentimes with a mere piece of rawhide stretched over a hoop, very much in the shape of a tambourine, and at other times are made in the form of a keg, with a head of rawhide at each end; on these they beat with a drum-stick, which oftentimes itself is a rattle, the bulb or head of it being made of rawhide and filled with pebbles. In other instances the stick has at its end a little hoop wound and covered with buckskin, to soften the sound, with which they beat on the drum with great violence as the chief and *heel-inspiring* sound for all their dances, and also as an accompaniment for their numerous and never-ending songs of amusement, of thanksgiving, and *medicine* or *metai*. The mystery whistle is another instrument of their invention, and very ingeniously made, the sound being produced on a principle entirely different from that of any wind instrument known in civilized inventions, and the notes produced on it by the sleight or trick of an Indian boy in so simple and successful a manner as to baffle entirely all civilized ingenuity, even when it is seen to be played. An Indian boy would stand and blow his notes on this repeatedly for hundreds of white men who might be lookers-on, not one of whom could make the least noise on it, even by practising with it for hour's. When I first saw this curious exhibition I was charmed with the peculiar sweetness of its harmonic sounds and completely perplexed (as hundreds of white men have no doubt been before me, to the great amusement and satisfaction of the women and children) as to the mode in which the sound was produced, even though it was repeatedly played immediately before my eyes and handed to me for my vain and amusing endeavors. The sounds of this little simple toy are liquid and sweet beyond description, and though among the Indians only given in harmonics, I am inclined to think might, by some ingenious musician or musical instrument maker, be modulated and converted into something very pleasing.

The war whistle is a well-known and valued little instrument of six or nine inches in length, invariably made of the bone of the deer or turkey's leg, and generally ornamented with porcupine quills of different colors which are wound around it. A chief or leader carries this to battle with him, suspended generally from his neck, and worn under his dress. This little instrument has but two notes, which are produced by blowing in the ends of it. The note produced in one end, being much more shrill than the other, gives the signal for battle, while the other sounds a retreat, a thing that is distinctly heard and understood by every man, even in the heat and noise of battle, where all are barking and yelling as loud as possible, and of course unable to hear the commands of their leader.

The signals in war are many and very intelligent as well as curious. The world-wide notorious war-whoop is one of these and is given by all tribes, both in North and South America, exactly alike when rushing into battle. It is a shrill, piercing note, sounded long, and with a swell on the highest key of the voice made by striking the palm or the fingers against the lips in order to produce the most rapid vibration possible.

There is nothing so frightful in the sound itself. There are many sounds more terrifying than the warwhoop. But no other sound can be so distinctly heard in the noise and confusion of battle. It is its association that gives it terror, for it is always the signal for attack, and is never made until the rush is made and weapons drawn for blood. No Indian is allowed to sound the war-whoop in time of peace, except in the war dance and countenanced by the chief, lest it be echoed by the sentinels, and hunting parties alarmed.

There is yet another wind instrument which I have added to my collection, and which from its appearance would seem to have been borrowed, in part, from the civilized world. This is what is often on the frontier called a "deer-skin flute," a "Winnebago courting flute," a "tsal-eet-quash-to," etc.; it is perforated with holes for the fingers, sometimes for six, at others for four, and in some instances for three only, having only so many notes with their octaves. These notes are very irregularly graduated, showing clearly that they have very little taste or ear for melody. These instruments are blown in the end, and the sound produced much on the principle of a whistle.

In the vicinity of the upper Mississippi, I often and familiarly heard this instrument called the Winnebago courting flute, and was credibly informed by traders and others in those regions that the young men of that tribe meet with signal success, oftentimes, in wooing their sweethearts with its simple notes, which they blow for hours together and from day to day from the bank of some stream, some favorite rock or log on which they are seated, near to the wigwam which contains the object of their tender passion, until her soul is touched, and she responds by some welcome signal that she is ready to repay the young Orpheus for his pains with the gift of her hand and her heart. How true these representations may have been I cannot say, but there certainly must have been some ground for the present cognomen by which it is known in that country.

CHAPTER XX
A DOG FEAST

IT WAS several weeks before the steamer "Yellowstone" arrived at Fort Pierre. The excitement and dismay among the six thousand Indians encamped here, as the puffing of the steam and the thundering of the cannon was heard, was very amusing. But when their old friend and agent, Major Sanford, stepped off the boat his presence seemed to restore courage, and they showed no further curiosity about it. We were now treated to numerous sights and amusements, some entertaining, others shocking.

It was announced that a grand feast would be held in honor of the great white chiefs. The two chiefs, Ha-wan-je-tah and Tchan-dee, brought their two tents together, forming a semicircle, enclosing a space sufficiently large to accommodate one hundred and fifty men, and sat down with that number of the principal chiefs and warriors of the Sioux nation, with Mr. Chouteau, Major Sanford, the Indian agent, Mr. McKenzie, and myself, whom they had invited in due time and placed on elevated seats in the centre of the crescent; while the rest of the company all sat upon the ground, and mostly cross-legged, preparatory to the feast being dealt out.

In the centre of the semicircle was erected a flagstaff, on which was waving a white flag, and to which also was tied the calumet, both expressive of their friendly feelings toward us. Near the foot of the flagstaff were placed in a row on the ground six or eight kettles, with iron covers on them shutting them tight, in which were prepared the viands for our *voluptuous* feast. Near the kettles and on the ground also, bottomside upward, were a number of wooden bowls, in which the meat was to be served out, and in front two or three men, who were there placed as waiters, to light the pipes for smoking, and also to deal out the food.

In these positions things stood, and all sat, with thousands climbing and crowding around for a peep at the grand pageant, when at length Ha-wan-je-tah (the one horn), head chief of the nation, rose in front of the Indian agent, in a very handsome costume, and addressed him thus: "My father, I am glad to see you here to-day. My heart is always glad to see my father when he comes. Our Great Father who sends him here is very rich and we are poor. Our friend Mr. McKenzie, who is here, we are also glad to see; we know him well, and we shall be sorry when he is gone. Our friend who is on your right hand we all know is very rich, and we have heard that he owns the great *medicine canoe;* he is a good man and a friend to the red men. Our friend the White Medicine, who sits with you, we did not know – he came among us a stranger and he has made me very well – all the women know it, and think it very good; he has done many curious things and we have all been pleased with him; he has made us much amusement and we know he is great medicine.

"My father, I hope you will have pity on us; we are very poor; we offer you to-day not the best that we have got, for we have plenty of good buffalo hump and marrow; but we give you our hearts in this feast – we have killed our faithful dogs to feed you – and the Great Spirit will seal our friendship. I have no more to say."

After these words he took off his beautiful war-eagle head-dress, his shirt and leggings, his necklace of grizzly bears' claws, and his moccasins, and, tying them together, laid them gracefully down at the feet of the agent as a present; and laying a handsome pipe on top of them, he walked around into an adjoining lodge, where he got a buffalo-robe to cover his shoulders, and returned to the feast, taking the seat which he had before occupied.

Major Sanford then rose and made a short speech in reply, thanking him for the valuable present which he had made him and for the very polite and impressive manner in which it had been done, and sent to the steamer for a quantity of tobacco and other presents, which were given to him in return. After this, and after several others of the chiefs had addressed him in a similar manner, and, like the first, disrobed themselves and thrown their beautiful costumes at his feet, one of the three men in front deliberately lit a handsome pipe and brought it to Ha-wan-je-tah to smoke. He took it, and, after presenting the stem to the north, to the south, to the east, and the west, and then to the sun that was over his head, he pronounced the words "How – how – how!" and drew a whiff or two of smoke through it. Then holding the bowl of it in one hand and its stem in the other, he held it to each of our mouths as we successively smoked it; after which it was passed around through the whole group, who all smoked through it, or as far as its contents lasted, when another of the three waiters was ready with a second, and at length a third one in the same way, which lasted through the hands of the whole number of guests. This smoking was conducted with the strictest adherence to exact and established form. After the pipe is charged and lighted, until the time that the chief has drawn the smoke through it, it is considered an evil omen for any one to speak; and if any one break silence in that time, even in a whisper, the pipe is instantly dropped by the chief, and their superstition is such that they would not dare to use it on this occasion; but another one is called for and used in its stead. If there is no accident of the kind during the smoking, the waiters then proceed to distribute the meat, which is soon devoured in the feast.

The lids were now raised from the kettles which were filled with dog meat. Being well cooked and made into a sort of stew, it sent forth a savory smell and promised to be a palatable food. Each of us civilized guests had a wooden bowl placed before us, the dog's flesh floating in rich gravy, with a large spoon of buffalo's horn in the dish. In this most painful dilemma we sat, knowing the solemnity and good feeling with which it was offered and the necessity of falling to and devouring at least a little of it. We tasted it a few times and then resigned our dishes, which were quite willingly taken and devoured by others. After eating, each one rose and walked off without uttering a word. In this way the feast ended, when the space was left to the waiters or officers who had charge of the occasion.

The dog feast, I feel competent to say, should be regarded as a religious ceremony in which the Indian sacrifices his most faithful companion to bear witness to the sacredness of his vows of friendship. The dog, among all Indian tribes, is more valued than in any part of the civilized world. The Indian has more time to devote to his company, and his untutored mind more nearly assimilates with that of his faithful servant. They hunt together and are equal sharers of the chase. Their bed is one, and on the rocks and on their coats of arms they carve his image as the symbol of fidelity. Yet he will end his affection with his faithful follower, and with tears in his eyes will offer him as a sacrifice to seal his friendship with man. A feast of venison or of buffalo meat is due to every one who enters his wigwam, and conveys no significance. I have seen the master take from the bowl the head of his victim and descant on its former affection and fidelity with tears in his eyes. I have also seen guests sneer and jest at the Indian's folly, and I have said in my heart that they did not deserve a name so good or so honorable as that of the poor animal whose bones they were picking.

The flesh of these dogs, though apparently relished by the Indians, is, undoubtedly, inferior to the venison and buffalo meat of which feasts are constantly made where friends are invited, as they are in civilized society, to a pleasant and convivial party. From this fact alone it would seem clear that they have some extraordinary motive, at all events, for feasting on the flesh of that useful and faithful animal, even when, as in the instance I have been describing, their village is well supplied with fresh and dried meat of the buffalo. The dog feast is given, I believe, by all tribes in North America; and by them all, I think, this faithful animal, as well as the horse, is sacrificed in several different ways to appease offended Spirits or Deities, whom it is considered necessary that they should conciliate in this way, and by giving the best in the herd or the kennel.

In the after-part of the day of the dog feast I was called to ride a mile or so to the base of the bluff near the Teton River, where on a little plain was a group of lodges of the Ting-ta-to-ah band of Sioux, to see a man "looking at the sun." We found him naked except for his breech-cloth, with splints or skewers run through the flesh of his breasts, and leaning back and hanging with the weight of his body to a pole, by a cord attached to the splints. The top of the pole was bent forward by the weight, allowing his body to sink about half-way to the ground. His feet were still upon the ground supporting a small part of his weight, and he held in his left hand his favorite bow, and in his right, with a desperate grip, his medicine-bag. In this condition, with the blood trickling down over his body, which was covered with white and yellow clay, and amid a great crowd who were looking on, sympathizing with and encouraging him, he was hanging and "looking at the sun," without paying the least attention to any one about him. In the group that was reclining around him were several mystery-men beating their drums and shaking their rattles, and singing as loud as they could yell, to encourage him and strengthen his heart to stand and look at the sun from its rising in the morning until its setting at night; at which time, if his heart and his strength have not failed him, he is "cut down," receives the liberal donation of presents (which have been thrown into a pile before him during the day), and also the name and the style of a doctor, or medicine-man, which lasts him and insures him respect through life.

This most extraordinary and cruel custom I never heard of among any other tribe, and never saw an instance of it before or after the one I have just named. It is a sort of worship or penance of great cruelty disgusting and painful to behold, with only one palliating circumstance about it, which is, that it is a voluntary torture and of very rare occurrence. The poor and ignorant, misguided and superstitious man who undertakes it puts his everlasting reputation at stake upon the issue; for when he takes his stand he expects to face the sun and gradually turn his body in listless silence till he sees it go down at night. If he faints and falls, of which there is imminent danger, he loses his reputation as a brave or mystery-man, and suffers a signal disgrace in the estimation of the tribe, like all men who have the presumption to set themselves up for braves or mystery-men, and fail justly to sustain the character.

During my stay with the Sioux I received many presents from them as tokens of friendship, and among these many pipes. Tobacco was made known to the Indians by the white man, who at the same time supplied them with whiskey. But smoking has always been one of their customs. There are leaves and the bark of many trees which grow wild that have mild narcotic properties. These the Indians dry, pulverize, and carry in their pouches. When thus prepared it is called "k'nick- k'neck," and is an innocent luxury, as its effect on the system is very feeble and harmless.

The Indian in his native state seems to be smoking one-half of his life. He has neither trade nor business, and he fills his leisure with amusement and smoking. The pipe is his constant companion through life. It is his messenger of peace, he pledges his friends through its stem and bowl, and when its care-drowning fumes cease to rise it takes a place with him in his solitary grave, with the tomahawk and war-club, on his journey to the "mild and beautiful hunting-grounds" of his fancy. The Indian accordingly spends much time on his pipe, which he makes himself. The bowls are generally made of red steatite, called in the language of the country pipe-stone. This stone is different from any other variety of steatite either in this country or Europe, and is traceable thus far to only one source, and that lies somewhere between these plains and the upper Mississippi.

According to the Sioux tradition : "Before the creation of man the Great Spirit, whose tracks are yet to be seen in the form of those of a large bird, used to slay the buffaloes and eat them on the ledge of the Red Rocks on the top of the Coteau des Prairies, and the blood running on the rocks turned them red. One day, when a large snake had crept into the nest of the bird to eat his eggs, one of the eggs hatched out in a clap of thunder. The Great Spirit then, picking up a piece of the stone to throw at the snake, moulded it into a man. This man's feet grew fast in the ground, where he stood for many ages like a great tree. He grew very old, older than a hundred men to-day. At last another tree grew up by the side of him, and the snake ate them both off at the roots, when they wandered off together, and from them sprang all the people on the earth."

This red stone the Indians say is great medicine, and has been given to them by the Great Spirit for their pipes, and it is strictly forbidden to use it for any other purpose. As yet the place has been visited only by the red man, but I shall certainly lay my course to it in time and make known its mysteries. The color of the stone is cherry red and admits of a beautiful polish. The Indian makes a hole in the solid stone, which is not quite as hard as marble, by drilling into it with a hard stick shaped to the desired size, using plenty of sharp sand and water in the hole; this is a work of great labor and much patience. Many of the bowls are afterward carved with much taste and skill with figures and groups in high relief.

The shafts or stems of these pipes are from two to four feet long, sometimes round, but usually flat, of an inch or two in breadth, and wound half their length or more with braids of porcupine quills, and often ornamented with the beaks and tufts from the woodpecker's head, with ermine-skins and long red hair, dyed from white horsehair or the white buffalo's tail.

The stems of these pipes will be found to be carved in many ingenious forms, and in all cases they are perforated through the centre, quite staggering the wits of the enlightened world to *guess how* the holes have been *bored* through them; until it is simply and briefly explained that the stems are uniformly made of the stalk of the young ash, which generally grows straight, and has a small pith through the centre, that is easily burned out with a hot wire, or with a piece of hardwood by a much slower process.

The *calumet,* or pipe of peace, ornamented with the war-eagle's quills, is a sacred pipe, and never allowed to be used on any other occasion than that of *peace-making,* when the chief brings it into treaty and, unfolding the many bandages which are carefully kept around it, has it ready to be mutually smoked by the chiefs after the terms of the treaty are agreed upon, as the means of *solemnizing* or *signing* by an illiterate people, who cannot draw up an instrument and sign their names to it as is done in the civilized world.

The mode of solemnizing is by passing the sacred stem to each chief, who draws one breath of smoke only through it, thereby passing the most inviolable pledge that they can possibly give for the keeping of the peace. This sacred pipe is then carefully folded up and stowed away in the chief's lodge, until a similar occasion calls it out to be used in a similar manner.

CHAPTER XXI
THE BUFFALO CHASE

IN THE heart of the buffalo country, where there are no extremes of heat and cold, the finest animals are to be found. I could never send from a better source some account of these noble animals that are being hurried to their final extinction. The Sioux are a a bold and desperate set of horsemen and great hunters. Here also in the midst of them is an extensive assortment of goods, of whiskey, and a number of indefatigable men, who are calling for every robe that can be stripped from these animals' backs. Like the poor savage himself, it is but a question of time when they will fade away before the approach of civilized man and exist only on canvas and in books.

The American bison, or buffalo, as I shall call him, is the largest of the ruminating animals on the prairie, where he seems to have been placed by the Great Spirit for the use and subsistence of the red men, who live almost exclusively upon his flesh and clothe themselves with his skin. Their color is dark brown, which changes with the seasons, exposure to the weather turning it quite light, while the new coat in the spring is jet black.

The buffalo bull often grows to the enormous weight of two thousand pounds, and shakes over his head and shoulders, and often down to the ground, a long and shaggy black mane. During the "running season," in August and September, they congregate in such masses as literally to blacken the prairie for miles. In these scenes the whole mass is in constant motion, and their bellows and roars at the distance of a mile or two sound like distant thunder. During this time the traveller may traverse miles of the vacated country without seeing a single buffalo. But a few weeks after, if he retraces his steps, he will find little flocks grazing in every direction, some at play and others indulging in their favorite wallows.

In the summer these animals suffer greatly from heat, and wherever there is a little stagnant water lying in the grass, and the ground underneath, the enormous bull, lowered down upon one knee, will plunge his horns, and at last his head, driving up the earth, and soon making an excavation in the ground. Into this the water filters from among the grass, forming for him in a few moments a cool and comfortable bath, into which he plunges like a hog in his mire.

In this delectable laver he throws himself flat upon his side, and forcing himself violently around, with his horns and his huge hump on his shoulders presented to the sides, he ploughs up the ground by his rotary motion, sinking himself deeper and deeper in the ground, continually enlarging his pool, into which he at length becomes nearly immersed. The water and mud about him mixed into a complete mortar, drips in streams from every part of him as he rises up on his feet, a hideous monster of mud and ugliness, too frightful and too eccentric to be described!

It is generally the leader of the herd that takes upon himself to make this excavation; but if another one opens the ground, the leader (who is conqueror) marches forward, and driving the other from it plunges in himself. Having cooled his sides and changed his color to a walking mass of mud and mortar, he stands in the pool until inclination induces him to step out and give place to the next in command, who stands ready, and another, and another, who advance forward in their turns to enjoy the luxury of the wallow, until the whole band (sometimes a hundred or more) will pass through it, each one throwing his body around in a similar manner, and each one adding a little to the dimensions of the pool, while he carries away in his hair an equal share of the clay, which dries to a gray or whitish color and gradually falls off. By this operation, which is done perhaps in the space of half an hour, a circular excavation of fifteen or twenty feet in diameter and two feet in depth is completed, and left for the water to run into, which soon fills it to the level of the ground.

To these sinks the waters lying on the surface of the prairies are continually draining and lodging their vegetable deposits. These after a lapse of years fill them up to the surface with a rich soil, which throws up an unusual growth of grass and herbage, forming conspicuous circles that arrest the eye of the traveller and are calculated to excite his surprise for ages to come.

A BUFFALO CHASE

Many travellers who have penetrated not quite far enough into the Western country to see the habits of these animals and the manner in which these *mysterious* circles are made, but who have seen the prairies strewn with bleached bones, and have beheld these strange circles, which often occur in groups and of different sizes, have come home with beautiful and ingenious theories (which *must needs be made)* for the origin of these singular and unaccountable appearances For want of a rational theory, these have generally been attributed to *fairy feet* and gained the appellation of "fairy circles."

Many travellers, again, have supposed that these rings were produced by the dances of the Indians, which are oftentimes (and in fact most generally) performed in a circle; yet a moment's consideration disproves such a probability, inasmuch as the Indians always select the ground for their dancing near the sites of their villages, and that always on a dry and hard foundation, while these "fairy circles" are uniformly found to be on low and wet ground.

The female buffalo is much smaller than the male, and always distinguishable by the peculiar shape of the horns, which are much smaller and more crooked, turning their points more in toward the centre of the forehead.

The horns of the male are short but very large, and have but one turn, *i. e.,* they are a simple arch, without the least approach to a spiral form, like those of the common ox or of the goat species.

One of the most remarkable characteristics of the buffalo is the peculiar formation and expression of the eye, the ball of which is very large and white and the iris jet black. The lids of the eye seem always to be strained quite open and the ball rolling forward and down, so that a considerable part of the iris is hidden behind the lower lid, while the pure white of the eyeball glares out over it in an arch, in the shape of a moon at the end of its first quarter.

The chief occupation of the Indian is the chase of the buffalo. He is mounted on the small but useful horse which is caught wild on the prairie running in numerous bands. When pursuing a large Herd, the Indian generally rides close in the rear until he selects the animal he wishes to kill, which he separates from the herd as soon as he can,' by dashing his horse between it and the herd and forcing it off alone, in order that he may not himself be trampled to death in the throng. No bridle whatever is used by the Indians as they have no knowledge of a bit. A short halter, however, which answers in place of a bridle, is in general use, of which they usually form a noose around the under jaw of the horse, by which they get great power over the animal, and which they use generally to *stop* rather than *guide* the horse. This halter is called by the French traders in the country *l'arrêt,* the stop, and has great power in arresting the speed of a horse, though it is extremely dangerous to use too freely as a guide, since it interferes too much with the freedom of his limbs for the certainty of his feet and security of his rider.

When the Indian then has directed the course of his steed to the animal which he has selected, the training of the horse is such that it knows the object of its rider's selection, and exerts every muscle to give it close company, while the halter lies loose and untouched upon its neck, and the rider leans quite forward and off from the side of his horse, with his bow drawn and ready for the deadly shot, which is given at the instant he is opposite to the animal's body. The horse, being instinctively afraid of the animal (though he generally brings his rider within the reach of the end of his bow), keeps his eye strained upon the furious enemy he is so closely encountering, and the moment he has approached to the nearest distance required and has passed the animal, whether the shot is given or not, he gradually sheers off, to prevent coming on to the horns of the infuriated beast, which often are instantly turned and presented for the fatal reception of its too familiar attendant. These frightful collisions often take place, notwithstanding the sagacity of the horse and the caution of its rider; for in these extraordinary (and inexpressible) exhilarations of chase, which seem to drown the prudence alike of instinct and reason, both horse and rider often seem rushing on to destruction, as if it were mere pastime and amusement.

I have always counted myself a prudent man, yet I have often waked, as it were, out of the delirium of the chase (into which I had fallen, as into an agitated sleep, and through which I had passed as through a delightful dream), where to have died would have been but to have remained riding on without a struggle or a pang.

BUFFALO HUNT ON SNOW-SHOES

In some of these, too, I have arisen from the prairie, covered with dirt and blood, having severed company with gun and horse, the one lying some twenty or thirty feet from me with a broken stock, and the other coolly browsing on the grass at half a mile distance, without man and without other beast remaining in sight.

For the novice in these scenes there is much danger to his limbs and his life, and he finds it a hard and a desperate struggle that brings him in at the death of these huge monsters, except where it has been produced by hands that have acquired more sleight and tact than his own.

With the Indian, who has made this the every-day sport and amusement of his life, there is less difficulty and less danger; he rides without "losing his breath," and his steady hand deals *certainty* in its deadly blows.

A part of the equipment I have not mentioned is the lasso, which is a long thong of rawhide ten or fifteen yards in length, made of several braids, which is chiefly used in catching wild horses. But in running buffaloes and in war the lasso is allowed to drag on the ground for several rods, so that if a man is dismounted, which is often the case, by the tripping or stumbling of the horse he can lay hold of the lasso and thus secure his horse and rejoin the chase.

In the winter, when horses, on account of the snow, are not available for the chase, the Indian uses snowshoes. These snow-shoes are made in many forms, generally two or three feet long, a foot wide, of bent hoops, with strips of rawhide netted across on which the feet rest and to which they are fastened with straps like a skate. With these the Indian will glide over the snow with astonishing quickness, while the great weight of the buffaloes sinks them down and insures their becoming an easy prey to the bow and lance of their pursuers.

As in winter the buffalo fur is at its thickest, it is in greatest demand and the slaughter is at its height. The carcass is quickly stripped, the fur taken and sold to the traders, and the flesh left for the wolves, inasmuch as the Indians generally kill and dry meat enough in the fall, when it is fat and juicy, to last them through the winter.

Thus at all seasons of the year the poor buffaloes have their enemy, man, devising ways for their destruction. He dashes among them on the plains with his wild horse, he chases them into the deep snowdrifts on his snow-shoes, where they fall an easy prey, and they unwittingly behold him under the skin of a white wolf, while they are peaceably grazing, and are shot down before they are aware of their danger. The white wolf sneaks about in gangs on the green prairie, looking like nothing so much as a flock of sheep. They are always seen following the herds ready to pick the bones of those the hunters leave on the ground or to slay and devour the wounded. So long as the herd of buffaloes is together they seem to have little dread of the wolf, and allow it to come near. The Indian takes advantage of this fact, and, hiding under, the skin of the wolf, will crawl a half-mile or more on his knees, until he gets within a few rods of the unsuspecting group, and easily shoots down the fattest of the herd.

The buffalo is a very timid animal, and shuns man, yet, when overtaken and harassed or wounded, turns in fury. In their desperate resistance the finest horses are often destroyed; but the Indian, with his superior sagacity and dexterity, generally finds some effective mode of escape.

During the season of the year while the calves are young the male seems to stroll about by the side of the dam, as if for the purpose of protecting the young, at which time it is exceedingly hazardous to attack them. The buffalo calf during the first six months is red, and has so much the appearance of a red calf in cultivated fields that it could easily be mingled and mistaken among them. In the fall, when it changes its hair, it takes a brown coat for the winter which it always retains. In pursuing a large herd of buffaloes in the season when their calves are but a few weeks old, I have often been exceedingly amused with the curious manoeuvres of these shy little things. Amid the thundering confusion of a throng of several hundreds or several thousands of these animals, there will be many of the calves that lose sight of their dams; and being left behind by the throng and the swift-passing hunters, they endeavor to secrete themselves, on the level prairie, where naught can be seen but the short grass of six or eight inches in height, save an occasional bunch of wild sage a few inches higher. To this the poor affrighted things will run, and, dropping on their knees, will push their noses under it and into the grass, where they will stand for hours, with their eyes shut, imagining themselves securely hid, while they are standing up quite straight on their hind feet and can easily be seen at several miles' distance. It is a familiar amusement for us, accustomed to these scenes, to retreat and approach these little trembling things, which stubbornly maintain their positions, with their noses pushed under the grass and their eyes strained upon us, as we dismount from our horses and are passing around them. From this fixed position they are sure not to move until hands are laid upon them, and then for the shins of a novice we can extend our sympathy; or, if he can preserve the skin on his bones from the furious buttings of its head, we know how to congratulate him on his signal success and good luck. In these desperate struggles, for a moment, the little thing is conquered and makes no further resistance. And I have often, in concurrence with a known custom of the country, held my hands over the eyes of the calf and breathed a few strong breaths into its nostrils, after which I have, with my hunting companions, ridden several miles into our encampment, with the little prisoner busily following the heels of my horse the whole way, as closely and as affectionately as its instinct would attach it to the company of its dam!

This is one of the most extraordinary things that I have met with in the habits of this wild country, and although I had often heard of it and felt unable exactly to believe it, I am now willing to bear destmony to the fact because of the numerous instances I have witnessed since I came to this country. In this way, before we left the head-waters of the Missouri, we had collected about a dozen of these little calves, which followed at our horses' heels even into the stables at the Fort, where our horses were led. With the aid of a good milch cow, Mr. Laidlaw was successfully raising them to be sent to Mr. Chouteau's plantation at St. Louis.

It is melancholy for the traveller in this country to perceive that the time is not far distant when these noble animals will at last perish before the cruel and improvident rapacity of the white men and the red. Only a few days before I arrived, an immense herd showing in the distance, a band of several hundred Sioux crossed the river at mid-

BUFFALO HUNT. WITH WOLF-SKIN MASK

day, and after a few hours brought in fourteen hundred fresh buffalo tongues for which they received a few gallons of whiskey. Not a skin did they bring; it was not the season for fur. Not a pound of flesh did they bring; the camp required no fresh meat. This is but one instance of the profligate waste of the buffalo.

The Indians look to the white men as beings wiser than they, and think it no harm to drink the beverage the white man offers and drinks himself. Thus the Indian easily acquires a taste for whiskey, and for it will strip the last buffalo of its skin, which his squaw will dress, that he may sell it for a pint of diluted alcohol.

On the other hand, under some great protecting policy of the government, how delightful to contemplate a magnificent park in this region, preserved in its pristine beauty and wildness, where the world could see in time to come the native Indian, his sports, his language, his manners and customs as they exist to-day in his isolation from the civilized world! What a beautiful and thrilling sight in the future would be the Indian, in his classic attire, with his sinewy bow, his shield and lance, on his wild horse chasing the fleeting herds of elk and buffalo! Such scenes might easily be preserved on the great plains of the West without detriment to the country or its borders, for those lands on which the buffaloes have assembled are uniformly sterile, and it is where the buffalo is found that the finest specimens of the Indian race are to be seen.

I would ask no other monument to my memory, nor any other enrolment of my name among the famous dead, than the reputation of having been the founder of such an institution.

CHAPTER XXII
A PRAIRIE FIRE

MY VOYAGE from the mouth of the Teton River to Fort Leavenworth has been the most rugged yet the most delightful of my whole tour. Our canoe was generally landed at night on the point of some projecting barren sand-bar, where we straightened our limbs on our buffalo-robes, secure from the annoyance of mosquitoes and out of the walks of Indians and grizzly bears. In addition to the opportunity which this descending tour has afforded me – of visiting all the tribes of Indians on the river and leisurely filling my portfolio with the beautiful scenery which its shores present – the sportsman's fever was roused and satisfied; the swans, ducks, geese, and pelicans, the deer, antelope, elk, and buffaloes were "stretched" by our rifles; and sometimes – "pull, boys, pull! a war party! for your lives, pull, or we are gone!"

I often landed my skiff and mounted the green-carpeted bluffs, whose soft, grassy tops invited me to recline, where I was at once lost in contemplation. Such a place was "Floyd's Grave," a name given to one of the most lovely and imposing bluffs on the Missouri River about twelve hundred miles above St. Louis.

Here was buried Sergeant Floyd, of the Lewis and Clarke expedition, in 1806, a cedar post bearing the initials of his name marking his grave. I landed my canoe in front of this grass-covered mound and we went into camp at its base. Several times I ascended the bluff and beheld the infinite windings of the Missouri and its thousand domes and hills of green vanishing into the blue distance. I could not hunt on this ground, but roamed from hill top to hill top gathering wild flowers, and seeing into the future when these hills and dales will be streaked by the plough, yellow with the harvest, and spotted with kine and groups of hamlets and villas.

This voyage in my little canoe afforded me infinite pleasure, mingled with pains and privations I shall never wish to forget. Gliding along from day to day, my merry voyageurs were continually chanting their cheerful boat songs, and every now and then taking up their rifles to bring down stately elks or antelopes.

But a few miles from "Floyd's Bluff" we landed our canoe and spent a day in the vicinity of "Black Bird's Grave." This is a celebrated point on the Missouri, which all the travellers in these realms, both white and red, are in the habit of visiting. This elevated bluff has received the name of "Black Bird's Grave" from the fact that a famous chief of the O-ma-has, by the name of the Black Bird, was buried on its top, over whose grave a cedar post was erected by his tribe, some thirty years ago, which is still standing. The O-maha village was about sixty miles above this place, and this very noted chief, who had been on a visit to Washington city in company with the Indian agent, died of the small-pox near this spot on his return home. When dying he requested his warriors to take his body down to the river to this, his favorite haunt, and on the pinnacle of this towering bluff to bury him on the back of his favorite war-horse, alive under him, from whence he could see, as he said, "the Frenchmen passing up and down the river in their boats."

He owned, among many horses, a noble white steed that was led to the top of the grass-covered hill, and with great pomp and ceremony, in presence of the whole nation and several of the fur traders and the Indian agent, he was placed astride of his horse's back, with his bow in his hand and his shield and quiver slung, with his pipe and his medicine-bag, with his supply of dried meat and his tobacco-pouch replenished to last him through his journey to the "beautiful hunting-grounds of the shades of his fathers," with his flint and steel and his tinder to light his pipes by the way. The scalps that he had taken from his enemies' heads were hung to the bridle of his horse; he was in full dress and fully equipped, and on his head waved to the last moment his beautiful head-dress of the war-eagle's plumes. In this plight, and the last funeral honors having been performed by the medicinemen, every warrior of his band painted the palm and fingers of his right hand with vermilion, which was stamped and perfectly impressed on the milk-white sides of his devoted horse. This all done, turf was brought and placed around the feet and legs of the horse and gradually laid up to its sides, and at last over the back and head of the unsuspecting animal, and last of all over the head and even the eagle plumes of its valiant rider, which have remained there undisturbed to the present day.

There have been some surprising tales told of this man. The traders say that his almost superhuman authority in his tribe was obtained by poisoning his enemies with arsenic. If this is true it is an instance of Indian depravity that in my travels I have never encountered. But I do know how Black Bird exposed his life and shed his blood rescuing victims from torture, and abolished that savage custom in his tribe; how he led on and headed his warriors against the Sacs and Foxes, and saved his women and children from butchery; how he received the Indian agent and entertained him in his hospitable wigwam, and how he conducted and acquitted himself in his embassy to the civilized world.

In this voyage Batiste and Bogard were my constant companions, and we all had our rifles and used them often. We often went ashore among the herds of buffaloes, and were obliged to do so for our daily food. We lived the whole way on buffaloes' flesh and venison – we had no bread – but laid in a good stock of coffee and sugar. These, however, from an unforeseen accident, availed us but little, as on the second or third day of our voyage, after we had taken our coffee on the shore and Batiste and Bogard had gone in pursuit of a herd of buffaloes, I took it into my head to have an extra fine dish of coffee for myself, as the fire was fine. For this purpose I added more coffee-grounds to the pot and placed it on the fire, which I sat watching, when I saw a fine buffalo cow wending her way leisurely over the hills but a little distance from me, for whom I started at once with my rifle trailed in my hand; and after creeping and running and heading for half an hour without getting a shot at her, I came back to the encampment, where I found my two men with meat enough, but in the most uncontrollable rage, for my coffee had all boiled out and the coffee-pot was melted to pieces!

This was truly a deplorable accident and one that could in no effectual way be remedied. We afterward botched up a mess or two of it in our frying-pan, but to little purpose, and then abandoned it to Bogard alone, who thankfully received the dry coffee-grounds and sugar at his meals, which he soon entirely demolished.

We met immense numbers of buffaloes in the early part of our voyage. In one instance, near the mouth of the White River, we met the

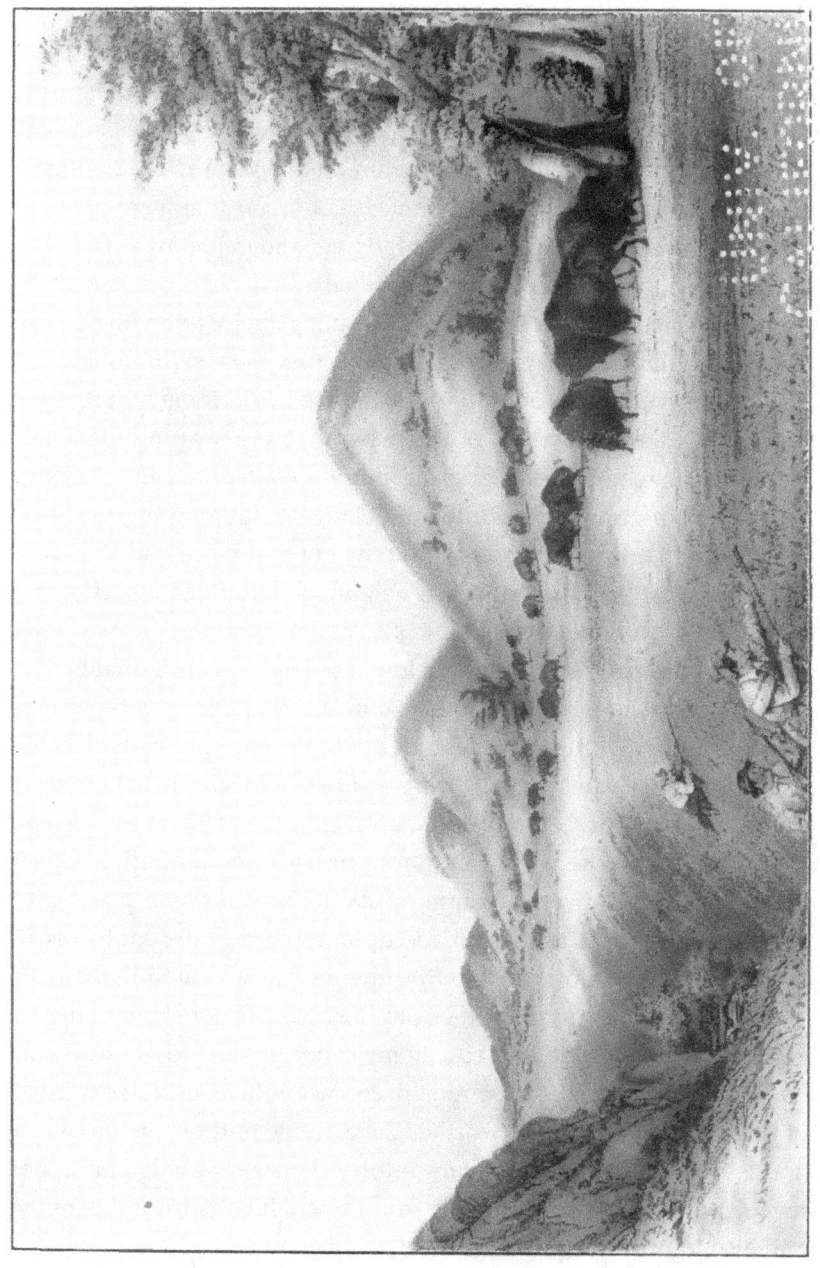

BUFFALO HUNT. APPROACHING IN A RAVINE

most immense herd crossing the Missouri River, and from an imprudence got our boat into imminent danger among them, from which we were highly delighted to make our escape. It was in the midst of the "running season," and we had heard the "roaring" (as it is called) of the herd when we were several miles from them. When we came in sight we were actually terrified at the immense numbers that were streaming down the green hills on one side of the river and galloping up and over the bluffs on the other. The river was filled and in parts blackened with their heads and horns as they were swimming about, following up their objects and making desperate battle while they were swimming.

    I deemed it imprudent for our canoe to be dodging among them, and ran it ashore for a few hours, where we lay, waiting for the opportunity of seeing the river clear; but we waited in vain. At length we pushed off, and successfully made our way among them. The immense numbers that had passed the river at that place had torn down the prairie bank of fifteen feet in height so as to form a sort of road or landingplace, where they all in succession clambered up. Many in their turmoil had been wafted below this landing, and, unable to regain it against the swiftness of the current, had fastened themselves along in crowds, hugging close to the high bank under which they were standing. As we were drifting by these, and supposing ourselves out of danger, I drew up my rifle and shot one of them in the head. He tumbled into the water, and brought with him a hundred others, which in a moment were swimming about our canoe and placing it in great danger. No attack was made upon us, and in the confusion the poor beasts knew not, perhaps, the enemy that was among them; but we were liable to be sunk by them, as they were furiously hooking and climbing on to each other. I rose in my canoe, and by my gestures and hallooing kept them from coming in contact with us until we were out of their reach. Fort Leavenworth is the extreme outpost on the frontier and is in the heart of the Indian country. This garrison is placed here for the purpose of protecting the frontier inhabitants from the Indians and also to preserve peace among the tribes.

    In this delightful cantonment there are generally stationed six or seven companies of infantry and ten or fifteen officers, several of whom have their wives and daughters with them, forming a very pleasant little community. Of pastimes they have many, such as riding on horseback or in carriages over the beautiful green fields of the prairies, picking strawberries and wild plums, deer-chasing, grouse-shooting, horse-racing, and other amusements of the garrison, in which they are almost constantly engaged. I have joined several times in the deer-hunts, and more frequently in grouse-shooting, which constitutes the principal amusement of this place.

This delicious bird, which is found in great abundance in nearly all the North American prairies, and most generally called the prairie hen, is, from what I can learn, very much like the English grouse, or heath hen, both in size, in color, and in habits. They make their appearance in these parts in the months of August and September, from the higher latitudes, where they go in the early part of the summer to raise their broods.

I was lucky enough the other day, with one of the officers of the garrison, to gain the enviable distinction of having brought in together seventy-five of these fine birds, which we killed in one afternoon; and although I am quite ashamed to confess the manner in which we killed the greater part of them, I am not so professed a sportsman as to induce me to conceal the fact. We had a fine pointer and had legitimately followed the sportsman's style for a part of the afternoon, but seeing the prairies on fire several miles ahead of us, and the wind driving the fire gradually toward us, we found these poor birds driven before its long line, which seemed to extend from horizon to horizon, and they were flying in swarms or flocks that would at times almost fill the air. They generally flew half a mile or so and lit down again in the grass, where they would sit until the fire was close upon them and then they would rise again. We observed by watching their motions that they lit in great numbers in every solitary tree, and we placed ourselves near each of these trees in turn, and shot them down as they settled in them, sometimes killing five or six at a shot by getting a range upon them.

In this way we retreated miles before the flames, murdering poor birds, and getting much credit at the Fort for our good shooting, as we were mutually pledged to keep our secret.

A burning prairie is one of the most sublime scenes in this country.

There are many ways in which fire is communicated to them by both the white men and the Indians – by accident, as they call it.

It is frequently done for the purpose of getting a fresh crop of grass for grazing, and also to secure easier travelling, inasmuch as the old grass is liable to entangle the feet of man and horse.

Over the high prairie, where the grass is short, the fire creeps with a flame so feeble that one can easily step over it. The wild animals often rest in their lairs until the flames touch their noses. Then they reluctantly rise, leap over the fire, and trot off among the cinders, where the fire has left the ground as black as jet. These scenes at night are indescribably beautiful, when the flames, seen from miles distant, appear to be sparkling and brilliant chains of liquid fire hanging in graceful festoons from the skies, for the hills are entirely obscured.

But the burning plain has another aspect when the grass is seven or eight feet high and the flames are driven by the hurricanes that often sweep over the meadows of the Missouri, the Platte, and the Arkansas. This grass is so high that we were obliged to stand in our stirrups to look over its waving tops. The fire in this grass before such a wind travels at a frightful speed, and often destroys parties of Indians on their fleetest horses who are so unlucky as to be overtaken by it. The high grass, being filled with wild-pea vines and other impediments, render it necessary to take the zigzag trails of the deer and buffalo. At length the dense column of smoke, which is swept along in advance of the fire, terrifies the horse, and he refuses to move until the burning grass is upon him, and he falls, while the swelling flood of smoke moves on like a thunder cloud rolling over the earth, with the glare of lightning and its thunder rumbling as it goes.

Batiste, Bogard, and Patrick Raymond, from the Fort, who, like Bogard, had been a free trapper in the Rocky Mountains, with our Indian guide Pah-me-o- ne-quah (the red thunder), were jogging back from a neighboring village over a high bluff which overlooked an immense valley of high grass, when I said to my comrades as we were about to descend the bluff: "We will take that buffalo trail, where the travelling herds have slashed down the high grass, and making for that blue point rising, as you can just discern, above this ocean of grass, a good day's work will bring us over this vast meadow before sunset." Soon after we entered my Indian guide dismounted slowly from his horse, and lying prostrate on the ground, with his face in the dirt, he *cried*, and was talking to the spirits of the brave – "For," said he, "over this beautiful plain dwells the Spirit of Fire! He rides in yonder cloud; his face blackens with rage at the sound of the trampling hoofs; the *fire-bow* is in his hand; he draws it across the path of the Indian, and quicker than lightning a thousand flames rise to destroy him. It was here," said he, "that the brave son of Wah-chee-ton and the strong-armed warriors of his band, just twelve moons since, licked the fire from the blazing wand of that great magician. A circular cloud sprang up from the prairie around them! it was raised, and their doom was fixed by the Spirit of Fire! Friends! it is the season of fire; and I fear, from the smell of the wind, that the Spirit is awake!"

Pah-me-o-ne-qua said no more, but mounted his wild horse and, waving his hand, glided through the thick mazes of waving grass. We were on his trail and busily traced him until the mid-day sun brought us to a halt. He stood like a statue, while his black eyes, in sullen silence, swept the horizon round; and then, with a deep-drawn sigh, he gracefully sunk to the earth, and lay with his face to the ground. Our buffalo tongues and pemmican and marrow-fat were spread before us, and we were in the full enjoyment of these dainties of the Western world when, quicker than the frightened elk, our Indian friend sprang upon his feet. His eyes skimmed again slowly over the prairie's surface, and then laid himself as before on the ground.

"Red Thunder seems sullen to-day," said Bogard; "he startles at every rush of the wind and scowls at the whole world that is about him."

"There's a rare chap for you, a fellow who would shake his fist at Heaven when he is at home, and here, in a grass-patch, must make his fire-medicine for a circumstance that he could easily leave at a shake of his horse's heels."

"I know by the expression of your face, mon, you neever have seen the world on fire yet, and therefore you know nothin' at all of a hurly burly of this kind – did ye ? Did ye iver see the fire in high grass, runnin' with a strong wind, about five mile and the half, and thin hear it strike into a slash of dry canebrake ? If I were advisin' I would say that we are gettin' too far in this imbustible meadow, for the grass is too dry to make a light matter of, at this season of the year. An' now I'll tell ye how McKenzie and I were served at this place about two years ago – hollo, what's that?"

Red Thunder was on his feet, his long arm was stretched over the grass, and his blazing eyeballs starting from their sockets.

"White man," said he, "see that small cloud rising from the prairie. He rises. The hoofs of horses have waked him. The Fire Spirit is awake; this wind is from his nostrils, and his face is this way."

He said no more, but his swift horse darted under him, and he slid over the waving grass as it was bent before the wind. We were quickly on his trail. The extraordinary leaps of his wild horse occasionally raised his shoulders to view, then he sank again in the waving billows of grass. On the wind above our heads was an eagle. His neck was stretched for the towering bluff, and his thrilling screams told of the secret that was behind him. Our horses were swift and we struggled hard, but our hope was feeble, for the bluff was yet blue and nature nearly exhausted. The cool shadow advancing over the plain told that the sun was setting. Not daring to look back we strained every nerve. The roar of a distant cataract seemed gradually overtaking us. The wind increased, and the swift winged beetle and the heath hens drew their straight lines over our heads. The fleet bounding antelope passed us, and the still swifter, long legged hare, who leaves but a shadow as he flies. Here was no time for thought, but I recollect that the heavens were overcast, the distant thunder was heard, and the lightning reddening the scene, and the smell that came on the wind struck terror to my soul.

The piercing yell of my savage guide at this moment came back on the wind, his robe was seen waving in the air, as his foaming horse leaped up the bluff.

Our breath and our sinews were just enough, in this last struggle for life, to carry us to the summit. We had risen from a sea of fire. Now looking back, still trembling from our peril, I saw beneath me a cloud of black smoke which extended from one extremity of this vast plain to the other, and seemed to roll over the surface of a bed of liquid fire. Above this mighty desolation the white smoke rose like magnificent cliffs to the skies. Then behind all this we saw the black and smoking desolation left by this storm of fire.

CHAPTER XXIII
SONGS AND DANCES OF THE IOWAS

THE INDIANS who belong to this neighborhood, and constantly visit the post, are such primitive tribes as the Iowas, Kansas, Pawnees, Omahas, Ottoes and Missouries, and the remnants of the semicivilized tribes, the Delawares, Kickapoos, Pottawa- tamies, Peorias, Shawnees, and Kaskaskias. These latter named tribes are becoming agriculturists, and now get their living by ploughing, raising corn, cattle and horses. They have been left on the frontier surrounded by civilized neighbors to whom they have been induced to sell their lands, or to exchange them for much larger tracts of wild lands which the government has purchased from the savage tribes.

Of the tribes first mentioned, the Iowas, a small tribe of about two thousand souls, have departed further from their primitive ways. Although their wigwams, dress, customs, and personal appearance are those of the wilder tribes, they depend chiefly on their cornfields for subsistence. The present chief is Notch-ce-ning-a (the white cloud). He is the son of the distinguished chief of the same name, who died recently, loved by his tribe and respected by all of the civilized world who knew him. The son of White Cloud is a young man thirty-two years old, who has performed many noble and humane acts since he inherited his office. I have painted him in a buffalo robe, with a necklace of the grizzly bear claws and a profusion of wampum strings around his neck, and armed with his shield, bow and quivers.

The Iowas have a peculiar way of wearing their hair, which I have seen only in two other tribes. They shave the hair from the entire head leaving only a patch the size of the hand on the top. In the centre of this is the scalp lock, which grows to its utmost length. The rest of the patch is cut to about two inches long, and to it is attached a crest made of the deer's tail and horse hair dyed the most brilliant vermillion. The scalp lock, which is kept braided, is passed through a curiously carved bone that holds the crest in place and distributes it uniformly. Outside this bone the scalp lock braid is again passed through a small wooden or bone key. The Iowas boast that this extravagant hair dressing, which resembles in effect a Grecian helmet, and is accompanied by the quills of the war eagle, is done that their enemies may "lose no time in hunting for the scalp lock." These same tribes ornament the greater part of the face with vermillion. Red, green, black and white are the colors of all the American Indians, and none use them more lavishly than the Iowas. These are put on in the morning, and arranged according to the business of the day, or the society they are to mingle with. In the evening the paint is carefully washed off. In moving their camps as do the other tribes, following the ranges of the buffalo, they halt upon the ground, and the doctor or medicine man invokes the favor and protection of the Great Spirit by throwing tobacco on the spot chosen for each wigwam. After this is done the women come, raise the wigwam, arrange the interior, and light the fires, while the men sit around in a circle smoking their pipes. As the other tribes, they are also very fond of amusements and dancing. Their principal musical instrument is the drum. This is made by hollowing out a log, leaving a thin rim around the outside, and stretching over each end of a section about as big as a keg a piece of rawhide. In the bottom of this they always have a quantity of water which sends out a remarkably rich and liquid tone.

Among their dances is the Welcome Dance given to strangers, to whom in respect all the spectators as well as the musicians rise to their feet. The song is at first a lament for the friends who have died or have gone away, but it ends in a gay and lively strain and step, announcing that their place is taken by the friend who has arrived. The War Dance as it is given by the Iowas is divided into a number of parts. The first of these is called Eh-ros-ka. The song in this dance seems to be addressed to the enemy, since the word means a body rather than an individual, and runs thus :

O-ta-pa.
Why run you from us when you
Are the most powerful ?
But it was not you.

O-ta-pa.
It was your body that ran,
It was your body, O-ta-pa,
It was your body that ran.

The War song, which is for the last part of this dance, is quicker and begins with the ejaculation:

How-a. How-a.
O-ta-pa.
I am proud of being at home.
I am proud, O-ta-pa.
I am at home, my enemy ran.
I am proud, I am proud, O-ta-pa.

This song is accompanied by many boasts and threats to the enemy to whom it is addressed. A spirited part of the dance is the approach, in which the dancers show their method of advancing on the enemy. The song which accompanies this dance is:

Oh-ta-pa.
I am creeping on your track.
Keep on your guard, Oh-ta-pa.
Or I will hop on your back.
I will hop on you, I will hop on you.
Stand back my friends, I see them.
The enemies are here, I see them.
They are in a good place, I see them.

War songs are many in each tribe and always consist of vaunts and self-praise, undervaluing the enemy and taunting him with past victories. Besides these each tribe has one war song which is as purely national as "God Save the Queen" or "Yankee Doodle." The War whoop is sounded at the instant the Indians rush into battle as the signal of attack, and thus gets its terror from association rather than from anything peculiarly terrifying in the sound itself. It is a shrill sounded note on a high key, given out with a gradual swell, and shaken by a vibration made by the four fingers of the right hand over the mouth. This note is not allowed to be given unless in battle or in the war dances where it has its place. The Death song is strictly national in every tribe, and is sung by any one in the tribe either resolved or condemned to die. It is generally sung the night previous to the execution, and is kept up to the last moment. It is very doleful, and is addressed to the Great Spirit, and offers back the soul, which "entered in at the breast, and is now going out at the toe."

The Wolf song is, I believe, peculiar to the Iowas, and belongs to the medicine or mystery man. When a party of young men, having fatigued the whole village for several days with the war dance and boasts of how they are going to kill their enemies, go to bed, in order to rise early for their expedition, they are serenaded in the dead of night just as they have got into a sound sleep. The serenading party is made up of young men who care more for fun than taking scalps. Stealing behind the wigwams of the "war party," they begin a song which has been taken from the howling of a gang of wolves. This is so admirably adapted for music that they make of it duet, quartet and chorus. With this song and its howling, barking chorus they make it impossible to sleep, and the warriors get up, light the fire, divide the luxuries they have prepared for their journey, and smoke until daylight, when they are thanked by their tormentors, and wished a successful campaign.

A very beautiful dance of the Iowas is the Eagle dance, and is generally made part of the war dance, since the war eagle conquers all other birds of its species. In this dance each dancer imagines himself a soaring eagle, and as they dance forward from behind the musicians, they take the positions of eagles heading against the wind, and looking down, prepare to swoop on their prey below. The wind seems too strong for them, and they fall back, advance again, imitating the chattering of the bird, with the whistles they carry in their hands, while they sing:

It's me. I am a war eagle.

The wind is strong, but I am an eagle.

I'm not ashamed. No, I am not.

The twisting eagle's quill is on my head.

I see my enemy below me. I am an eagle, a war eagle.

Of Indian games I have previously spoken of the game of the Moccasin, called in the Iowa tongue Ing- kee-ko-kee. This is played by two, four or six persons seated in a circle on the ground with three or four moccasins lying in the centre. The player lifts each moccasin in turn, and leaves under one a small stone about the size of a hazel nut. The game is for his opponent to determine under which moccasin the stone is hid. Accompanying the game is this song:

Take care of yourself. Shoot well or you lose.
You warned me, but see, I have defeated you.
I am one of the Great Spirit's children.
Wakonda, I am. I am Wakonda.

This is sung with perfect rhythm, suiting the movements of the game, and often for hours without intermission, for this is one of the principal gambling games of a people fond of gambling.

The women have a game exclusively their own called Kon-tho-gra, or the game of the platter. This is played with a number of blocks the size of a half dollar, marked with certain points for counting the game. These are shaken in a bowl, and the bowl is turned over on a sort of pillow. After the bowl is turned the bets are made, and decided by the number of points and colors that appear.

The Kickapoos have long lived in alliance with the Sacs and Foxes, and speak a language so similar that they seem almost to be of one family. The present chief of this tribe, whose name is Kee-an-ne-kuk (the foremost man), usually called the Shawnee Prophet, is a very shrewd and talented man. When he sat for his portrait, he took the attitude of prayer. And I soon learned that he was a very devoted Christian, regularly holding meetings in his tribe on the Sabbath, preaching to them and exhorting them to a belief in the Christian religion, and to an abandonment of the fatal habit of whiskey drinking, which he strenuously represented as the bane that was to destroy them all, if they did not entirely cease to use it. I went on the Sabbath to hear this eloquent man preach when he had his people assembled in the woods, and although I could not understand his language, I was surprised and pleased with the natural ease and emphasis and gesticulation, which carried their own evidence of the eloquence of his sermon.

How far the efforts of this zealous man have succeeded in christianizing I cannot tell, but it is quite certain that his constant endeavors have completely abolished the practice of drinking whiskey in his tribe.

It was told to me in the tribe by the Traders (though I am afraid to vouch for the whole truth of it) that while a Methodist preacher was soliciting him for permission to preach in his village, the Prophet refused him the privilege, but secretly took him aside and supported him until he learned from him his creed, and his system of teaching it to others, when he discharged him, and commenced preaching among his people himself; pretending to have had an interview with some superhuman mission or inspired personage. If there was anything to be gained he concluded he might as well have it as another person; and with this view he instituted a prayer which he ingeniously carved on a maple stick of an inch and a half in breadth, in characters somewhat resembling Chinese letters. These sticks, with the prayers on them, he has introduced into every family of the tribe, and into the hands of every individual, and as he makes them all, he sells them at his own price, and has thus added lucre to fame. Every man, woman and child in the tribe, so far as I saw them, were in the habit of saying their prayer from this stick when going to bed at night, and also when rising in the morning, which was invariably done by placing the forefinger of the right hand under the upper character, until they repeat a sentence or two, which it suggests to them, and then slipping it under the next, and the next, and so on, to the bottom of the stick, which altogether required about ten minutes, as it was sung over in a sort of a chant, to the end. In any case he has effectually turned their attention toward temperance and industry in the pursuits of agriculture and the arts.

Among the Omahas I painted the portrait of a young man which was generally approved. A few days after I saw him looking at the portrait, and then walking surlily away. At length he came back with the interpreter and told me that I had painted all the others looking straight forward. He, too, had always looked the white man straight in the face, but I had shown him looking the other way, as if he was ashamed. I learned shortly afterward, that if I did not alter it and make his eyes look straight in front of him, I must fight him. He was even then in front of my wigwam and ready for me.

Palette in hand, I went out and found him sure enough, naked and ready. I explained that I loved him too much to fight him, but if he only wanted me to change his eyes I could easily do it the next day. The next day he promptly presented himself, and with some water colors and white lead, I painted him a new pair of eyes, while he sat staring over the bridge of his nose in a most extraordinary manner. These pleased him greatly, since they were looking straight forward. He then shook hands with me and presented me with a pair of leggings. A sponge and some clean water were only necessary afterward to take off the new pair of eyes from a portrait which is one of the most interesting I painted.

CHAPTER XXIV
PAINTING BLACK HAWK AND HIS WARRIORS

MY LITTLE bark has been soaked in the water again, and Batiste and Bogard have paddled, and I have steered and dodged our little craft among the snags and sawyers until at last we landed the humble little thing among the huge steamers and floating palaces at the wharf of this bustling and growing city of St. Louis.

And first of all I must relate the fate of my little boat, which had borne us safe over two thousand miles of the Missouri's turbid and boiling current, with no fault, excepting two or three instances, when the waves became too saucy, and she, like the best of boats of her size, went to the bottom and left us soused, to paddle our way to the shore and drag out our things and dry them in the sun.

When we landed at the wharf my luggage was all taken out and removed to my hotel, and when I returned a few hours afterward to look for my little boat, some *mystery* or *medicine* operation had relieved me from any further anxiety or trouble about it – it had gone and never returned, although it had safely passed the countries of mysteries, and had often lain weeks and months at the villages of red men, with no laws to guard it; and had also often been taken out of the water by *mysterymen,* and carried up the bank and turned against my wigwam, and by them again safely carried to the river's edge, and put afloat upon the water when I was ready to take a seat in it.

St. Louis, which is fourteen hundred miles west of New York, is a flourishing town of fifteen thousand inhabitants, and destined to be the great emporium of the West – the greatest inland town in America.

This is the great depot of all the fur trading companies to the Upper Missouri and Rocky Mountains, and their starting-place; and also for the Santa Fé, and other trading companies, who reach the Mexican borders overland to trade for silver bullion from the extensive mines of that rich country.

In my sojourn in St. Louis, among many other kind and congenial friends I met, I have had daily interviews with Governor Clarke, who, with Captain Lewis, were the first explorers across the Rocky Mountains and down the Columbia river to the Pacific ocean thirty-two years ago. He is now Superintendent of Indian Affairs for all the western and north-western regions, and the interests of these people could not be in better hands. His whitened locks are still shaken with roars of laughter and jests among the numerous citizens, who all love him and rally around him continually in his hospitable mansion.

Batiste and Bogard, I found, after remaining here a few days, had been about as unceremoniously snatched off as my little canoe. Bogard particularly had hard luck, as he had made a show of a few hundred dollars which he had saved of his hard earnings in the Rocky Mountains. He came down with a liberal heart, which he had gained in an Indian life of ten years, and a strong taste, which he had acquired for whiskey in a country where it was sold for twenty dollars a gallon, and with an independence which illy harmonized with the rules and regulations of a country of laws. The consequence was that by the "Hawk and Buzzard" system, and Rocky mountain liberality and Rocky mountain prodigality, the poor fellow was soon "jugged," where he could dream of beavers and the free and cooling breezes of the mountain air, without the pleasure of setting his trap for the one or the hope of ever having the pleasure of breathing the other.

Mr. Catlin's narrative was here broken off by a visit to Pensacola, but elsewhere in his notes it appears that this was not his first acquaintance with Governor Clark. In the notes to his Indian catalogue, it appears that he had accompanied Governor Clarke on one of his visits to the Kansas tribe, and, returning to St. Louis, painted the portraits of Black Hawk and five of his warriors, who at the time were prisoners at Jefferson Barracks.

The Black Hawk war, of which every school boy has heard, was fought in the summer of 1832. Black Hawk was the old chief of the Sacs and Foxes. These were once two distinct tribes, but having a similar language, at some time not very remote, were united and afterward known under their joint name. Keokuk, one of the younger chiefs, with others of the tribe, made a treaty of sale of their lands in Illinois, and agreed to move further west. Black Hawk was not only not a party to the treaty, but opposed it, and subsequently, with others of his tribe, recrossed the Mississippi, and recovered their corn fields, that were then owned and cultivated by the whites.

General Scott accordingly sent out a detachment of regulars from Fort Dearborn (Chicago) and called for volunteers. Among the regulars was Lieutenant Jefferson Davis, and among the volunteers, private Abraham Lincoln, of Captain Iles's Company of Illinois Mounted Rangers. The rendezvous was John Dixon's Ferry, now Dixon, Illinois. On the 27th of August, 1832, Black Hawk, with several of his warriors, was captured at Bad Axe by two Winnebago Indians, and was taken to General Street at Prairie du Chien, where he made his memorable speech.

With other prisoners Black Hawk was taken by Lieutenant Jefferson Davis to Jefferson Barracks at St. Louis, where Mr. Catlin painted them during this visit. Of them he says:

We were immediately struck with admiration at the gigantic and symmetrical figures of these warriors, who seemed, as they reclined in native ease and gracefulness, with their half-naked bodies exposed to view, rather like statues from some master hand than like beings of a race called degenerate and debased. We extended our hands, which they rose to grasp, and to our greeting 'How d' ye do?' they responded in the same words, accompanying them with a hearty shake of the hand. They were all clad in leggings and moccasins of buckskin, and wore blankets thrown around them like a Roman toga, which leaves one arm bare. The youngest of them had their necks painted bright vermillion, and their faces transversely streaked with alternate stripes of red and black. From their faces and eyebrows the hair was carefully plucked out. They had also shaved or pulled it from their heads, with the exception of a tuft about three inches wide from the crown to the back of the head. This was plaited in a queue, with the edges cut down to an inch in length, and was plastered with vermillion until it stood up like a cock's comb.

Muk-a-ta-mish-a-kah-kaik (the black hawk) was the leader of the Black Hawk War [Mr. Catlin continues.] Although his name has carried terror through the country, he has heretofore been distinguished as a speaker and councillor rather than as a warrior. I believe it has been pretty generally admitted that Nah-pope and the Prophet were, in fact, the instigators of the war. Both of these had much higher claims to the name of warrior than Black Hawk ever had. This chief, Black Hawk, I painted in a plain suit of buckskin, with strings of wampum in his ears and on his neck. He held in his hand his medicine-bag, which was the skin of a black hawk, from which he had taken his name, and the tail of which made him a fan that he was constantly using.

The eldest son of Black Hawk, Nah-see-us-kuk (the whirling thunder), is a very handsome young warrior, and one of the finest looking Indians I ever saw. There is a strong party in the tribe that is anxious to make this young man chief, and I think it is more than likely that Keokuk may meet his fate by his hand, or by some of the tribe, who are anxious to reinstate the family of Black Hawk.

Of this young man the Hon. Augustus Murray writes in 1837:

"Whirling Thunder is a fine young chief. . . . After the defeat of his tribe in 1832 he was taken prisoner with his father and paraded through the Atlantic states. One evening he was present at a party where a young lady sang a ballad with much taste and pathos. Nah- see-us-kuk, who was standing at a distance, listened with profound attention, and at the close of the song took an eagle's feather from his head-dress, and giving it to a by-stander said: 'Take that to your mocking-bird squaw.'"

Wah-pi-kee-suck (the white cloud), and more widely known as the Prophet, was an even more important historical character painted at this time by Mr. Catlin, since he was believed to be the principal mover in the Black Hawk war. He was distinguished by the white cloth head-dress he wore in fight, when he also carried a white flag in his hand, and dressed in very white deerskin with fringed seams. In his portrait he carried a pipe over à yard long, the stem of which was ornamented with the neck feathers of the duck and beads and ribbon streamers. According to Mr. Catlin's notes, he was endeavoring to secure the favor of the whites by letting his hair grow out like that of the white men.

Nah-pope (the soup) was the brother of the Prophet, and Black Hawk's second in command. Drake in his *Book of the Indians* relates that when Mr. Catlin was about to paint Nah-pope he seized the chain and cannon ball that were fastened to his leg, and, holding them up, said : "Make me so, and show me to the Great Father." When Mr. Catlin refused to do as he wished he made grimaces to prevent the artist from catching his likeness. Mr. Catlin merely remarks in his notes that he wished to be painted with a white flag in his hand. His own narrative is resumed in the next chapter.

CHAPTER XXV
WITH THE ARMY AT FORT GIBSON

FORT GIBSON is the extreme south-western post on the United States frontier. It is beautifully situated on the Arkansas river, in the midst of an extensive and lovely prairie, and is at present occupied by the Seventh Regiment of Infantry under the command of General Arbuckle, one of the oldest officers on the frontier, and the builder of the fort.

Having the permission of Secretary of War Cass I accompanied the dragoons in their summer campaign. The object of this campaign seems to have for its object a better acquaintance with the Pawnees and Camanches. These are two large tribes of roaming Indians, who have not yet recognized the United States through treaty, and have accordingly struck frequent blows on the prairie and plundered the traders. For this I cannot much blame them, for the Spaniards advancing gradually on one side and the Americans on the other, are fast destroying the fur and game of the country, which furnish them their subsistence. The movement of the dragoons seems to be most humane, and I hope may prove so both for ourselves and the Indians.

The regiment of eight hundred men with whom I am to travel is composed of young men of respectable families, who would act on all occasions from feelings of pride and honor, in addition to those of the common soldier. After many difficulties they have had to encounter they have at length all assembled, and the grassy plains are resounding with the trampling hoofs of the prancing war horse, and already the hills are echoing back the notes of the spirit-stirring trumpets. Day before yesterday the troops were reviewed by General Leavenworth, who has just arrived to take command.

Both regiments were drawn up in battle array, in fatigue dress, and passing through a number of the manœuvres of battle, of charge and repulse, etc., presenting a novel and thrilling scene in the prairie, to the thousands of Indians and others who had assembled to witness the display. The proud and manly deportment of these young men remind one forcibly of a regiment of Independent Volunteers, and the horses have a most beautiful appearance from the arrangement of colors. Each company of horses has been selected of one color entire. There is a company of bays, a company of blacks, one of whites, one of sorrels, one of grays, one of cream color, etc., etc., which render the companies distinct, and the effect exceedingly pleasing. This regiment goes out under the command of Colonel Dodge, and from his well-tested qualifications, and from the beautiful equipment of the command, there can be little doubt but that they will do credit to themselves and honor to their country, so far as honors can be gained and laurels can be plucked from their wild stems in a savage country.

It is a pretty thing for an army of mounted men to be gayly prancing over the boundless green fields of the west. Although the first part of the journey will be picturesque and pleasing, the after part will be fatiguing and tiresome in the extreme. As the troops advance the grass, and consequently the game, will diminish, and water in many places will not be found. Meanwhile, with half famished horses and exhausted men, we may have to contend with an enemy on its own ground, with horses fresh and ready for action. The plan to be pursued is to send out runners to the different bands, explaining the friendly intentions of our government, and to invite them to a meeting. For this purpose several Camanche and Pawnee prisoners have been bought from the Osages, who may be of service in securing a friendly interview. During the delay I have been recording the deeds and looks of the Osages.

The Osages, or as they call themselves, the Wa-waw- see, are a tribe of about five thousand members, living on the head-waters of the Arkansas and Grand rivers.

The Osages may justly be said to be the tallest race of men in North America, either of red or white skins; there being very few indeed of the men, at their full growth, who are less than six feet in stature, and very many of them six and a half, and others seven feet. They are at the same time well-proportioned in their limbs, and good looking; being rather narrow in the shoulders, and, like most all very tall people, a little inclined to stoop; not throwing the chest out and the head and shoulders back quite as much as the Crows and Mandans and other tribes among which I have been familiar. Their movement is graceful and quick, and in war and the chase I think they are equal to any of the tribes about them.

This tribe, though living, as they long have, near the borders of the civilized community, have studiously rejected everything of civilized customs, and are uniformly dressed in skins of their own dressing, strictly maintain- / ing their primitive looks and manners, excepting in the blankets, which have been recently admitted to their use instead of the buffalo robes that are now getting scarce among them.

The Osages are one of the tribes who shave the head, as I have before described, and they decorate and paint it with great care and some considerable taste. There is a peculiarity in the heads of these people which is very striking to the eye of a traveller, and which I find is produced by artificial means in infancy. Their children, like those of all the other tribes, are carried on a board and slung upon the mother's back. The infants are lashed to the boards, with their backs upon them, apparently in a very uncomfortable condition; and with the Osages, the head of the child bound down so tight to the board as to force in the occipital bone, and create an unnatural deficiency on the back part, and consequently more than a natural elevation of the top of the head. This custom they told me they practised because "it pressed out a bold and manly appearance in front"

These people, like all those tribes who shave the head, cut and slit their ears, and suspend from them great quantities of wampum and tinsel ornaments. Their necks are generally ornamented also with a profusion of wampum and beads; and as they live in a warm climate, where there is not so much necessity for warm clothing, as among the more northern tribes, of whom I have been heretofore speaking, their shoulders, arms, and chests are generally naked, and painted in a great variety of picturesque ways, with silver bands on the wrists, and oftentimes a profusion of rings on the fingers.

The head chief of the Osages at this time is a young man by the name of Clermont, the son of a very distinguished chief of that name who recently died. I painted the portrait of this chief at full length, in a beautiful dress, his leggings fringed with scalp-locks, and in his hand his favorite and valued war-club.

By his side I have painted also at full length his wife and child. She was richly dressed in costly cloths of civilized manufacture, which is almost a solitary instance among the Osages, who so studiously reject every luxury and every custom of civilized people; and, among those, the use of whiskey, which is on all sides tendered to them – but almost uniformly rejected! This is an unusual and unaccountable thing, unless the influence which the missionaries and teachers have exercised has brought about this result.

Three of the braves came to me and asked to be painted together. It was explained to me that they were of the best families of the Osage nation, and having a peculiar attachment for one another, they desired me to paint them all on one canvas, which I did. These portraits fairly set forth the dress and ornaments of the young men of the tribe. The only dress they wear in warm weather is the breech-cloth, leggings, and moccasins of dressed skins, with garters worn below the knee that are ornamented lavishly with beads and wampum.

Their names are Ko-ha-tun-ka (the big crow), Nah- com-e-shee (the man of the bed), and Mun-ne-pus-kee (he who is not afraid). These three young men have been, with eight or ten others, set aside by Black Dog to accompany the dragoons as guides and hunters, so I shall doubtless see much of them. Joseph Chadwick, a young man from St. Louis, whom I have long known and greatly esteem, and myself will be the only guests on this campaign. Although I have an order from the Secretary of War to the commanding officer to protect and supply me, I shall ask but for protection, as I have, with my friend Joe, laid in our own supplies for the campaign, not putting the government to any expense when I am in pursuit of my own private objects.

Again I am in the land of the buffalo and the fleet bounding antelope. We are in camp on the point of land between the Red River and its junction with the False Wachita, and in a country too beautiful to be adequately described with the pen. The verdure about us is of the deepest green, and the plains literally speckled with buffalo. Lieutenant Wheelock, Joseph Chadwick and I rode to the top of some of the prairie bluffs, and we agreed that even our horses looked and admired. They gave no heed to the rich herbage under their feet, but, with deep-drawn sighs, curved their necks loftily, and with wide-open eyes gazed over the landscape beneath us. There over the pictured vales, bounded by mountain streaks of blue, the "bold dragoons" were marching in beautiful order, forming a train a mile in length. From the point where we stood the line was seen in miniature, and, bending its way over the undulating hills, looked like a huge black snake gracefully gliding over a carpet of green.

Scarcely a day has passed in which we have not crossed oak ridges where the ground was almost literally covered with vines of delicious grapes, five-eighths of an inch in diameter, and hanging in endless clusters.

The next hour we would be trailing through broad and verdant valleys of green prairies, and oftentimes find our progress completely arrested by hundreds of acres of small plum-trees of four or six feet in height, so closely woven and interlocked as to dispute our progress, and send us several miles around. Every bush that was in sight was so loaded with the weight of its delicious wild fruit that they were without leaves on their branches and bent quite to the ground. Among these, and in patches, were beds of wild roses, wild currants, and gooseberries; and underneath them huge masses of the prickly pears, and beautiful and tempting wild flowers that sweetened the atmosphere above; while an occasional huge yellow rattlesnake or a copperhead could be seen gliding over or basking across their tendrils and leaves.

On the eighth day of our march we met, for the first time, a herd of buffaloes, being in advance of the command in company with General Leavenworth, Colonel Dodge, and several other officers. General Leavenworth and Colonel Dodge, with their pistols, gallantly and handsomely belabored a fat cow, and were in together at the death. I was not quite so fortunate in my selection, for the one which I selected of the same sex, younger and coy, led me a hard chase, when, at length, the full speed of my horse forced us to close company, and she desperately assaulted his shoulders with her horns. My gun was aimed, but, missing its fire, and the muzzle becoming entangled in her mane, was instantly broken in two in my hands, and fell over my shoulder. My pistols were then brought to bear upon her, and, though severely wounded, she succeeded in reaching the thicket, and left me without "a deed of chivalry to boast."

We are halting here for a few days to recruit horses and men, and if the Pawnees are as near to us as we have strong reason to believe, from their recent trails and fires, it is probable that within a few days we shall "thrash" them or "get thrashed," unless they elude our search by flying before us to their hiding-places.

Colonel Dodge had employed two famous Delaware Indians, semi-civilized, as guides and hunters. They entertained Chadwick and myself by the ingenious preparations they were making for decoying and trapping game. Among these was a sort *of* whistle made of the bark of a young sapling, two or three inches long, which they carried in their pouches, and with it could imitate exactly the bleating of a young fawn. Being impatient with the delay, we concluded to do a little deer stalking on Maple Ridge, in a heavy timbered country said to be full of deer and turkeys. Taking with us a half-breed Indian, we drove, approached, and saw their white flags many times, but could not get near enough for a shot.

At length at the edge of a small prairie I heard the sudden "ma, ma, ma," the sound of the bleating of the small fawn. I was sure the little creature was in the shade of a small copse, so I dropped into the grass to wait until it came out. Presently I began to creep slowly on my hands and knees toward the bushes, sure that I would get a shot at one or both of its parents. I was now quite near, with my rifle cocked and drawn to my shoulder, when to my surprise the little thing called out "ma" directly behind me. I turned, and there within two feet of me lay the Delawares laughing at me. My hunting pretensions were a good deal cut down by this occurrence.

We are in camp on the ground on which Judge Martin and servant were killed, and his son kidnapped by either the Pawnees or Camanches but a few weeks ago.

Judge Martin, living on the lower part of the Red River, was in the habit of taking his children and a couple of black men-servants with him every summer into these wild regions, where he spent several months in killing buffaloes and other wild game. The news came to Fort Gibson but a few weeks before we started that he had been set upon by a party of Indians. A detachment of troops was speedily sent to the spot, where they found his body horridly mangled, and also that of one of his negroes; and it is supposed that his son, a fine boy of nine years of age, has been taken home to their villages by them, where they still retain him, and where it is our hope to recover him.

It belongs now to the regiment of dragoons to demand the surrender of the murderers. The moment the Indians discover us in a large body they will probably think that we are seeking revenge, and will either attack us or will elude our search. As enemies I do not believe they will stand to meet us. But as friends I think we may bring them to a talk, if the proper means are adopted.

CHAPTER XXVI
LASSOING WILD HORSES

GENERAL LEAVENWORTH, Colonel Dodge, Lieutenant Wheelock and myself were jogging along, and all in turn complaining of the lameness of our bones, when the General, who had long ago had his surfeit of the chase on the Upper Missouri, remonstrated in the following manner: "Well, Colonel, this running for buffaloes is bad business for us – we are getting too old; I have had enough of this fun in my life; it is the height of folly for us, but will do well enough for boys." Colonel Dodge assented at once, while I, who had tried it in every form on the Upper Missouri, joined my assent to the folly of our destroying our horses.

In the midst of this conversation, as we were jogging along in "Indian file," General Leavenworth taking the lead, when just rising to the top of a little hill, over which it seems he had had an instant peep, he dropped himself suddenly upon the side of his horse and wheeled and told us with an agitated whisper that a snug little band of buffaloes was quietly grazing just over the knoll, and that if I would take to the left and Lieutenant Wheelock to the right and let him and the Colonel dash right into the midst of them we could play the devil with them. One half of this at least was said after he had got upon his feet and taken off his portmanteau and valise. I am almost sure nothing else was said, and if it had been I should not have heard it, for I was too eagerly gazing and plying the whip to hear or to see anything but the trampling hoofs and the blackened throng and the darting steeds and the flashing of guns! As my horse was darting into the timber the limb of a tree scraped me into the grass, from which I soon raised my head, and all was silent and all out of sight save the dragoon regiment, which I could see in the distance creeping along on the top of a high hill. I found my legs under me in a few moments, and at last got them to work, and brought "Charley" out of the bushes, where he had "brought up" in the top of a fallen tree without damage.

Neither buffalo, horse, nor rider was harmed in this attack. Colonel Dodge and Lieutenant Wheelock had joined the regiment, when General Leavenworth joined me, with too much game expression *yet* in his eye to allow him more time than to say, "I'll have that calf before I quit!" and away he sailed in pursuit of a fine calf that had been hidden on the ground during the chase, and was now making its way over the prairies in pursuit of the herd. I rode to the top of a little hill to witness the success of the General's second effort, and after he had come close upon the little affrighted animal, it dodged about in such a manner as evidently to perplex his horse, which at last fell in a hole, and both were instantly out of my sight. I ran with all possible speed to the spot, and found him on his hands and knees, endeavoring to get up. I dismounted and raised him on to his feet, when I asked him if he was hurt, to which he replied "no, but I might have been," when he instantly fainted. I had left my canteen with my portmanteau, nor was there water near us. I took my lancet from my pocket and was tying his arm to open a vein when he recovered, assuring me that he was not in the least injured. I caught his horse and after two or three hours we joined the regiment.

We had been gayly advancing, although in some apprehension from the Indians, when on the second night, when we were in camp and sound asleep, there was the flash and the sound of a gun within a few paces of us, followed by frightful groans. In an instant we were all upon our hands and knees, and our snorting horses, breaking their lassos, were over our heads in full speed, and the cries of "Indians! Pawnees! Indians!" from every part of the camp. In a few moments quiet was restored, and a general inquiry revealed that a raw recruit standing sentry saw, as he supposed, an Indian creeping through the bushes. As he did not, when called, advance and give the countersign, the sentry "let off" his rifle and shot a poor dragoon horse that had strayed away the day before, but had faithfully followed our trail, and poking through the bushes had come up to rejoin his comrades and take up his army life again. In the meanwhile we could hear the trampling hoofs of our horses, which were making off in all directions.

Our camp was usually in four lines forming a square of fifteen or twenty rods in diameter. On these lines our packs and saddles were

WILD HORSES AT PLAY

laid about five feet apart. Each man, after grazing his horse, tied it to a stake a little distance from his feet, thus inclosing the horses within the square to secure them in case of attack or alarm. In this manner we lay at the time of the alarm, and our horses, breaking their ropes, dashed out over the heads of their masters.

It took us two days after this disaster to recover them, with the exception of about thirty, who took up again their free life on the plains. Indian trails began to grow fresh, and their smoke was seen in various directions ahead of us. On the fourth day of our march at noon we discovered a large party at several miles distance, sitting on their horses and looking at us. From the glistening of the blades of their lances, which were blazing as they turned them in the sun, it was at first thought that they were Mexican cavalry, who might have been apprized of our approach into their country. On drawing a little nearer, however, and scanning them closer with our spy-glasses, they were soon ascertained to be a war-party of Camanches, on the lookout for their enemies.

The regiment was called to a halt, and the requisite preparations having been made and orders issued, we advanced in a direct line toward them until we were within two or three miles of them, when they suddenly disappeared over the hill, and soon after showed themselves on another mound further off. The course of the regiment was then changed, and another advance toward them was commenced, and as before they disappeared and showed themselves in another direction. After several such efforts, which proved ineffectual, Colonel Dodge ordered the command to halt, while he rode forward with a few of his staff and an ensign carrying a white flag. I joined this advance, and the Indians stood their ground until we had come within half a mile of them. We then came to a halt, and the white flag was sent a little in advance, at which one of their party galloped out in advance of the war-party, on a milk white horse, carrying a piece of white buffalo skin on the point of his long lance in reply to our flag.

This moment was the commencement of one of the most thrilling and beautiful scenes I ever witnessed. All eyes, both from his own party and ours, were fixed upon the manoeuvres of this gallant little fellow, and he well knew it.

The distance between the two parties was perhaps half a mile, and that a beautiful and gently sloping prairie, over which he was for the space of a quarter of an hour reining and spurring his maddened horse, and gradually approaching us by tacking to the right and the left, like a vessel beating against the wind. He at length came prancing and leaping along till he met the flag of the regiment, when he leaned his spear for a moment against it, looking the bearer full in the face, wheeled his horse, and dashed up to Colonel Dodge, with his extended hand, which was instantly grasped and shaken. We all had him by the hand in a moment, and the rest of the party seeing him received in this friendly manner, instead of being sacrificed, as they undoubtedly expected, started under "full whip" in a direct line toward us, and in a moment gathered, like a black cloud, around us! The regiment then moved up in regular order, and a general shake of the hand ensued, which was done by every warrior riding along the ranks and shaking the hand of every one as he passed. This took some time, but during it my eyes were fixed on the gallant and wonderful appearance of the little fellow who bore us the white flag on the point of his lance. He rode a fine and spirited wild horse, which was as white as the drifted snow, and had a luxuriant mane, and a long and bushy tail that swept the ground. In his hand he tightly drew the reins upon a heavy Spanish bit, and at every jump plunged into the horse's side a huge pair of spurs, plundered doubtless from the Spaniards in the border wars which are continually waged on the Mexican frontiers. The eyes of this noble little steed seemed to be squeezed almost out of its head, and its fright had brought out a perspiration fretted into white foam and lather. The warrior's quiver was slung on the warrior's back, and his bow, grasped in his left hand, was ready for instant use. His shield was on his arm, and across his thigh, in a beautiful buckskin cover, his gun was slung. In his right hand he held a lance fourteen feet long.

Thus armed and equipped was this dashing cavalier, and the rest of the party in much the same manner. Many of them were leading an extra horse, which we learned was the favorite war horse, for this was a war party in search of the enemy. After a shake of the hand we dismounted, the pipe was lit and passed around. Afterward Colonel

Dodge explained, through a Camanche who spoke some Spanish, that we were sent by the President to see the chiefs of the Camanches and Pawnee Picts, shake hands, smoke the pipe of peace, and establish an acquaintance with them, and a system of trade that would benefit both.

They listened attentively, and taking Colonel Dodge at his word with perfect confidence, told him that their great town was within a few days march, and pointing in the direction, offered to abandon their war excursion and escort us to it. This they did in good faith. During this march over one of the loveliest countries in the world we had much to amuse and excite us. The whole country seemed to be alive with buffaloes and bands of wild horses. There is no other animal on the prairie so wild and so sagacious as the horse. So remarkably keen is their eye that they will generally run "at sight" a mile distant. There is no doubt but that they are able to distinguish the character of the enemy approaching, and, when off, will generally run three or four miles before they stop. I made many attempts to approach them by stealth, when they were grazing or gambolling, and never succeeded but once.

On this occasion I left my horse, and, with my friend Chadwick, skulked through a ravine for a couple of miles until within gun shot of a fine herd, when under the cover of a little hedge I used my pencil sketching them. In this herd we saw all the colors that can be seen in a kennel of English hounds. Some were milk white, some jet black, others were sorrel, bay and cream color, many were iron gray, others were pied. Their manes were very thick, and hanging in the wildest confusion over their necks and faces. Their long tails swept the ground. After we had satisfied our curiosity in looking at these proud and playful animals, we agreed that we would try the experiment of "creasing" one, as it is termed in this country. This is done by shooting them through the gristle on the top of the neck, which stuns them so that they fall, and are secured with the hobbles on the feet, after which they rise again without fatal injury. This is a practice often resorted to by expert hunters, with good rifles, who are not able to take them in any other way. My friend Joe and I were armed on this occasion, each with a light fowling-piece, which has not quite the preciseness in throwing a bullet that a rifle has, and having both levelled our pieces at the withers of a noble, fine-looking iron gray, we pulled trigger, and the poor creature fell, and the rest of the herd were out of sight in a moment. We had the most inexpressible mortification of finding that we never had thought of hobbles or halters to secure him, and in a few moments more had the still greater mortification, and even anguish, to find that one of our shots had broken the poor creature's neck, and that he was quite dead. The laments of poor Chadwick for the wicked folly of destroying this noble animal were such as I never shall forget.

The usual mode of taking the wild horses is by throwing the lasso, while pursuing them at full speed, and dropping a noose over their necks, by which their speed is soon checked, and they are "choked down." The lasso is a thong of rawhide, some ten or fifteen yards in length, twisted or braided, with a noose fixed at the end of it. This, when the coil of the lasso is thrown out, drops with great certainty over the neck of the animal, which is soon conquered.

The Indian, when he starts for a wild horse, mounts one of the fleetest he can get, and coiling his lasso on his arm, starts off under the "full whip," till he can enter the band, when he soon gets it over the neck of one of the number, when he instantly dismounts, leaving his own horse, and runs as fast as he can, letting the lasso pass out gradually and carefully through his hands, until the horse falls for want of breath, and lies helpless on the ground, at which time the Indian advances slowly toward the horse's head, keeping his lasso tight upon its neck, until he fastens a pair of hobbles on the animal's two forefeet, when he loosens the lasso (giving the horse chance to breathe), and gives it a noose around the under jaw, by which he gets great power over the affrighted animal, which is rearing and plunging when it gets breath, and by which, as he advances, hand over hand, toward the horse's nose, he is able to hold it down and prevent it from throwing itself over on its back, at the hazard of its limbs. By this means he gradually advances, until he is able to place his hand on the animal's nose, and over its eyes, and at length to breathe in its nostrils, when it soon becomes docile and conquered, so that he has little else to do than to remove the hobbles from its feet, and lead or ride it into camp.

It is a curious fact known to all the Indians that the wild horse, the deer, elk and other animals never run in a straight line, but curve almost invariably to the left. The Indian, seeing the direction in which the horse is "leaning," knows just about the point where it will stop, and steers in a straight line to it, where they will arrive at about the same time, the horse having run a mile, and his pursuer a little more than half the distance. The alarmed animal is then off again, and, by a series of such curves, before sundown the horse's strength is about gone, and it is easy to get near enough to throw the lasso. One must imagine the rest – what kindness and caressing during the night, for they camp on the spot, enables the Indian to ride his captured horse into the village the next morning.

I have said that the horse and other animals generally turn to the left. How curious this fact, and from what cause ? All animals bend their course, because they wish to return to their wonted abodes; but why bend to the left ? Once on the Upper Missouri with one man I started thirty miles over the prairie to a Sioux village. The second day being cloudy we had nothing to guide us. Everywhere was short grass, and the horizon a straight line. Late in the afternoon, very tired, we found ourselves at the same camp we had made the night before. All the time we thought we were walking in a straight line we were traveling in a circle. The next day, the sun shining, we kept our course. On arriving at the Sioux village the Indians laughed heartily at our adventure, and all the chiefs agreed in telling me that when a man is lost on the prairie he travels in a circle and invariably to the left.

The "breaking down" or taming is not, however, without the most desperate trial on the part of the horse, which tries in every manner to escape, until at last its power is exhausted, and the poor animal seems to be so completely conquered that it submits quietly, and is led or ridden away with but little difficulty. Great care, however, is taken not to destroy the spirit of the animal, which is carefully preserved, although the Indians are cruel masters.

The wild horse of these regions is a small but very powerful animal, with a prominent eye, sharp nose, high nostril, small feet and delicate leg. Undoubtedly it sprang from stock introduced by the Spaniards at the time of the invasion of Mexico, which having strayed off

CATCHING THE WILD HORSE

to the plains, has stocked them as far north as Lake Winnipeg. Many of the Indian tribes have their traditions about the first appearance of horses. The Sioux call the wild horse Shonk-a-wa-wakon (the medicine dog). To the Indian the wild horse is very important. Vast numbers are killed by them for food when game is scarce. But their chief use is in enabling him to take his game more easily and to carry his burdens.

While on our march we had several times the opportunity of seeing the Indians take them with the lasso. But the first successful attempt was by one of our guides named Beatté, a Frenchman, whose parents had lived nearly all their lives in an Osage village, where he had been reared from infancy, and had acquired all the skill and tact of his Indian teachers. This took place at noon one day while the regiment halted. Beatté and several others had asked Colonel Dodge's permission to pursue a drove of horses then in sight. They started off, and, by following a ravine, got near the unsuspecting animals and chased them for several miles in full view of the regiment. After a race of two or three miles Beatté was seen with his wild horse down, and the band and the other hunters rapidly leaving him.

Seeing him in this condition I galloped off to him as rapidly as possible, and had the satisfaction of seeing the whole operation of "breaking down," and bringing in the wild animal. When the command resumed its march, Beatté, astride of his wild horse, rode quietly and without difficulty, until night, the whole thing, the capture, and breaking, all having been accomplished within the space of one hour, our usual and daily halt at midday.

CHAPTER XXVII
VISITING THE CAMANCHES

AT LAST our Camanche guides told us we were approaching their village. From the top of the gentle elevation to which they led us, in the midst of this lovely valley, we could just discern in the midst of the shrubbery that lined the watercourse the tops of the wigwams and their curling smoke.

The chiefs of the war party asked us to halt so they could ride on and tell their people we were coming. We dismounted for an hour or more, and could see them hurrying to catch their horses, and at length several hundreds of the braves came dashing on at full speed to welcome us. We immediately mounted, and they, wheeling their horses, formed a line "dressed" like well disciplined cavalry. Our regiment was drawn up in three columns, with a line in front formed of Colonel Dodge and his staff. In this rank my friend Chadwick and I were also paraded, and had a fine view of the whole manœuvre, which was most picturesque and thrilling.

In the centre of our advance was our white flag, and the Indians responded by planting by its side one they had sent forward. A fact that I think here worth noting is that, even among the most primitive tribes I have visited, the white flag is always the flag of truce, and is inviolable. The chief going to war always carries in some form or other a piece of white skin or bark wrapped around a stick under his arm. He also carries a red flag which is to be unrolled if the occasion calls for "blood."

The two lines were thus drawn up, face to face, within twenty or thirty yards of each other, and, to the everlasing credit of the Camanches, whom the world had always looked upon as murderous and hostile, they had all come out, with their heads uncovered, and without a weapon of any kind, to meet a war-party bristling with arms, and trespassing to the middle of their country. They had every reason to look upon us as their natural enemy, and yet, instead of arms or defences, or even of frowns, they galloped out without an expression of fear or dismay, and evidently with expressions of joy and impatient pleasure, to shake us by the hand, on the bare assertion of Colonel Dodge, which had been made to the chiefs, that "we came to see them on a friendly visit."

After we had sat and gazed at each other in this way for some half an hour or so, the head chief of the band came galloping up to Colonel Dodge, and having shaken him by the hand, passed on to the other officers in turn, and then rode alongside of the different columns, shaking hands with every dragoon in the regiment; he was followed in this by his principal chiefs and braves, which took up nearly an hour longer. Then the Indians escorted us to the banks of a fine clear stream, a half mile from their village, suitable for our camp, and we were soon bivouacked.

No sooner were we in camp than Major Mason, Lieutenant Wheelock, Captains Brown and Duncan, and Chadwick and myself galloped off to the village, and through it to the prairie, where at least three thousand horses were grazing, eager to see the splendid Arabian horses we had heard were owned by the Camanche warriors. We returned to camp quite crestfallen. Although there were some tolerable nags among this motley group of all colors and shapes, the beautiful Arabian must be further south than this, or it must be a horse of the imagination. The Camanche horses are generally small, all of them being of wild breed, and are tough and serviceable. From what I can learn there are better horses near the Mexican border. But this information may be no more correct than that we had in the East of the horses here. Among these immense herds we found many mules, and these are more valuable than the horses.

The officers and men have bought a number of horses by giving for them a cheap blanket and a butcher knife, both worth about four dollars. In the East these horses would be worth from eighty to a hundred dollars. If we had goods to trade for them great profit could be made. A fine looking Indian was hanging about my tent for several days, scanning an old half-worn cotton umbrella that I carried to keep off* the sun, as I was suffering from ague. At last he offered to buy it with a neat limbed and pretty pied horse, if I would throw in a knife. I refused, for I did not know whether there was another umbrella in the regiment, and I needed this one. He came a second time and offered the horse for the umbrella alone. This offer I rejected. He seemed to think that the horse was not good enough, and returned with another of better quality. I tried to make him understand that I was sick and could not part with it. He rode back to the village and in a short time returned with one of the largest and finest mules I ever saw. This too I refused, and he disappeared. Captain Duncan coming in, I told him the circumstance, when he sprang to his feet.

"Where has the fellow gone? Here, Gosset, get my old umbrella out of the pack. I rolled it up with my wiper and the frying-pan. Get it as quick as lightning."

With the umbrella the Captain ran and overtook the Indian, and went with him to the village, but returned not with the mule, but with the second horse offered me.

The village of the Camanches, by the side of which we are in camp, is composed of six or seven hundred skin-covered lodges, like those of the Sioux and the other Missouri tribes. This village, with its thousands of wild inmates, horses and dogs, wild sports and domestic occupations, and the manners and looks of the people, presents a most curious scene.

We white men, strolling among the wigwams, are looked on with as much curiosity as if we had come from the moon, and evidently send a chill through the blood of the children and dogs when we appear. I was pleased to-day with the simplicity of a group which came out of the chief's lodge, and sketched it as quick as lightning, while Joe captured their attention by some trick I did not see, for I had no time to turn around. These were the younger members of the chief's family, left at home, while he and his wives had gone to visit the camp. I have also had the chance to see and sketch one of those extraordinary and amusing scenes which daily happen where so many dogs and so many squaws are traveling in such a confused mass. Each horse drags his load, and each dog, *i. e.* each dog that *will* do it, also dragging his wallet on a couple of poles, and each squaw with her load, and each ready for a quarrel, there is generally a fight. It commences usually among the dogs, and is sure to result in fisticuffs of the women; while the men, riding leisurely on the right or the left, take infinite pleasure in overlooking these desperate conflicts, at which they are sure to have a laugh, and in which as sure never to lend a hand.

The Camanches, like the northern tribes, have many games. In their ball-plays and some other games they are far behind the Sioux and others of the northern tribes, but in racing horses and riding they are not equalled by any other Indians on the Continent. Racing horses is their chief exercise and their principal mode of gambling; perhaps a more finished set of jockeys are not to be found. Among their feats of riding there is one that has astonished me more than anything of the kind I have ever seen, or expect to see, in my life: a stratagem of war, learned and practised by every young man in the tribe, by which he is able to drop his body upon the side of his horse at the instant he is passing, effectually screened from his enemies' weapons as he lies in a horizontal position behind the body of his horse, with his heel hanging over the horse's back, by which he has the power of throwing himself up again, and changing to the other side of the horse if necessary. In this wonderful condition he will hang while his horse is at fullest speed, carrying with him his bow and his shield, and also his long lance of fourteen feet in length, all or either of which he will wield upon his enemy as he passes, rising and throwing his arrows over the horse's back, or with equal ease and equal success under the horse's neck. This astonishing feat, which the young men have been repeatedly playing off to our surprise as well as amusement, while they have been galloping about in front of our tents, completely puzzled the whole of us, and appeared to be the result of magic rather than of skill through practise. I tried several times to get near them in order to see by what means their bodies could be suspended in this manner, where nothing could be seen but the heel hanging over the horse's back. But I was continually frustrated until I coaxed a young fellow within a short distance of me by a few plugs of tobacco. I found, on examination, that a short halter was passed around the neck of the horse, and both ends tightly braided into the mane near the withers. This left a loop hanging under the neck and on the breast, which being caught up in the hand made a sling into which the elbow fell, taking the weight of the body on the middle of the upper arm. Into this loop the rider drops suddenly and fearlessly, leaving his heel to hang over the back of the horse to steady him, and also to enable him to recover an upright position when he desires. This solved the matter, but left it an extraordinary result of persistent practice.

The Camanches are rather low in stature and approach corpulency. In their movements they are heavy and ungraceful, and on their feet one of the most unattractive and slovenly looking tribes of Indians I have ever seen. Indeed a Camanche on his feet is as awkward as a monkey on the ground without a limb to cling to. But the moment he lays his hand upon his horse, his face even becomes handsome, and he flies away a different being, surprising one with the ease and elegance of his movements. These people have several other feats of horsemanship, that are both pleasing and wonderful, of which they are very proud, and are always showing off. A people who spend the greater part of their lives on their horses' backs must become expert in everything that pertains to riding, and I can say that the Camanches are the most extraordinary horsemen I have seen, and I doubt whether they can be surpassed in any other part of the world.

For several days after we arrived there was a huge mass of flesh Ta-wah-que-nah (mountain of rock), who was put forward as the chief of the tribe, and all honors were paid to him by the regiment of dragoons. A perfect personification of Jack Falstaff in size and figure, he had an African face and a beard on his chin two or three inches long. His name he told me he got from having conducted a large party of Camanches through a secret and subterraneous passage in a mountain of granite rock lying back of the village, thus saving their lives from a more powerful enemy from whom there was no other escape. But it seems his name would have been more appropriate if it had been "mountain of flesh," for he weighs quite three hundred pounds. He proved to be, however, not the head chief, who was away on a war-party, and when he arrived the Mountain of Rock stepped quite into the background.

The head chief is Ee-shah-ko-nee (the bow and quiver). He is a mild and pleasant looking gentleman, dressed in a humble manner, with few ornaments and his hair carelessly falling about his face and over his shoulders, and seems to have the confidence of the entire tribe. Ish-a-ro-yeh (he who carries the world) and Is-sa-wah-tam-ah (the wolf tied with hair) are also chiefs of standing and of influence, as they were put forth by the head chiefs to be painted. The first of the two was the leader of the war-party that brought us here, and Colonel Dodge has presented him with a very fine gun. One of the most distinguished men in this country, and one of the leading warriors, is His-oo-san- ches (the Spaniard). He is a Spanish half-breed, for whom the Indians generally have only contemptuous feeling. But this man has always been in the front of battle and danger, and commands the highest respect and admiration of the tribe. It was he who dashed out so boldly from the war-party with the white flag on the point of the lance I have before described, and of whom I have made a sketch. This extraordinary little man, whose figure was slight, seemed to be all bone and muscle, and exhibited immense power by the curve of the bones in his legs and his arms. We had many exhibitions of his extraordinary strength as well as agility, and of his gentlemanly politeness and friendship we had as frequent evidences. As an instance of this, I will recite an occurrence which took place but a few days since, when we were moving our encampment to a more desirable ground on another side of their village. We had a deep and powerful stream to ford, when we had several men who were sick and obliged to be carried on litters. My friend "Joe" and I came up in the rear of the regiment where the litters with the sick were passing, and we found this little fellow up to his chin in the muddy water, wading and carrying one end of each litter on his head, as they were in turn passed over. After they had all passed, this gallant little fellow beckoned to me to dismount, and take a seat on his shoulders, which I declined, preferring to stick to my horse's back, which I did, as he took it by the bridle and conducted it through the shallowest ford. When I was across, I took from my belt a handsome knife and presented it to him, which seemed to please him very much.

CHAPTER XXVIII
THE STOLEN BOY

SO MANY of the men and officers fell sick that, after building a sort of fort with breastworks of timbers and bushes, we left them, and, much crippled in numbers, set out for the village of the Pawnee Picts, with several Camanches who agreed to pilot us.

We were four days marching over a fine country, mostly prairie, for the most part along the base of a stupendous range of mountains of reddish granite. These were without a tree or shrub, and looked as if they had dropped from the clouds and lay in a confused mass just where they had fallen. These mountains inclosed the Pawnee village on the bank of the Red River, about ninety miles from the Camanche town. The dragoons were drawn up within a half mile of the village, and camped in a square, where we remained three days. We found a numerous village of five or six hundred wigwams made of prairie grass thatched over poles, which are fastened in the ground and bent over at the top, resembling nothing so much as straw beehives.

To our great surprise we found these people cultivating extensive fields of corn, pumpkins, melons, beans and squashes. With these and an abundant supply of buffalo meat, they may be said to live very well. The next day after our arrival here Colonel Dodge opened a council with the chiefs in the chief's lodge, with most of his officers around him. He first explained to them the friendly intentions which brought him, and the wish of the government to establish a lasting peace with them. This they seemed at once to appreciate and regard with favor. The head chief is a very old man, and several times replied to Colonel Dodge in a very eloquent manner.

After Colonel Dodge had explained in general terms the objects of our visit, he told them that he should expect from them some account of the foul murder of Judge Martin and his family on the False Wachita, which had been perpetrated but a few weeks before, and which the Camanches had told us was done by the Pawnee Picts. The Colonel told them, also, that he learned from the Camanches that they had the little boy, the son of the murdered gentleman, in their possession, and that he should expect them to deliver him up, as an indispensable condition of the friendly arrangement that was now making. They positively denied the fact and all knowledge of it. The demand was repeatedly made, and as often denied, until at length a negro was discovered living with the Pawnees, who spoke good English, and coming into the council house said that such a boy had recently been brought into their village, and was now a prisoner among them. This excited great surprise and indignation in the council, and Colonel Dodge then informed the chiefs that the council would not take place until the boy was brought in. In this alarming dilemma all remained in gloomy silence for awhile, when Colonel Dodge further informed the chiefs that, as an evidence of his friendly intentions toward them, he had, on starting, purchased, at a very great price, from their enemies the Osages, two Pawnee (and one Kiowa) girls, who had been held by them for some years as prisoners, and whom he had brought the whole way home, and had here ready to be delivered to their friends and relations, but whom he certainly would never show until the little boy was produced. He also made another demand, which was for the restoration of a United States ranger, by the name of Abbé, who had been captured by them during the summer before. They acknowledged the seizure of this man, and all solemnly declared that he had been taken by a party of the Camanches, over whom they had no control, and carried beyond the Red River into the Mexican provinces, where he was put to death. They held a long consultation about the boy, and seeing their plans defeated by the evidence of the negro, and also being convinced of the friendly disposition of the Colonel, by bringing home their prisoners from the Osages, they sent out and had the boy brought in from the middle of a corn-field where he had been secreted. He is a smart and very intelligent boy of nine years of age, and when he came in he was entirely naked, as they keep their own boys of that age. There was a great excitement in the council when the little fellow was brought in, and as he passed amongst them, he looked around and exclaimed with some surprise, "What! are there white men here?" to which Colonel Dodge replied, and asked his name, and he promptly answered, "My name is Matthew Wright Martin."

He was then received into Colonel Dodge's arms, and an order was given for the Pawnee and Kiowa girls to be brought in. When they entered the council house they were at once recognized by their friends and relatives, who embraced them with the most extravagant expressions of joy and satisfaction.

The heart of the old chief was melted at this evidence of the white man's friendship. He rose to his feet and, taking Colonel Dodge in his arms, placed his left cheek against the left cheek of the Colonel, and held him for some minutes without saying a word, while the tears were flowing from his eyes. He then embraced each officer in turn, in the same silent and affectionate manner. This form took half an hour before it was finished.

From this moment the council, which before had been very grave and uncertain, became familiar and pleasing, and this excellent old man ordered the women to supply the dragoons with food. The little camp was indeed hungry, as they had eaten their last rations twelve hours before. The soldiers were now gladdened by the approach of a number of women, who brought their "back loads" of dried buffalo meat and green corn and threw it down among them.

The council thus proceeded successfully and pleasantly for several days, while the warriors of the Kiowas and Wicos, two adjoining and friendly tribes, and a number of Camanche bands who had heard of our arrival, were coming in. At length over two thousand of these wild and fearless looking fellows were assembled, and all from their horse's backs, with weapons in hand, saw our pitiful little encampment in a state of dependence and almost of starvation, for the country between this place and the Camanche village had been destitute of game. In addition, nearly one-half of our two hundred men were sick, and would have been incapable of resistance if we had been attacked.

These Pawnee Picts are undoubtedly a numerous and powerful tribe, and with Kiowas and Wicos, occupy the whole country on the head-waters of the Red River, and quite into and through the southern part of the Rocky Mountains. The old chief told me by signs, enumerating with his hands and fingers, that they had altogether three thousand warriors. These then, in an established alliance with the great tribe of Camanches, hunting and feasting together, and ready to join in common defence of their country, become a very formidable enemy when attacked on their own ground.

The name of the Pawnee Picts, we find to be in their own language, Tow-ee-ahge, the meaning of which I have not yet learned. I have ascertained, also, that these people are in no way related to the Pawnees of the Platte, who reside a thousand miles or more north of them, and know them only as enemies. There is no family or tribal resemblance, nor any in their language or customs. The Pawnees of the Platte shave the head, and the Pawnee Picts abominate the custom, allowing their hair to grow like the Camanches and other tribes.

The Pawnee Picts, as well as the Camanches, are generally a very clumsy and ordinary looking set of men, when on their feet, but being fine horsemen, are equally improved in appearance as soon as they mount upon their horses' backs.

Among the women of this tribe there were many that were exceedingly pretty in feature and in form, and also in expression, though their skins are very dark. The dress of the men in this tribe, as among the Camanches, consists generally in leggings of dressed skins and moccasins, with a flap or breech-clout, made also of dressed skins or furs, and often very beautifully ornamented with shells. Above the waist they seldom wear any drapery, owing to the warmth of the climate, which will rarely justify it, and their heads are generally without a head-dress, unlike the northern tribes who live in a colder climate, and actually require them for comfort.

The women of the Camanches and Pawnee Picts are always decently and comfortably clad, being covered generally with a gown or slip, that reaches from the chin quite down to the ankles, made of deer or elk skins, often garnished very prettily, and ornamented with long fringes of elk's teeth, which are fastened on them in rows, and more highly valued than any other decoration.

The two Pawnee girls, who had been purchased as prisoners from the Osages by the Indian Commissioner, the Rev. Samuel Schemmerhorn, and given to their friends, were Kah-kee-tsee (the thighs) and She-de-a (the wild sage). Wun-pan-to-me (the white weasel) and Tunk-aht-o-ye (the thunderer) were a Kiowa boy and girl bought at the same time and taken to their tribe by the dragoons. The girl was taken with us the whole distance on horseback to the Pawnee village. The boy, unhappily, was killed at Fort Gibson by being butted by a ram. He was a beautiful boy of nine, whose portrait I painted the day before he was killed.

The Kiowas are a much finer looking tribe than either the Camanches or the Pawnees. They are tall, erect, with an easy, graceful gait, and cultivate their hair so as to nearly reach the ground. They have for the most part that fine and Roman outline of head that is found among the northern tribes, and that is very unlike that of the Camanches and Pawnee Picts. Their language, moreover, is so different that they appear quite like strangers. The head chief of the Kiowas, Teh-toot-sah, we found to be a gentlemanly, high-minded man, who treated the dragoons and officers with great kindness while in his country. His long hair was put up in several long club-like divisions, and he wore many silver brooches extending quite down to his knees.

The chief of the Wicos is Ush-ee-kitz (he who fights with a feather). He is a very polite and polished Indian and very remarkable in his manner of embracing the officers and others in council. In all our talks and councils this man has been a conspicuous speaker. At the close of his speeches he steps forward and, taking each person, friend or foe, holds them closely and affectionately in his arms for several minutes. Another of the extraordinary men of this tribe is Kots-a-to-ah (the smoked shield). This man is seven feet tall, and is not only a great warrior, but so swift a runner that he chases the buffalo on foot and slays it with his knife.

Smoking the shield is one of the most curious as it is one of the most important of the Indian customs. A young man about to make him a shield digs a hole two feet deep in the ground and as large in diameter as he means to make his shield. In this he builds a fire, and over it a few inches higher than the ground he stretches the rawhide horizontally over the fire by means of little pegs driven through holes made near the edges of the skin. This skin is at first twice as large as the size of the shield is to be. Having got together his especial friends in a ring, they dance and sing around it, begging the Great Spirit to instil into it the power to protect him from his enemies. While these sing he spreads glue over the skin which is rubbed and dried in as the skin is heated. As the skin contracts the pegs are drawn out and others inserted. This process is continued until the skin, taking up the glue and increasing in thickness, his friends think they have sung and danced long enough to make it almost arrow and bullet proof. The dance then ceases and the fire is put out. When the skin, now half the original size, is cooled, it is cut into the desired shape, and painted with the figure of an eagle, owl, buffalo, or whatever may be the bird or animal he has chosen to keep him from harm.

CHAPTER XXIX
A CRUEL MARCH

FROM THE Camanche village to Fort Canadian, Texas, was a six days severe march. The country was entirely prairie, the most of it high and dry ground, without water, for lack of which we suffered greatly. From day to day we have dragged along, exposed to the hot and burning rays of the sun, without a cloud to relieve its intensity, or a bush to shade us, or anything to cast a shadow except the bodies of our horses. The grass for a great part of the way was dried up, scarcely affording a bite for our horses, and sometimes, for the distance of many miles, the only water we could find was in stagnant pools, lying on the highest ground, in which the buffaloes had been lying and wallowing like hogs in a mud-puddle, and into which our poor and almost dying horses ran and plunged their noses, sucking up the dirty and poisonous draught, until, in some instances, they fell dead in their tracks. The men also (and oftentimes the writer of these lines) sprang from their horses, and ladled up and drank the disgusting and tepid draught, and with it filled their canteens, from which they were sucking the bilious contents during the day.

In our march we found many deep ravines, in the bottoms of which there were the marks of wild and powerful streams, except an occasional one, where we found the water dashing along in the coolest and clearest manner, but so *salt* that even our horses could not drink it.

This poisonous and indigestible water, with the intense rays of the sun in the hottest part of the summer, is the cause of the sickness of the horses and men.

During this march over these dry and parched plains we picked up many curious things of the fossil and mineral kind, and besides them a number of the horned frogs. In our portmanteaux we had a number of tin boxes in which we had carried Seidlitz powders, in these we caged a number of them safely in hopes to carry them home alive. My friend Joe has secured several remarkable specimens with horns three-quarters of an inch in length and very sharp at the points. Joe's fancy for horned frogs has grown into a sort of frog-mania, and his eyes are strained all day gazing into the grass and pebbles as he rides along for his little prizes.

We have just learned of the deaths of General Leavenworth, Lieutenant McClure, and ten of the fifteen men we left at the mouth of the False Wachita. It seemst that the General had moved on our trail a few days after we left, to the Cross Timbers, a distance of fifty or sixty miles, where he died. I am inclined to believe that his death is in consequence of the injury he received in falling from his horse when running a buffalo calf. From that moment he was different. Riding by his side several days after I said: "General, you have a bad cough!" "Yes," he replied, "I have killed myself in running that devilish calf. It was a lucky thing, Catlin, you painted that portrait of me before we started. It is all my dear wife will ever see of me."

Of the four hundred and fifty fine fellows who started from Fort Gibson four months since about one-third have died, and I believe the fates of as many more are sealed. After leaving the head-waters of the Canadian River my illness so increased that I had to be lifted on and off my horse. At length I could not ride at all, and was put in the baggage wagon with several sick soldiers, and for eight days, the most of the time delirious, I was jolted on the hard planks until the skin from my elbows and knees was worn through. At length we reached Fort Gibson, where I heard the sound of "Roslin Castle" with muffled drums six or eight times a day under my window, and could see as I lay each poor fellow lowered into his silent and peaceful habitation.

During my illness my friend Joe has been almost constantly at my bedside, and has given me every aid and every comfort that has been in his power. Such tried friendship as this one must always remember. When we started we were fresh and eager for the adventures before us. Our little pack-horse carried our bedding and culinary articles, among which we had a frying-pan and a coffee pot, coffee in good store and plenty of sugar. When we spread our bear-skin by night and kindled our fire in the grass we were sure of a delightful repast together and a refreshing sleep. During the march, as we were subject to no military subordination, we galloped about as we saw fit, and popped away at whatever we chose to spend our ammunition upon, and ran our noses into every wild crevice we chose. One of the most curious places we met in all our route was a mountain ridge of fossil shells. This was several hundred feet high and from a quarter to a half mile in breadth, composed of nothing but clam and oyster shells in a perfect state of petrifaction. Seen either individually or in the mass they were nothing but pure shells both in color and shape. In many instances they had never been opened, and taking out our knives and splitting them as one would an oyster, the fish was seen petrified in perfect form. By dipping it in water it showed the color and freshness of an oyster just opened and laid upon a plate ready to be eaten. In my opinion this is one of the greatest geological curiosities in this country, as it lies some thousands of feet above the level of the ocean, and seven hundred miles at least from the sea coast.

In another section over which we passed was a ridge of several miles running parallel to this ridge with neither grass nor earth under our feet. Our horses tread on a solid reddish rock. Dismounting I struck it with a hatchet and it resounded like an anvil. I found it to contain from sixty to eighty per cent. of solid iron. In other parts between the Camanche village and the Canadian River we found miles of surface entirely denuded except for small patches of grass and wild sage. This was a solid surface of dark gray gypsum, in which, from west to east, were streaks from three to five inches wide literally as white as the drifted snow. So it will be seen that the savage, who never converts these inexhaustible mineral resources of this wild country to his own use, must in time yield them to the enlightened and cultivating white man.

Since we came in from the prairies Colonel Dodge, Major Armstrong, the Indian Agent, and General Stokes, the Indian Commissioner, have been in council, with seven or eight of the neighboring Indian tribes invited to meet the Pawnee Picts, Camanches and Kiowas who came back with us. I cannot think of a scene more interesting than this in which the civilized, halfcivilized, and wild have met, embraced, smoked the calumet together for the first time, and pledged lasting peace and friendship. Here were three stages of man fearlessly asserting their rights, their happiness, and their friendship for each other. The vain orations of the half-polished and half-breed Choctaws and Cherokees, with all their finery and art, found their match in the brief and jarring gutturals of the wild and naked men.

Bringing these unknown people to a knowledge of one another and a general peace has been a handsome achievement. Yet I have strong doubts whether it will better their condition unless they are protected by the strong arm of the government in their rights. There is already a company of men fitted out which will start to-morrow to overtake these Indians and accompany them home with a large stock of goods, with traps for catching beavers, intending to build a trading house among them, where they, being the first traders in that country, will immediately amass a large fortune.

I have travelled too much among Indian tribes and seen too much not to know the evil consequences of such a system. Goods are sold at such exorbitant prices that the Indian gets a mere shadow for his peltries. If the government would promptly prohibit such establishments, and invite these Indians to our frontier posts, they would bring in their furs, their robes, horses, mules, etc., to this place, where there is an honorable competition, and where they would get four or five times as much for their articles of trade as they would get from a trader in the village, out of the reach of competition, and out of sight of the civilized world.

At the same time they would be continually coming where they would see good and pciished society, they would be gradually adopting our modes of living, introducing to their country our vegetables, our domestic animals, poultry, etc., and at length, our arts and manufactures. They would then see and estimate our military strength and advantages, and would be led to fear and respect us. In short, it would undoubtedly be the quickest and surest way to a general acquaintance – to friendship and peace, and at last to civilization.

CHAPTER XXX
A CHOCTAW BALL GAME

IN THE Indian country I have always attended every ball game I could hear of, if I could manage it by riding twenty or thirty miles. My custom has been to straddle the back of my horse and look on to the best advantage. In this way I have sometimes sat, oftentimes reclined, and sometimes almost dropped from my horse's back in laughing at the droll tricks, kicks and scuffles that follow in these almost superhuman struggles for the ball. These plays generally begin about nine o'clock in the morning. More than once I have balanced myself on my pony from that time until sundown, without one minute of intermission, before the game has been decided.

While at the Choctaw agency it was announced that there was to be a great play on a certain day within a few miles. Of course I attended. Monday afternoon at three o'clock I rode out to a very pretty prairie, about six miles distant, to the ball playground of the Choctaws, where we found several thousand Indians encamped. There were two points of timber about half a mile apart, in which the two parties for the play, with their families and friends, were encamped. My companions and myself, although we had been apprised that to see the whole of a ball play we must remain on the ground all the night previous, had brought nothing to sleep upon, resolving to keep our eyes open and see what happened through the night. During the afternoon we loitered about and afterward, at sundown, witnessed the ceremony of measuring out the ground, and erecting the "byes" or goals which were to guide the play. Each party had their goal made with two upright posts, about twenty-five feet high and six feet apart, set firm in the ground, with a pole across at the top. These goals were about forty or fifty rods apart, and at a point just half-way between was another small stake driven down, where the ball was to be thrown up at the firing of a gun. All this preparation was made by some old men who were, it seems, selected to be the judges of the play. They drew a line from one bye to the other, to which a great concourse of women and old men, boys and girls, with dogs and horses, came to make their bets. The betting was all done across this line, and seemed to be chiefly left to the women. Goods and chattels, knives, dresses, blankets, pots and kettles, dogs and horses and guns were placed in the possession of *stake-holders,* who sat by them and watched them on the ground all night preparatory to the play.

The sticks with which this tribe play are bent into an oblong hoop at the end, with a sort of slight web of small thongs tied across to prevent the ball from passing through. The players hold one of these in each hand, and by leaping into the air, they catch the ball between the two nettings and throw it, without being allowed to strike it or catch it in their hands.

In every ball-play of these people it is a rule of the play that no man shall wear moccasins on his feet, or any other dress than his breech-cloth around his waist, with a beautiful bead belt and a "tail," made of white horsehair or quills, and a "mane" on the neck of horsehair, dyed of various colors.

This game had been arranged and "made up" three or four months before the parties met to play it, and in the following manner: The two champions who led the two parties, and had the alternate choosing of the players through the whole tribe, sent runners, with the ball-sticks most fantastically ornamented with ribbons and red paint, to be touched by each one of the chosen players, who thereby agreed to be on the spot at the appointed time and ready for the play. The ground having been all prepared and preliminaries of the game all settled, and the bets all made, and goods all "staked," night came on without the appearance of any players on the ground. But soon after dark a procession of lighted flambeaux was seen coming from each encampment to the ground, where the players assembled around their respective byes, and at the beat of the drums and chants of the women, each party of players commenced the "ball-play dance." Each party danced for a quarter of an hour around their respective byes in their ballplay dress, rattling their ball-sticks together in the most violent manner, and all singing as loud as they could raise their voices, while the women of each party who had their goods at stake formed into two rows on the line between the two parties of players and danced also, in a uniform step, and all their voices joined in chants to the Great Spirit, in which they solicited his favor in deciding the game to their advantage, and also encouraged the players to exert every power they possessed in the struggle that was to ensue. In the meantime, four old medicine-men, who were to start the ball, and who were to be judges of the play, were smoking to the Great Spirit that they might judge rightly and impartially in so important an affair.

This dance was one of the most picturesque scenes imaginable, and was repeated at intervals of every half hour during the night, and exactly in the same manner. In the morning, at the hour, the two parties and all their friends were drawn out and over the ground, when at length the game commenced by the judges throwing up the ball at the firing of a gun. The players, who were some six or seven hundred in numbers, endeavored to catch the ball in their sticks and throw it home and between their respective stakes, which counts one for game. In this game every player was dressed alike, that is, divested of all dress except the girdle and the tail which I have before described. In these desperate struggles, when the ball is up, hundreds are running, leaping over one another's heads, and darting between their opponents' legs, tripping, and throwing, and foiling each other in every possible way, and every voice raised to the highest key in shrill yelps and barks; the rapid succession of feats and incidents is astonishing. Frequently there is individual resistance, which ends in violent scuffles and fisticuffs. At such times their sticks are dropped and they fight it out unmolested. Every weapon, by a rule in all ball games, is left in their camps, and no one is allowed to go for one, so their broils are settled without much personal injury.

There are times when the ball falls to the ground, that for a quarter of an hour a confused mass of ballsticks, shins, bloody noses are carried around to different parts of the grounds, without any one of the players being able to see the ball. For each time the ball was passed between the stakes of either side one was counted for game and a halt of a minute given. The judges then started the play again, and a similar struggle was carried on until the successful party gained one

DANCE BEFORE THE BALL-PLAY

hundred, which was the limit, and took the stakes. These, then, by previous agreement, produced several jugs of whiskey, which sent them all home merry but not drunk.

After this exciting day we went to the agency house where we had a number of dances. One I had not seen before was the Eagle dance, and a very pretty scene. This is got up by the young men in honor of that bird, for which they seem to have a religious regard. This picturesque dance was given by twelve or sixteen men, whose bodies were almost naked and painted white with white clay. Each dancer held in his hand the tail of an eagle, while his head was decorated with an eagle's quill. Spears were stuck in the ground around which the dance was performed by four men at a time, who had simultaneously, at the beat of the drum, jumped up from the ground where they had all sat in rows of four, one row immediately behind the other, and ready to take the place of the first four when they left the ground fatigued, which they did by hopping or jumping around behind the rest, and taking their seats, ready to come up again in their turn, after each of the other sets had been through the same forms.

In this dance the steps, or rather jumps, were different from anything I had ever witnessed before, as the dancers were squat down, with their bodies almost to the ground, in a severe and most difficult posture.

From Ha-tchoo-tuck-nee (the snapping turtle), whom the whites call familiarly Peter Pinchlin, a gentlemanly and well educated man, I have heard several of the curious traditions of this tribe, which I will try to give in his own words.

The Deluge. "Our people have always had a tradition of the Deluge, which happened in this way: there was total darkness for a great time over the whole of the earth; the Choctaw doctors or mystery-men looked out for daylight for a long time, until at last they despaired of ever seeing it, and the whole nation was unhappy. At last a light was discovered in the North, and there was great rejoicing until it was found to be great mountains of water rolling on, which destroyed them all except a few families who had expected it and built a great raft, on which they were saved."

Future State. "Our people all believe that the spirit lives in a future state, that it has a great distance to travel after death toward the West, that it has to cross a dreadful deep and rapid stream, which is hemmed in on both sides by high and rugged hills; over this stream, from hill to hill, there lies a long and slippery pine-log, with the bark peeled off, over which the dead have to pass to the delightful hunting-grounds. On the other side of the stream there are six persons of the good huntinggrounds, with rocks in their hands, which they throw at them all when they are on the middle of the log. The good walk on safely to the good hunting-grounds, where there is one continual day, where the trees are always green, where the sky has no clouds, where there are continual fine and cooling breezes, where there is one continual scene of feasting, dancing and rejoicing, where there is no pain or trouble, and people never grow old, but forever live young and enjoy the youthful pleasures.

"The wicked see the stones coming and try to dodge, by which they fall from the log, and go down thousands of feet to the water which is dashing over the rocks. There the trees are all dead, and the dead are always hungry and have nothing to eat, are always sick and never die. There thousands crawl up the sides of a high rock where they can overlook the good huntinggrounds they can never reach.

"Our people have a crawfish band. A long time ago they lived under the ground, and used to come up out of the mud as crawfish, and go about on their hands and feet. They spoke no language at all, nor could they understand any. The entrance to their cave was through the mud, so for a long time the Choctaws were unable to molest them. The Choctaws used to lie and wait for them to come out and lie in the sun, where they would try to make their acquaintance.

"One day a party of them were run upon so suddenly by the Choctaws that they had no time to go through the mud to their cave, but were driven into another entrance they had through the rocks. The Choctaws then determined to smoke them out, and at last succeeded. They afterward treated them very kindly, taught them the Choctaw language, made them walk on two legs, cut their toe-nails, and pluck the hair from their bodies. Then they adopted them into

AN INDIAN BALL-PLAY

the nation. The remainder of the crawfish band is living underground to this day."

The tradition among the Choctaws is that they came from the region beyond the Rocky Mountains. "Many winters ago," said Peter Pinchlin, "the Choctaws began moving from the country where they then lived, which was a great distance to the west of the great river and the mountains of snow. They were many years on the way. A big medicine-man led them by going before with a long red pole. This he stuck in the ground every night when they went into camp. Every morning this pole was found leaning to the east. Then he told them they must keep on traveling until the pole stood upright in camp. There the Great Spirit meant that they should live. Finally they came to a place called Nah-ne-wa-ye (the sloping hill). There the pole stood upright. They then pitched their camp a mile square, with the men outside and the women in the centre. This is the centre of the old Choctaw nation to this day."

CHAPTER XXXI
ALONE WITH CHARLEY

AS SOON as I recovered sufficient strength I made up my mind that if I could get out on the prairies and move northward I could save myself from that voracious burial ground that lay in front of my window, and where for so long I lay and imagined myself going with the other poor fellows, whose mournful dirges were played from day to day under my window. Rather die on the prairies and be devoured by wolves, rather fall in fight with the Indians and be scalped, than the lingering death that would consign me to that insatiable grave.

So having packed my canvases and brushes to be sent by river to St. Louis, one fine morning my horse Charley was brought up and saddled. A bearskin and a buffalo robe being spread on the saddle, and a tin coffee pot and cup tied to it, with a few pounds of hard biscuit in my portmanteau, with my fowling piece in my hand and my pistols in my belt, with my sketch book slung across my back, and my little compass in my pocket, I took leave of Fort Gibson against the advice of my surgeon and all the officers of the garrison, who gathered around me to bid me farewell.

Thus alone, without any other companion than my affectionate horse, Charley, I turned my face northward, to find my way over the five hundred miles of prairie that lay between me and the Missouri river. No one can ever know the pleasure of that moment which placed me alone upon the boundless sea of waving grass, over which my proud horse was prancing, and I with my life in my own hands.

Day by day I thus pranced and galloped along the whole way, through waving grass and green fields, occasionally lying in the grass an hour or so, until the grim shaking and chattering of an ague chill had passed off, and through the nights slept on my bearskin spread upon the grass, with my saddle for my pillow, and my buffalo robe drawn over me for my covering. My horse Charley was picketed near me at the end of his lasso, which gave him room for his grazing, and thus we snored and never were denied the doleful serenades of the gangs of sneaking wolves that in the morning we saw gazing at us, impatient to pick up the crumbs and bones that were left when we moved away from our feeble fire that, in the absence of timber, had been made of dried buffalo dung.

Charley was a noble animal, a wild Camanche halfbreed, the color of a clay bank, and with a sweeping black mane and tail. I had bought him from Colonel Burbank of the Ninth Infantry before the journey to the Camanche village, and he was considered the finest, as he was the best known horse in that part of the country. Charley and I, although heretofore the best of friends, had always too much company to fully realize how much we loved one another. We both required the solitary and mutual dependence we were now entering upon to fully develop the actual strength of the sympathy that had long existed between us. Another advantage arose from the fact that we were old campaigners, and knew exactly how to go at our work. There was yet another advantage that helped us very much. Twenty-five days is a long time to be without speaking to any one, or hearing the cheering sound of a human voice. From our long companionship and practice Charley and I had established a sort of language that was very significant, and helped to break the awful monotony of a solitary campaign on the prairie.

When I went into the field to catch Charley after a separation of two months, I said, "Charley, is that you ?" He instantly replied, "Ee-gh-ee-e-eeh" (yes). This was distinctly an affirmative. Some might call this gibberish, but it had its meaning, and he was always sure to be right provided I put to him the right sort of questions. He had one agreeable trait which does not always belong to those one meets in far-away countries, he always answered immediately.

I generally halted on the bank of some little stream, at half an hour's sun, where feed was good for Charley, and where I could get wood to kindle my fire and water for my coffee. The first thing was to undress "Charley" and drive down his picket, to which he was fastened, to graze over a circle that he could describe at the end of his lasso. In this wise he busily fed himself until nightfall, and after my coffee was made and drank, I moved him up, with his picket by my head, so that I could lay my hand upon his lasso in an instant, in case of any alarm that was liable to drive him from me. On one of these evenings, when he was grazing as usual, he slipped the lasso over his head, and deliberately took his supper at his pleasure, wherever he chose to prefer it, as he was strolling around. When night came I went as usual to catch him, but he evaded me. He led me a chase for a half-mile, and it seemed that I would have to make the rest of my journey on foot. At last I went back and laid myself on my bearskin and went to sleep.

In the middle of the night I half opened my eyes and saw a huge figure leaning over me, which I took to be an Indian about to take my scalp. I was too paralyzed to move, but at length I realized that it was my faithful horse, Charley, who, whether from fear or affection, stood with his forefeet at the edge of my bed, his head hanging over me, and fast asleep.

The next morning I saw him some distance off browsing, and after breakfast started to catch him. But he refused to be caught. I recalled the affection he had shown me in the night, so I thought I would try a new method. Slinging my saddle on to my back and trailing my gun I started on. After I had gone about a quarter of a mile I looked around, and there by our camp fire Charley stood, with his head and tail on high, gazing over the prairie. Presently I heard him neighing loudly behind me, and galloping at full speed he passed me, when suddenly he wheeled and stood before me, trembling like an aspen. I walked up to him, and he held down his head for the bridle, and literally stooped for the saddle, both of us equally pleased at being together again.

On the night of this memorable day Charley and I stopped in an enchanting little lawn of five or six acres, on the banks of a cool and rippling stream, that was alive with fish, and every now and then a fine brood of young ducks, just old enough for delicious food, and too unsophisticated to avoid an easy and simple death. This little lawn was surrounded by bunches and copses of the most luxuriant foliage, spreading out their branches as if offering protection, groups of cherry and plum trees that supported festoons of purple grapes. Everywhere the green carpet was decked out with wild flowers, from the drooping head of the modest sunflower to the erect lilies and violets that crept beneath them. By the side of this cool stream Charley was fastened, and near him my bearskin was laid. I soon brought a fine string of perch from the brook for my little fire, and had with it a broiled duck and a fine cup of coffee for my dinner and supper united, at half an hour's sun. After this I strolled about this sweet little paradise, which I found was chosen, not only by myself, but by the wild deer.

The Indians also, I found, had loved it once and left It, for here and there were their solitary and deserted graves which told, though briefly, of former chants and sports, and perhaps of wars and deaths, that had once rung and echoed through this little silent vale.

On my return to my camp I lay down and looked awhile into the blue sky above, over which the milk-white clouds were passing, with the sun setting in the west, and the silver moon rising in the east, and felt anew my own insignificance as I contemplated that wonderful clock whose time is infallible and whose motion is eternal. At last I trembled at the expanse of my thoughts, and turning, my eyes rested on a newspaper I had brought from the garrison. This was *The National Intelligencer* I had read for years, but never with the zest and relish as now, in this clean sweet valley of dead silence.

After reading it I laughed at what I had almost forgotten while among the Minatarees on the Upper Missouri. I had in my painting kit a copy of the *Commercial Advertiser*, edited by my friend, Colonel Stone. The Minatarees thought me mad when they saw me for hours poring over its columns. They had various conjectures, but the most popular was that I was looking at it to cure my sore eyes, and they called it the "medicine cloth for sore eyes." I had several liberal offers for it but I had already accepted a beautiful painted robe for it from a young medicine-man, who told me that if he could employ a good interpreter, he could travel among the Minatarees, Mandans, and Sioux after I left, and it would make him a great medicine-man. Just before I left I saw him taking it from some eight or ten folds of birch bark and deer-skins, all of which were carefully enclosed in a sack made of a pole-cat skin, and undoubtedly destined to become his mystery or medicine- bag.

With the exception of one night in twenty-five I managed to bivouac on the bank of some little stream or river, where there was water to make my coffee and wood to make a fire. We generally halted a little before sundown, so as to give Charley plenty of time to get his supper before I took up his picket and brought him in. The moment his saddle was off I drove his picket down where the grass was plenty and fresh, and gave him the full length of his lasso. I would then gather my wood, make my fire, and that well going, I would dress my prairie hen or prepare my venison steak, and fasten them on top of litttle sharpened stakes before the fire. Then I would put my little tin coffee pot on the fire, and spread out all my traps, such as a tin cup, a bowie knife, an iron spoon, a little sack of salt, some sugar, and a slice or two of cold ham.

It was a habit of Charley's and mine at this time to take him a little salt, of which he was very fond, and which he took with added relish out of my hand. This might have been possibly one of the causes of Charley's affectionate attachment to me, and, on this occasion, I took care to lay in enough salt to keep up friendly feelings between us during our campaign. He was so accustomed to receiving this little attention when his meal was half over, and mine just to begin, and he had learned the time so well, that if I was not ready at the moment, his head was up and his tail spread out like a turkey cock while he stood and gazed inquiringly at me. I would say to him "Charley, do you want your salt?" "Eegh-ee-e," he never failed to answer.

Once we crossed a large prairie of many miles in extent, without a tree or bush in sight, and so perfectly level that, in the language of the region, we were "out of sight of land." Here night overtook us, and we were obliged to bivouac without water. I had no coffee that night, but I cooked very nicely a venison steak with a fire of dried buffalo dung which I gathered from the prairie.

In the middle of the night I was awakened by a terrific thunder storm. I got up and drove Charley's picket doubly strong, and folding up one of my robes, laid it across the saddle to sit upon, and spread the other robe over my head. This fell all around me to the ground and formed a tent that not only sheltered me, but all my things from the rain. This fell in torrents, and the flashes of lightning seemed to run like fiery snakes over the prairie, as if they were hunting for something to strike. At every flash I feared that Charley and I might be snapped up. Notwithstanding I had to sit upright all night, I got some sleep,

The monotony of these broad level prairies was sometimes not only tedious, but doleful. I repeatedly fell asleep while riding, and when waking found Charley not only going forward, but keeping the course. Some- • times for hours together, creeping along without a bird or beast in sight, while both were in deep thought, I would say, "Charley, a penny for your thoughts." "Eegh-ee-e," Charley would reply. Thus we both braced up our nerves and moved along with new life.

One day while we were thus jogging along, suddenly a stately buck, with a pair of horns that looked as if he had a chair on his head, sprang up before us. While I was getting my left barrel to bear upon him, Charley trembled so I could scarcely get my aim. When I fired, the deer staggered back a little but recovered, and bounded off. A few rods took him over the hill, and he was out of sight. I pushed Charley up to where he stood, and seeing the blood on the grass, knew I had hit him. We could easily track him by the blood, but at length struck the high grass, which came quite up to Charley's back. But I could feel by his movements and the extraordinary excitement he was under that he was tracing the deer. I had the curiosity to slacken rein and let him take his course. He went on in an unnaturally fast walk, snuffing and smelling as precisely as a hound could have done. We went on for a half-mile or more, when breaking out of the grass at the foot of a small hill, he suddenly turned and raised his head to the left, his ears pointing forward. "Eegh-ee-e," he exclaimed. I looked in the direction, and there lay our noble buck with his frightful horns, quite dead.

I did not straighten the rein even then, but Charley started up on a trot, with his head and tail up, and bringing me within a few paces of him, stopped. I then pushed him up, and he smelled of the animal's nose and bleeding wound. "Are you sorry, Charley?" said I. "Eegh-ee-e." "No, you are not. I put the question wrong." "Eegh-ee-e." "That's right." I dismounted, and Charley looked on while I cut a nice steak, and looked and smelled back at me while I was tying it to the saddle. He knew as well as I that he was going to carry it home, and I was going to have it for supper.

Sometimes we came upon deep sunken streams, like ditches, when I was within a few steps of plunging into them from their perpendicular sides, which were overhung with long wild grass. Into one of these canals which I had followed for several miles in the vain hope of finding a shoal or an accustomed ford, I plunged with Charley where it was about six or eight yards wide (and God knows how deep, for we did not go to the bottom), and swam him to the opposite bank, to which I clung, and which being perpendicular and of clay, and three or four feet higher than the water, was an insurmountable difficulty to Charley. I led the poor fellow at least a mile as I walked on the top of the bank, with the bridle in my hand, holding his head above the water as he was swimming, and I at times almost inextricably entangled in the long grass that was often higher than my head. I at length (and just before I was ready to drop the rein of faithful Charley in hopeless despair) came to an old buffalo ford, where the banks were graded down, and the poor exhausted animal at last got out, and was ready and willing to take me and my luggage (after I had dried them in the sun) on the journey again.

The Osage River, which is a powerful stream, I struck at a place which was sixty or eighty yards in width, with a current that was sweeping along at a rapid rate. I stripped everything from Charley and tied him with his lasso until I travelled the shores up and down for some distance and collected drift wood enough for a small raft which I constructed to carry my clothes and saddle and other things safe over. I then took up Charley's picket, and leading him to the water's edge and taking off his lasso, I said, "Charley, do you know what you have to do?" "Eegh-ee-e." There was no mistake about this, as it was a thing he was used to. I pointed to the other bank and drove him in, and he started for the other shore. The current swept him down some distance, but he got to the bank and out upon the prairie. Then he turned about and looked at me with a tremendous "eegh-ee-eh," and went to grazing.

Having arranged my things on it I moved my raft into the stream, and swimming behind, with one hand on it, proceeded very slowly down the stream. Approaching the opposite shore, I saw with alarm that the rotten timbers of my raft were absorbing the water so fast that some of my things were already under water. Meanwhile the shore was lined with logs and tree tops where I was to land. Some of the long timbers of my raft, as I had no axe to make them of equal length, caught in the limbs of a tree, and whirling it around the raft, began to go to pieces, and I was thrown again out into the stream. A second effort got me a better landing, and at length I got myself and my traps safely on to the ground. I was then in front of a dense forest, and full a mile below where I had last seen Charley standing, with his head and tail up and watching me as I disappeared behind a point of timber. I was just making ready to go in search of him when I was startled by a cracking noise behind me, and as I turned around "Eegh-ee-e" said Charley, as he crowded through the thick weeds and nettles.

Such are a few incidents of this journey of five hundred miles which I made entirely alone, and which at last brought me out at Boonville, on the western bank of the Missouri River.

CHAPTER XXXII
CANOEING ON THE UPPER MISSISSIPPI

AFTER RECRUITING my health during the winter in recreation and amusement on the coast of Florida, like a bird of passage I started, at the rallying notes of the swan and the wild goose, for the cool, fresh North. But the gifted passengers soon left me behind. I found them here, their nests built, their eggs hatched, and their offspring fledged and figuring in the world before I arrived at Fort Snelling, on the Falls of St. Anthony, from which place I will begin my summer's campaign.

With several hundred of the wildest of the Chippewas, and as many Sioux, we celebrated the Fourth of July in an unusual and interesting manner. To aid me in getting sketches of the customs and manners of these Indians, Major Talliaferro, the Indian agent at this place, told them I was a great medicine-man who had visited many of the tribes and witnessed their sports, and I had come to see if the Indians of this region were their equals in ball-play and other games. If they would come on the next day, which was the Fourth of July, and give us a ball-play and some of their dances, he would have the big gun fired twenty-one times.

This they easily construed into a great compliment to themselves. I gave them an even stronger inducement in a barrel of flour and a quantity of pork and tobacco. Accordingly, on the Day of Independence, about eleven o'clock, which is the hour the Indians usually make their appearance on great occasions, the young men who were to play came onto the ground. Their dress consisted of the flap, and attached to their girdle a tail reaching nearly to the ground, made of the choicest arrangement of quills and feathers, or of the hair of the tails of white horses, with the ball-sticks in their hands. After an excited and warmly contested play of two hours they gave a number of their most fanciful and picturesque dances. The most beautiful of these was the Dance of the Braves.

During this dance, at intervals, they stop, and one of them steps into the ring, and as loud as possible, with the most significant gestures, relates the feats of bravery he has performed, boasts of the scalps he has taken, of the enemies he has vanquished, going through all the motions which accompanied these scenes he described. At the end of his boasting all assent to the truth of his story, and give in their approbation by the guttural "waugh!" and the dance again commences. At the next interval another makes his boasts, and another, and another, and so on.

During this scene a little trick was played off in the following manner, which produced much amusement and laughter. A woman of goodly size, and in woman's attire, danced into the ring (which seemed to excite some surprise, as women are never allowed to join in the dance), and commenced "sawing the air," and boasting of the astonishing feats of bravery she had performed, of the incredible number of horses she had stolen, of the scalps she had taken, etc., until her feats surpassed all that had ever been heard. They all gave assent, however, to what she had said, and apparently *credence,* too, and to reward so extraordinary a feat of female prowess, they presented to her a kettle, a cradle, beads, ribbons, etc. After getting her presents and placing them safely in the hands of another matron for safekeeping, she commenced disrobing herself, and, almost instantly divesting herself of a loose dress, in the presence of the whole company, came out in a *soldier s coat* and *pantaloons!* and laughed at them excessively for their mistake! She then commenced dancing and making her boasts of her exploits, assuring them that she was a man, and a great brave. They all gave unqualified assent to this, acknowledged their error, and made her other presents of a gun, a horse, of tobacco, and a war-club. She then deliberately threw off the pantaloons and coat, and presented herself at once, and to their great astonishment and confusion, in a beautiful woman's dress. The tact with which she performed these parts so uniformly pleased, that it drew forth thundering applause from the Indians as well as from the spectators, and the chief stepped up and crowned her head with a beautiful plume of the eagle's quill, rising from a crest of the swan's down.

**THREE DISTINGUISHED BALL-PLAYERS.
PORTRAITS FROM LIFE, IN THE BALL-PLAY DRESS**

The Sioux occupy all the country on the west bank of this river, while the Chippewas claim all lying east from the Chippewa River at the mouth of Lake Pepin to the source of the Mississippi. These two tribes are hostile, and from time out of mind have been at war. They are now encamped on different sides of the fort, and at present their difficulties have been arranged by the Indian agent, whom they call Great Father, and whose advice they listen to with the greatest attention. For two weeks past they have been making speeches before him, and have united in their dances, games, feasts and smokes. But this does not mean that when again on their hunting-grounds the war cry and tomahawk will not be raised.

I have been a daily visitor to the camp of the Chippewas. Their wigwams are made of slight poles stuck in the ground and bent over so as to give a roof-like shape to the lodge. This framework is then covered with birch bark. I was strolling through the village with my wife when the Indian women gathered around her, anxious to shake hands with her and show her their children, of which she took especial notice. They literally filled her arms with muk-kuhs of maple sugar, of which they make great quantities for sale.

The Sioux in this region who are out of the reach of beavers and buffaloes are poor and meanly clad, compared to their tribe on the Missouri, where the skins of the wild animals supply them with picturesque and comfortable dresses. The same deterioration is also seen in the morals and constitutions of these, as of all the other Indians who live on the frontier, owing to whiskey, small-pox, and other diseases that shorten their lives.

After the great business of the treaty between the Sioux and Chippewas was over the Chippewas struck their tents by taking them down and rolling up their bark coverings and packing them, with women, dogs and all, into their canoes.

The bark canoe of the Chippewas is perhaps the most beautiful and light model of all the water crafts that were ever invented. It is generally made entirely of the rind of one birch tree, so ingeniously shaped and sewed together with the roots of tamarack that the canoes are water-tight, and ride the water as light as cork. Under the skilful guidance of the Indian or the ugliest squaw, they gracefully dodge about, but, like everything wild, are timid and treacherous with the white man, who, unless he is very skilful in balancing, is pretty sure to get soused a few times in his first efforts to make their acquaintance.

A few days after these scenes, I embarked in a light birch canoe with one companion, Corporal Allen, a young man of considerable taste, who thought he would relish the transient scenes of such a voyage with a painter down the Mississippi for Prairie du Chien.

In the afternoon of the first day of our journey we discovered three lodges of Sioux on the bank, hallooing and waving their blankets for us to come in shore. As we had no business with them we held to our course, when one of them ran into his lodge, and, coming out with his gun, levelled it at us and gave us a charge of buckshot about our ears. One of them passed through several folds of my cloak lying in front of my knee, and several others so near as to spatter our faces with water. There was no fun in this. I ran the canoe to the shore as fast as possible, and men, women and children ran to the shore to meet us with yells and laughter as we landed. As the canoe struck the shore I rose, and throwing all the infuriated demon I could into my countenance, thrust my pistols into my belt, a half dozen bullets into my mouth, and my doubled barrel gun in my hand, I leaped ashore. By a nearer route I got between them and their wigwams, where, with my barrels presented, I made them understand I could annihilate the whole of them in a minute. I slipped my sketch book and pencil into my hand, and, under the muzzle of my gun, each fellow stood for his likeness, which I made them understand by signs were to be sent to "Muzzabucksa" (iron cutter), the name they gave to Major Talliaferro, their agent at St. Peters.

We went on peaceably and pleasantly during the rest of our voyage, having ducks, deer, and bass for our game and our food, and for our bed the grass at the foot of some towering bluff. Our light bark ran to every ledge, dodged into every cut-off, every cave was explored, and almost every great bluff ascended. One of these is "The Lovers' Leap" on Lake Pepin, a bold projecting rock six or seven hundred feet high. From the summit of this, it is said, a beautiful Indian girl, the daughter of a chief, threw herself off in the presence of the tribe, some fifty years ago, and dashed herself to pieces rather than marry a man her father had decided should be her husband.

In the midst, or half-way of Lake Pepin, Corporal Allen and I hauled our canoe out upon the beach of Point aux Sables, where we spent a couple of days, feasting on plums and fine fish and wild fowl, and filling our pockets with agates and carnelians we picked up along the pebbly beach, at last started on our way for the outlet of the lake, with a fair north-west wind, as I sat in the stern and steered, while the corporal was "catching the breeze" in a large umbrella which he spread open and held in the bow.

This has been one of the earliest trading-posts of the Fur Company. The prairie is a beautiful elevation of several miles above the river, with a picturesque range of grassy bluffs in the rear. The government has built a substantial fort in which generally several companies are stationed for the purpose of keeping peace among the hostile tribes and to protect the inhabitants of the frontier.

While I was there Wabesha's band of Sioux came to get their annuities, which came very far from paying off their accounts, which the traders take care to have standing against them for the goods furnished on a year's credit. However, whether they pay or not, they can always get whiskey enough for a carouse and a brawl, which lasts a week or two. At the end of this time it was announced that the women were going to have a ball game. A pole was stretched on crotches, and on this was hung the ribbons and calicoes and other presents that would appeal to women. These were guarded by an old man who was to umpire the game.

In this game the women have two balls attached to the ends of a string about a foot and a half long. Each woman has in each of her hands a short stick. With these she endeavors to catch the string wich the two balls, and throws them over toward her own goal. This game sometimes lasts for hours; meanwhile the men, who are often half-drunk, roll over the ground, shouting with laughter at the women who are tumbling about in every direction and in all attitudes, scuffling for the ball.

CHAPTER XXXIII
PAINTING THE PORTRAIT OF KEOKUK

MY CANOE I beached at Dubuque. This is a small town of two hundred houses, all built within two years, in the heart of the richest part of this mining region. It has the advantage over other mining districts, inasmuch as the soil overlying the lead mines produces the finest of corn. Here I met my wife, and we proceeded to Camp Des Moines, the winter post of Colonel Kearney and three companies of dragoons. Then placing my wife and two friends in my bark, I paddled them fourteen miles through the Des Moines rapids, that they might take the steamer for St. Louis, while I returned to the wild and romantic life I love to lead.

At Camp Des Moines I joined General Street, the Indian agent, in a tour to Keokuk's village of Sacs and Foxes. Colonel Kearney gave us a corporal's command of six or eight dragoons, and in two days we reached the village, sixty miles up the Des Moines River, finely situated on a prairie as rich as a garden. We found Keokuk (running fox) to be a chief of fine and portly figure, with a good countenance, a dignified and proud man, yet very vain, and of great grace of movement.

General Street had some messages from Washington to read to him. To these he and his chiefs listened patiently, after which he placed before us some good brandy and wine, and invited us to lodge with him. He then called up five runners, to whom in low and emphatic tones he told the substance of General Street's talk and communication. These started off at full gallop, one to proclaim it through the village, the others to carry his message to the other villages of the nation.

It is with Keokuk that the treaty was made by General Scott at the close of the Black Hawk war. This was owing to the fact that during the war he had kept two-thirds of the warriors neutral, and thus averted much bloodshed. The poor dethroned monarch, Black Hawk, was at Rock Island at the time, and an object of pity. With an old frock coat and brown hat on, and a cane in his hand, he stood outside of the group in dumb and dismal silence, his two sons by his side.

They were not allowed to speak nor to sign the treaty. Nah-pope, the Prophet, however arose, and commenced a very earnest speech on the subject of temperance. But Governor Dodge ordered him to sit down, being out of order. This saved him a much more peremptory order from Keokuk, who was rising at that moment with a look on his face that the devil might have shrunk from.

During this time I painted his portrait. He brought in all his costly wardrobe that I might select the dress that suited me; but, at once, of his own accord, named the dress that was most purely Indian. In that he paraded for several days, and in it I painted him at full length. He was vain enough to say to me that he made a fine appearance on horseback, and that he wished me to paint him mounted. The horse that he rode was the finest on the frontier. It was a black, blooded horse, beautifully caparisoned, with his scalps attached to the bridle bits. He rode and nettled his prancing steed in front of my door until its sides were covered with blood, making a great display, until the picture was finished. He expressed much satisfaction, and after finishing him I painted the portrait of his favorite wife, the oldest of seven, and the only one that could be painted. This seemed to be an honor accorded to her because she was the mother of his favorite son. Her dress, of civilized stuffs, had been made and ornamented by herself. It was truly a splendid affair, the upper part being almost entirely covered with silver brooches. I also painted this son, who is to be his successor, and eight or ten of his principal men and women.

When General Street and I arrived at Keokuk's village we were just in time to see one of the very curious customs of the Sacs and Foxes. This is called "smoking horses." The Foxes were just making up a war party to go against the Sioux, and lacked twenty horses. Accordingly they had sent word to the Sacs, the day before, that they were coming at a certain hour on that day to "smoke" that number of horses, and they must not fail to have them ready. At that hour the twenty young men, who needed the horses, were on the spot, and seated themselves on the ground, in a circle, and began smoking. The villagers flocked around them in a dense crowd, and soon after appeared on the prairie, at half a mile distance, an equal number of young men of the Sac tribe, who had agreed, each to give a horse, and who were then galloping them about at full speed, and gradually, as they went around in a circuit, coming in nearer to the centre, until they were at last close around the ring of young fellows seated on the ground. While dashing about thus, each one, with a heavy whip in his hand, as he came within reach of the group on the ground, selected the one to whom he decided to present his horse, and as he passed him gave him the most tremendous cut with his lash over his naked shoulders, and as he darted around again he plied the whip as before, and again and again, with a violent "crack!" until the blood could be seen trickling down over his naked shoulders, upon which he instantly dismounted, and placed the bridle and whip in his hands, saying, "here, you are a beggar; I present you a horse, but you will carry my mark on your back." In this manner they were all in a little time "whipped up," and each had a good horse to ride home and into battle.

The dances among this tribe were exceedingly spirited and amusing. The slave dance is a picturesque scene, and the custom on which it is founded a very curious one. This tribe has a society called "The Slaves," composed of a number of young men of the best families, who volunteer to be slaves for two years, when they will, at the order of the chief, perform any service, no matter how humiliating or degrading it may be. One of the number is the master, and he receives the commands of the chief. On one day in the year they have a feast, and before it perform this dance. After serving two years they are exempt from labor for the rest of their lives.

A very droll dance is called the Discovery dance. In this there is a great deal of pantomine, and no music or noise except the patting of the feet. They advance two and four at a time, as if stealing secretly along overlooking the country, and, professing to announce the discovery of animals and enemies, signal back to the leader of the dance.

The dance to the medicine of the brave is worth recording for its beautiful moral. When a party of Sac warriors, returning with scalps, have lost one of their number, they appear and dance in front of his wigwam fifteen days in succession, about an hour on each day, when the widow hangs his medicine-bag on a green bush which she erects before her door, and under which she sits and cries, while the warriors dance and brandish the scalps they have taken, and at the same time recount the deeds of bravery of their deceased comrade in arms, while they are throwing presents to the widow to heal her grief and afford her the means of a living.

The Sacs and Foxes draw from the government twenty-seven thousand dollars annually. By treaty they conveyed to the government two hundred and fifty- six thousand acres of land on the Iowa River, known as the Black Hawk purchase, for seventy-five cents an acre. The price paid for this tract is a liberal one, although even one dollar an acre would not have been too much to have paid for it, since every acre of it can be sold to actual settlers in one year for one dollar and a quarter an acre.

After the treaty was signed the Indians were told that one month would be given them to wind up their affairs, move their families and property from the tract before the white settlers arrived. Considerable excitement was created among the chiefs and braves by this suggestion, and a hearty laugh ensued, the cause of which was soon after explained by one of them in the following manner:

"My father, we have to laugh; we require no time to move; we have all left the lands already, and sold our wigwams to Chemokemons (white men) – some for one hundred and some for two hundred dollars – before we came to this treaty. There are already four hundred Chemokemons on the land, and several hundred more on their way moving in; and three days before we came away one Chemokemon sold his wigwam to another Chemokemon for two thousand dollars, to build a great town."

CHAPTER XXXIV
THE LAND OF THE RED-PIPE STONE[2]

DO NOT be amazed if I now invoke the Indian Muse, for here she dwells, nor if my story savors of poetry or has the air of romance.

Here, according to the traditions, happened the mysterious birth of the red pipe, which has blown its fumes of peace and war to the remotest corners of the continent, which has visited every warrior and passed through its reddened stem the irrevocable oath of war and desolation. Here, also, the peace-breathing calumet was born and, fringed with eagles' quills, has soothed the savage fury.

In my varied wanderings among the Indian tribes, everywhere I had heard of this sacred spot. When on the upper Missouri a distinguished Knisteneaux presented me with a handsome red-stone pipe, he told me:

"In the time of a great freshet, which took place many centuries ago and destroyed all the nations of the earth, all the tribes of the red men assembled on the Coteau du Prairie to get out of the way of the waters. After they had all gathered here from all parts, the water continued to rise, until at length it covered them all in a mass, and their flesh was converted into red-pipe stone. Therefore it has always been considered neutral ground; it belonged to all tribes alike, and all were allowed to get it and smoke it together.

"While they were all drowning in a mass, a young woman, K-wap-tah-w (a virgin), caught hold of the foot of a very large bird that was flying over, and was carried to the top of a high cliff, not far off, that was above the water. Here she had twins, and their father was the wareagle, and her children have since peopled the earth.

"The pipe stone, which is the flesh of their ancestors, is smoked by them as the symbol of peace, and the eagle's quill decorates the head of the brave."

When I painted the portrait of a Mandan chief four years ago, he said:

---

2   The red-pipe stone is now known as Catlinite. — ED.

"My brother, I am a young man, but my heart is strong. I have jumped on to the medicine-rock; I have placed my arrow on it and no Mandan can take it away. The red stone is slippery, but my foot was true; it did not slip. My brother, this pipe which I give to you I brought from a high mountain; it is toward the rising sun. We left our *totems* or marks on the rocks; we cut them deep in the stones, and they are there now. The Great Spirit told all nations to meet there in peace, and all nations hid the war-club and the tomahawk. My friend, we want to visit our medicines; our pipes are old and worn out. My friend, I wish you to speak to our Great Father about this."

The chief of the Puncahs, on the upper Missouri, also made the following allusion to this place in a speech which he made to me on the occasion of presenting me a very handsome pipe about four years since:

"My friend, this pipe which I wish you to accept was dug from the ground, and cut and polished, as you now see it, by my hands. I wish you to keep it, and when you smoke through it recollect that this red stone is a part of our flesh. This is one of the last things we can ever give away."

The tradition of the Missouri Sioux I have given elsewhere. The Sioux of the Mississippi, who live in the region of the Pipe Stone Quarry, have not a less strange tradition, which says : "Many ages after the red men were made, when all the different tribes were at war, the Great Spirit sent runners and called them all together at the 'Red Pipe.' He stood on the top of the rocks and the red people were assembled in infinite numbers on the plains below. He took out of the rock a piece of the red stone and made a large pipe; he smoked it over them all; told them that it was part of their flesh; that though they were at war they must meet at this place as friends; that it belonged to them all; that they must make their calumets from it and smoke them to him whenever they wished to appease him or get his good-will. The smoke from his big pipe rolled over them all, and he disappeared in its cloud. At the last whiff of his pipe a blaze of fire rolled over the rocks and melted their surface. At that moment two squaws went in a blaze of fire under the two medicine-rocks, where they remain to this day, and must be consulted and propitiated whenever the pipe stone is to be taken away."

Such are a few of the traditions of this curious place which long ago determined me to visit it. With an English traveller, Mr. Robert Serril Wood, for my companion, and an Indian guide, O-kup-pee, I left the Falls of St. Anthony for the Coteau du Prairie, where the Pipe Stone Quarry is to be found. We traversed the beautiful shores of the St. Peters River, which we crossed at a place called Traverse des Sioux. Here, while halting at the hut of a trader named Le Blanc, we were held up by a band of Sioux for daring to approach the sacred source of the pipe.

A murky crowd of dark-visaged warriors and braves gathered around the house, cramming and closing every means of escape, while one of them, in an insulting harangue, informed us that we were prisoners. About twenty spoke in turn, and we were doomed to sit the entire afternoon without being allowed to speak in our own behalf until they were through, while they brandished their fists in our faces and overwhelmed us with threats. After these copper-visaged advocates of their country's rights had assembled about us and filled up every avenue of the cabin, the grave council was opened in the following manner. Te-o-kun-hko (the swift man) first rose and said:

"My friends, I am not a chief but the son of a chief, and when he is gone away it is my duty to speak for him; he is not here, but what I say is the talk of his mouth. We have been told that you are going to the Pipe Stone Quarry. We come now to ask for what purpose you are going and what business you have to go there. ("How! how!" vociferated all of them, thereby approving what was said, giving assent by the word *how*, which is their word for yes.)

"Brothers, we look at you and we see that you are Che-mo-ke-mon capitains (white men officers); we know that you have been sent by your government to see what that place is worth, and we think the white people want to buy it. ('How! how!')

"Brothers, we have seen always that the white people, when they see anything in our country that they want, send officers to value it, and then if they can't buy it they will get it some other way. ('How! how!')

"Brothers, we know that the whites are like a great cloud that rises in the East and will cover the whole country. We know that they will have all our lands; but if ever they get our Red Pipe Quarry they will have to pay very dear for it. ('How! how! how!')

"Brothers, we know that no white man has ever been to the Pipe Stone Quarry, and our chiefs have often decided in council that no white man shall ever go to it. ('How! how!')

"Brothers, you have heard what I have to say, and you can go no further, but you must turn about and go back. ('How! how! how!')

"Brothers, you see that the sweat runs from my face, for I am troubled."

Then I commenced to reply in the following manner: "My friends, I am sorry that you have mistaken us so much and the object of our visit to your country. We are not officers; we are two poor men travelling to see the Sioux and shake hands with them. This man who is with me is my friend; he is a Sa-ga-nosh (Englishman). ('How! how! how!' All rising and shaking hands with him, and a number of them taking out and showing British medals which were carried in their bosoms.)

"We have heard that the Red Pipe Quarry was a great curiosity, and we have started to go to it and we will not be stopped." (Here I was interrupted by a grim and black-visaged fellow, who shook his long, shaggy locks as he rose, with his sunken eyes fixed in direst hatred on me and his fist brandished within an inch of my face.)

"*Pale faces,* you cannot speak till we have all done; you are our *prisoners;* you must listen to what we have to say. What has been said to you is true; you must go back. ('How! how!')

"I brought a large piece of the pipe stone and gave it to a white man to make a pipe; he was our trader, and I wished him to have a good pipe. The next time I went to his store I was unhappy when I saw that stone made into a dish! ('Eugh!')

"This is the way the white men would use the red- pipe stone if they could get it. Such conduct would offend the Great Spirit and make a red man's heart sick." ('How! how!')

To this I replied in the following manner:

"My friends, I think as you do that the Great Spirit has given that place to the red men for their pipes. ('How! how!') But we have started to go and see it, and we cannot think of being stopped."

During this scene the son of M. le Blanc was standing by, and, seeing this man shaking his fist in my face, told him to stand back at a respectful pace or he would knock him down. Le Blanc advised us that these were the most treacherous part of the Sioux nation and we had better go back as they ordered. But I made a few remarks declaring our intention of going on, for this we intended to do even at the risk of our lives, and this we did the next morning, riding off through the midst of them.

On our way we were notified at several villages through which we passed to go back. But we kept our way over a hundred miles of beautiful prairie until we reached the trading-house of an old friend of mine, M. la Framboise, where we rested pleasantly a couple of days. La Framboise has some good Indian blood in his veins, and from his mode of life, as well as from a natural passion that seems to belong to these French adventurers, is fond of songs and stories, of which he has many, and which makes him a most amusing companion. My friend Wood sings delightfully, and as I cannot sing, but now and then can tell a story, we passed our evenings in our humble bivouac over buffalo meat and prairie-hens with much fun and amusement.

We were now but forty or fifty miles from the base of the Coteau des Prairie, and, with our kind companion La Framboise, pushed on. For many miles we had the Coteau before us like a blue cloud settling down on the horizon. When we had arrived at its base we were scarcely sensible of it from the graceful and almost imperceptible terraces gently rising one above the other until we reached the summit. Bivouacked on its ridge, the air as light to breathe as nitrous oxide, nothing could be seen in the distance but a thousand treeless, bushless, weedless hills of vivid green vanishing into an infinity of blue and azure.

Such is the Coteau des Prairie, the dividing ridge between the St. Peters and the Missouri Rivers, equidistant from both. This wonderful feature is several hundred miles in length, and, varying from fifty to a hundred miles in width, is perhaps the noblest mound of its kind in the world. On the very top of the ridge we found the famous quarry of the red pipe. Its most striking feature is a perpendicular wall of close-grained compact quartz, thirty feet high, nearly two miles long, with its face to the west and its ends disappearing by running under the prairie. This rock, and the only rock in view, is as polished as if a liquid glazing had been poured over its surface. Not far from our camp in the solid rock are the deep "footsteps of the Great Spirit," in the forms of the tracks of a large bird, where he formerly stood when the blood of the buffaloes he was eating ran into the rocks and turned them red.

A few yards distant leaped a beautiful little stream from the top of the precipice into a deep basin below. Here among rocks of the loveliest hues but of the wildest contour a poor Indian was bathing. At a little distance beyond, at the base of five huge granite bowlders, he humbly propitiates the guardian spirits of the place by sacrifices of tobacco for permission to take away a small piece of the red stone for a pipe. The surface of these five bowlders is in every part covered with a gray moss which gives them a very venerable appearance. It is under these blocks that the two holes, or ovens, are seen in which the two old women, according to Indian tradition, as guardian spirits of the place, reside.

The fact alone that these blocks differ in character from all other specimens which I have seen in my travels among the thousands of bowlders which are strewed over the great valley of the Missouri and Mississippi, from the Yellowstone almost to the Gulf of Mexico, raises in my mind an unanswerable question as regards the location of their native bed and the means by which they have reached their isolated position, like five brothers, leaning against and supporting each other, without the existence of another bowlder within many miles of them. Further on are seen, like gopher hills, the excavations of the Indians, ancient and recent, and on the surface of the rocks their sculptured hieroglyphics – their wakons, totems, and medicines. Graves, mounds, and fortifications lay in sight, and above all the medicine or leaping rock. This is a part of the precipice that has become severed from the main part, and, about seven feet in diameter, stands about seven feet from the wall, its equal in height. This is to say that it stands like an immense column thirty-five feet high, and highly polished on its top and sides. It requires a bold heart to leap on to its top from the main wall and back again. This is the ambition of the young brave. Some have tried it with success and have left their arrows in its crevices. Others have tried it and, unable to cling to its slippery surface, have been dashed to pieces on the crags and rocks below. Those who have succeeded are allowed to boast of the feat for the rest of their lives.

While there a Sioux chief with thirty of his tribe came to visit the Pipe Stone Quarry and weep over the grave of his son. This was a conical mound near by, where we stood with him as he told the story of the daring leap and death of his son two years before.

While at the Pipe Stone Quarry the Indians told us we were within twenty miles of the "Thunder's Nest." "'Thunder's Nest!' What on earth is that ?" "It is the place where the thunders are hatched out," said the medicine-man.

"The thunder comes out of an egg? It must be a very large egg?"

"No, it is a very small egg, about the size of your finger," said the Sioux. "Most of the medicine-men of the Sioux have seen it."

Our interpreter and guide told us that this was on the highest ridge of the Coteau, and the Indians believed that in the very hottest days, before the thunder showers, the bird sits on her eggs, and when they hatch out they make the thunder. Accordingly, we took an early start the next morning, with three of the Indians, to the Thunder's Nest and the Stone Man medicine. We reached the latter first, and found on a couple of acres of lightly rounded surface the Stone Man medicine. It was the figure, tolerably well-proportioned, of a man lying on his back, some three or four hundred feet long, made entirely of flat stones that had been brought by Indians, probably through centuries, and deposited there. The Indians tell us that every hunting party coming in this direction brings a flat stone and adds to it. No stone lies on top of another; the number is countless, and in size and color represent the features and even the toes and fingers. I could not discover a stone the size of a pigeon's egg within several miles of it.

The Thunder's Nest was on the top of a high prairie mound where was a group of hazel bushes. Blue Mountain, who led the party, requested us all to dismount and wait a little. The Indians took all the plumes out of their heads, and, placing them under their robes, smoothed out their black locks and took a squint at their faces in their little looking-glasses to see if the paint was all right. Then wrapping their robes around them, with the medicine-man at their head, all marched slowly toward the bushes leading the horses.

Within two or three rods of the bushes the Indians halted and each tossed a plug of tobacco into the grass. I started with my gun in my hand, as if to shoot a bird on the wing, toward the hallowed ground, when deep groans caused me to look back, and I saw the Indians in great distress, with their hands over their mouths. I retreated without seeing anything except some hundreds of bits of tobacco lying on the grass, that had been thrown as sacrifices to the Thunder Spirit in dread of which they always live,

CHAPTER XXXV
THE SAD FATE OF OSCEOLA

OVER TWO thousand miles I have wandered to paint the portrait of that great Seminole, Osceola, who, with two hundred and fifty warriors, is imprisoned at Fort Moultrie, South Carolina. With the Seminoles the government has been at war for four or five years in the endeavor to remove them from their lands, in compliance with a treaty stipulation, which the government claims was justly made and which the Seminoles aver was not.

The Cherokees, the Creeks, the Choctaws, and the Seminoles are semi-civilized tribes that owned valuable tracts of the best cotton lands in Georgia and Alabama, and were therefore rich. These lands are too valuable for Indians to own, and Indians are bad neighbors. General Jackson was elected President, and decided that all the Indian tribes should be removed west of the Mississippi. The Seminole chiefs, however, refused to sign the treaty. One day the eleven subordinate chiefs of this tribe were told that on the next day the treaty was to be signed by Charley Omalatla, the head chief. With their rifles in their hands they went to the government agent's office at the appointed time to see for themselves if their chief was capable of such treachery to his tribe. With these chiefs came Osceola.

The treaty was spread upon the table, and Charley Omlatla, according to the agreement, stepped forward and made his signature, expecting the other chiefs to follow him. As he rose from the table Osceola fired, and before the body of the chief could fall to the ground the bullets of six other chiefs went through him. The treaty went to Washington and was there ratified, notwithstanding that it was proven that Charley had received a bribe of seven thousand dollars. The tribe was now removed by force to the West. Osceola, however, fled to the Everglades of Florida, the other chiefs following him as their leader; for, by the custom of all the tribes, he who kills the chief of his own tribe is the leader, if his act is approved. If it is not approved he is immediately put to death.

For six years Osceola kept an army of ten thousand men at bay. At last he was captured by a stratagem that I doubt if any Indian tribe would practise. Under a flag of truce Osceola, with two hundred of his warriors, advanced, unarmed, carrying a white flag. They were at once surrounded, made prisoners of war, and, tied to the backs of horses, were sent to Fort Moultrie. This disgraceful act, I am glad to say, was condemned by every officer of the United States Army except the one that was guilty of it.

Summoned to paint his portrait, I found an extraordinary character. Osceola is a half-breed, his father being white, his mother a Creek. The word Seminole is a Creek word, meaning "runaway," and was given to that part of the Creek nation that emigrated further South. Osceola, who was commonly called Powell, has always been a leader and master-spirit in his tribe, although not a chief. From boyhood he had led an active, desperate sort of life, and in some way, whether he deserved it or not, had acquired an influence and a name that was known even among the remote tribes of the Rocky Mountains.

I found him an easy, affable man. He is only of medium height, elastic and graceful in his movements, very good-looking, with rather an effeminate smile, but of so peculiar a character that I doubt if its like could be found elsewhere. He is polite and gentlemanly in manner, and spoke English well enough to describe to me many of the events of the Seminole war and the shameful manner in which he had been entrapped. At Fort Moultrie I occupied a large room in the officers' quarters, where I painted the portraits of Osceola, Mick-e-no-pa, Ye-how-lo-gee (the cloud), King Philip, and others. As Osceola stood for his portrait he wore three ostrich feathers in his head and a turban made of a varicolored cotton shawl. His dress was of calico, with a handsome dead belt around his waist and his rifle in his hand. Thus I painted him to every string and trinket.

Mick-e-no-pa took great pleasure in being in my room while I was painting the others. When at length he agreed to be painted, it was on the condition that I could make a fair likeness of his legs, which he had tastefully dressed in a handsome pair of red leggings. As he sat cross-legged, I began on these at once, painting them on the lower part of the canvas, leaving room above in which to get his body and head. The Cloud I found to be a very good-natured, jolly man, growing fat in his imprisonment, where he gets enough to eat and is a great favorite with the officers.

One of the young men of the party, and one of the handsomest men I ever saw, was one morning accused by a white man of having stolen a chicken from him the night before. The matter was laid before the chiefs, who heard the evidence, which the white man made very conclusive. The young man had no evidence to give, only asking the chiefs, "Did any Seminole ever know Chee-ho-ka to steal?"

However, the white man's story was so strong that the Indian was convicted, and the sentence of the chiefs was that he should be publicly whipped the next morning at nine o'clock. But the next morning at seven o'clock his body was found hanging from a spike in the wall of the Fort by a thong of rawhide, quite dead. Not long after, while the officers and the Indians were still grouped about him, the white man came up with the chicken under his arm and admitted that it had not been stolen.

The wretch was standing by my side, and from an impulse, without thought, I seized his throat with both hands, and with a grip that I was never capable of before or since. The officers came up and begged me to use no violence, but what had ten times more effect was the hand of Osceola laid lightly on my shoulder, and his whisper in my ear, "Don't, don't, my friend; don't hurt him – don't strike a dog."

It was apparent then that Osceola was brokenhearted and ready to die. I myself saw his rapid decline, and Dr. Weedon, the surgeon of the post, who had charge of him, said that he did not think he would live many weeks. I had scarcely reached New York with my portraits when I received word that he had died the morning after I left Fort Moultrie.

CHAPTER XXXVI
THE INDIAN AS AN ALL-AROUND MAN

HAVING NOW a little leisure, and no particular tribes before my eye, I will take a brief survey of the Indian, and write of the things I have seen but have yet only told in part. I have had toils, difficulties, and dangers to encounter in visiting these wild people, yet I have had my pleasures as I went along in shaking the friendly hands that never knew the contaminating touch of money or the withering embrace of pockets. I have shared the comforts of their hospitable wigwams and have always been preserved unharmed in their country. If I have spoken or am to speak of them with a seeming bias, you will know what allowance to make for me, who am standing as the champion of a people who have treated me kindly, of whom I feel bound to speak well, and who have no means of speaking of themselves.

Of the general appearance of the Indians it may be said that their average in height is about equal to that of their fellow-men in the civilized world. In girth they are less, lighter in limb, and almost free from useless flesh. Their bones are lighter, their skulls are thinner, and their muscles, except in the legs and feet are less hard than those of the white men. Their continual and violent exercise on foot and horseback gives them great strength of leg, and swells the muscles as conspicuously as those in the shoulders and arms of our laboring men.

Although the Indians are narrow in the shoulder and less powerful with their arms, yet it does not always happen that these are as effeminate as they look or so inferior in strength as the smooth and rounded surface seems to indicate.

The Indian who exercises his limbs for the most of his life, denuded and exposed to the air, gets over his muscles a thicker and more compact layer of integuments, which hide them from view, leaving the casual spectator, who sees them only at rest, to suppose them too decidedly inferior to those which are found among people of his own color. Of muscular strength in the legs, I have met many of the most extraordinary instances in the Indian country that ever I have seen in my life; and I have watched and studied such for hours together, with utter surprise and admiration, in the violent exertions of their dances, where they leap and jump with every nerve strung and every muscle swelled, till their legs will often look like a bundle of ropes rather than a mass of human flesh. And from all that I have seen I am inclined to say that whatever differences there may be between the North American Indians and their civilized neighbors in the above respects, they are decidedly the results of different habits of life and modes of education rather than of any difference in constitution. And I would also venture the assertion that he who would see the Indian in a condition to judge of his muscles must see him in motion, and he who would get a perfect study for a Hercules or an Atlas should take a stone-mason for the upper part of his figure and a Camanchee or a Blackfoot Indian from the waist downward to the feet.

There is a general and striking character in the facial outline of the North American Indians, which is bold and free and would seem at once to stamp them as distinct from natives of other parts of the world. Their noses are generally prominent and aquiline, and the whole face, if divested of paint and of copper-color, would seem to approach to the bold and European character. Many travellers have thought that their eyes were smaller than those of Europeans; and there is good cause for one to believe so, if he judges from first impressions without taking pains to inquire into the truth and causes of things. I have been struck, as most travellers no doubt have, with the want of expansion and apparent smallness of the Indians' eyes, which I have found, upon examination, to be principally the effect of continual exposure to the rays of the sun and the wind, without the shields that are used by the civilized world; and also when in-doors, and free from those causes, subjected generally to one more distressing and calculated to produce similar results, the smoke that almost continually hangs about their wigwams, which necessarily contracts the lids of the eyes.

The teeth of the Indians are generally regular and sound, and wonderfully preserved to old age, owing, no doubt, to the fact that they live without the spices of life, without saccharine, and without salt, which are equally destructive to teeth in civilized communities. Their teeth, though sound, are not white, having a yellowish cast; but for the same reason that a negro's teeth are "like ivory," they look white, set as they are in bronze, as any one with a *tolerable* set of teeth can easily test by painting his face the color of an Indian and grinning for a moment in his looking-glass.

Beards they generally have not, esteeming them great vulgarities, and using every possible means to eradicate them whenever they are so unfortunate as to be annoyed with them.

From the best information that I could obtain among forty-eight tribes that I have visited, I feel authorized to say that, among the wild tribes, where they have made no efforts to imitate white men, at least the proportion of eighteen out of twenty by nature are entirely without the appearance of a beard; and of the very few who have them by nature, nineteen out of twenty eradicate it by plucking it out several times in succession, precisely at the age of puberty, when its growth is successfully arrested; and occasionally one may be seen who has omitted to destroy it at that time, and subjects his chin to the repeated pains of its extractions, which he is performing with a pair of clam-shells or other tweezers nearly every day of his life. Wherever there is a cross of the blood with the European or African, which is frequently the case along the frontier, a proportionate beard is the result, and it is allowed to grow or is plucked out with much toil and with great pain.

There has been much speculation and great variety of opinions as to the results of the intercourse between the European and African population with the Indians on the borders. The finest-built and most powerful men that I have ever yet seen have been some of the last-mentioned, the negro and the North American mixed, of equal blood. These instances are rare, to be sure, yet are occasionally to be found among the Seminoles and Cherokees, and also among the Camanchees, even, and the Caddoes, and I account for it in this way: From the slave-holding States to the heart of the country of a wild tribe of Indians, through almost impassible wilds and swamps for hundreds of miles, it requires a negro of extraordinary leg as well as courage and perseverance to travel. Stealing from his master's fields to throw himself among a tribe of wild and hostile Indians in order to enjoy their liberty, such a negro, when he succeeded, was admired by the Indians. As they come with a good share of the tricks and arts of civilization, they are at once looked upon by the tribe as important personages, and generally marry the daughters of chiefs, thus uniting with theirs the best blood in the nation, and thus are produced those remarkably fine and powerful men I have mentioned.

The Indian women live lives of drudgery, but they give strong constitutions to their children. I feel that Nature deals impartially, and that if from their childhood our mothers had, like Indian women, carried loads like beasts of burden in long journeys and over high mountains; if they had swum broad rivers and galloped about for months and even years of their lives astride the backs of horses, we should have taxed them as little in stepping into the world as an Indian pappoose does its mother, who ties her horse under the shade of a tree for a half an hour, and before night overtakes her travelling companions with her infant in her arms.

An Indian family rarely consists of over four or five children; there are generally but two or three. The childish diseases of these are few and simple. I asked the chief of a Guarani village in South America how many children under ten had died in his recollection. He talked with his wife, who said but three. One was drowned, another kicked by a horse, and a third bitten by a rattlesnake.

Sleepy Eye, the chief of a band of fifteen hundred Sioux, told me that they never lost a child from teething but had lost several through accidents. The Mandans preserve the skulls of their dead, and among these I found but eleven skulls of children. Nor in visiting over two millions of Indians have I ever seen a hunchback, an idiot, or one deaf and dumb. I have heard of several lunatics and as many deaf and dumb. It has been said that the reason of this is that such unfortunates are not allowed to live. This is untrue, for in every such case that I heard of they were cared for superstitiously as receptacles of some medicine or mystery bequeathed by the Great Spirit for the benefit of their families. Shah-ra-tar-rusti, chief of the Pawnee Picts, and Clermont, chief of the Osages, told me the same thing.

The savage has the advantage of moving about and sleeping in the open air. The civilized races have the advantages of houses and comfortable beds, also of skilled physicians, surgeons, and dentists. The Indian mother straps her child to a board and preserves its back and limbs straight. From the first sleep of its existence, the pappoose has its mouth closed. When I have seen a poor Indian woman in the wilderness press the lips of her child together as it falls asleep, and swing its cradle in the open air, I have said, "Here is the nurse for emperors."

The consequence is that while the teeth are forming they meet and feel one another, and, taking their natural positions, they form that healthful and pleasing regularity which has given to the Indian, as a race, the most beautiful mouths perhaps in the world. The American savage often smiles but rarely laughs. He meets most of the emotions of life, however sudden or exciting, with his mouth closed. He is garrulous, fond of anecdote and fun at his fireside, but he feels and expresses his pleasures without the explosive action of the muscles of his face and without gesticulation. If by extreme excitement he is forced to laugh or cry, he invariably hides his mouth behind his hand.

In England I asked one of the Iowas who had come over what he thought of the people. "Well, white man – suppose mouth shut – putty coot," he said; "mouth open – no coot; me no like um – not much." The chief then told me that nothing astonished an Indian so much as any derangement or absence of the teeth. This they believed was caused by the number of lies that had passed over them.

In the mechanic arts the Indians have advanced but little, probably because they have had but little use for them. In the fine arts they are still more rude. The materials and implements they work with are rare and simple. Their principal efforts at pictorial effects are found on their buffalo-robes.

I have been unable to find anything like a system of hieroglyphic writing among them, yet their picturewriting on the rocks and on their robes approaches somewhat toward it. I have satisfied myself that they are generally the totems (symbolic names), merely, of Indians who have visited those places, and, from a similar feeling of vanity that everywhere belongs to man much alike, have been in the habit of recording their names or symbols, such as birds, beasts, or reptiles.

I was able also to secure a copy of an Indian song written, or rather drawn, on a piece of birch bark. This was used by the Chippewas before starting on a medicine hunt. For the bear, the moose, the beaver, and for nearly every animal they hunt, they have a certain season to commence and for which they "make medicine" for several days, in order to conciliate the bear or other spirit. For this purpose the doctors, to the beat of the drum, come forth and sing these songs, to the chorus of which all sing and dance, although they have no idea of the meaning of the words. These are the secret of the doctors.

Their governments, if they have any, are generally alike, each tribe having at its head a chief (and most generally a war and a civil chief), who, it would seem, alternately hold the ascendency, as the circumstances of peace or war may demand their respective services. These chiefs, whose titles are generally hereditary, hold their offices only as long as their ages will enable them to perform the duties of them by taking the lead in war parties, etc., after which these devolve upon the next incumbent, who is the eldest son of the chief, provided he is as worthy of it as any other young man in the tribe. If he is not worthy, a chief is elected from among the sub-chiefs, so that the office is *hereditary on condition* and *elective in emergency*.

The chief has no control over the life or limbs or liberty of his subjects, nor other power whatever, excepting that of *influence*, which he gains by his virtues and his exploits in war, and which induces his warriors and braves to follow him, as he leads them to battle, or to listen to him when he speaks and advises in council. In fact, he is no more than a *leader*, whom every young warrior may follow, or turn about and go back from, as he pleases, if he is willing to meet the disgrace that awaits him who deserts his chief in the hour of danger.

The influence of names and families is strictly kept up and preserved in heraldic family arms. Wealth is seldom amassed by any persons in Indian communities, and most sure to slip from the hands of chiefs who often-times, for the sake of popularity, render themselves the poorest of any in the tribe.

These people have no written laws, nor others, save the penalties affixed to certain crimes by long-standing custom or by the decisions of the chiefs in council, who form a sort of court and congress too for the investigation of crimes and transaction of the public business. For the sessions of these dignitaries each tribe have, in the middle of their village, a government or council house, where the chiefs often try and convict for capital offences, leaving the punishment to be inflicted by the nearest of kin, to whom all the eyes of the nation are turned, and who has no means of evading it without suffering disgrace in his tribe.

In their treatment of prisoners they are in the habit of inflicting cruel tortures; but these are always in retaliation for similar treatment to relatives, whose spirits they thus appease. Other prisoners are adopted into the tribe or are married to the widows of those who have fallen in battle. These are respected and enjoy all the rights and immunities of the tribe. If these punishments are certain and cruel, they are few, and confined only to their enemies.

No man in their communities is subject to any restraints upon his liberty or to any corporal or degrading punishment, each one valuing his limbs and his liberty to use them as his inviolable right, which no power in the tribe can deprive him of, while each one holds the chief as amenable to him as the most humble individual in the tribe.

On an occasion when I had interrogated a Sioux chief on the upper Missouri about their government – their punishments and tortures of prisoners, for which I had freely condemned them for the cruelty of the practice – he took occasion when I had got through to ask *me* some questions relative to modes in the *civilized world*, which, with his comments upon them, were nearly as follows, and struck me, as I think they must every one, with great force:

"Among white people, nobody ever take your wife – take your children – take your mother; cut off nose – cut eyes out – burn to death?" No! "Then *you* no cut off nose – *you* no cut out eyes – *you* no burn to death – very good."

He also told me he had often heard that white people hung their criminals by the neck and choked them to death like dogs, and those their own people, to which I answered "yes." He then told me he had learned that they shut each other up in prisons, where they keep them a great part of their lives *because they can't pay money* ! I replied in the affirmative to this, which occasioned great surprise and excessive laughter, even among the women.

For their religion, which is chiefly Theism, they are indebted to the Great Spirit. I can fearlessly assert that the North American Indian, in his native state, is a moral and religious being, endowed by his maker with an intuitive knowledge of some great author of his being and of the universe, in the dread of whose displeasure he constantly lives, since ne expects to be rewarded or punished according to the merits he has gained or forfeited in this world. Of the sincerity of his worship I speak with equal confidence. I never saw any people of any color who spend so much time in humbling themselves before and worshipping the Great Spirit as some of these tribes do, nor any whom I would not as soon suspect of insincerity and hypocrisy.

By nature the Indians are decent, modest, and inoffensive, and all history proves them at first to have been friendly and hospitable. I am proud to add out of my experience my testimony to that which was given by the immortal Columbus, who wrote back to his royal master and mistress :

"I swear to your Majesties that there is not a better people in the world than these – more affectionate, affable, or mild. They love their neighbors as themselves, and they always speak smilingly."

ADVENTURE AND EXPLORATION

Beyond the Old Frontier
Adventures of Indian Fighters, Hunters, and Fur Traders
By GEORGE BIRD GRINNELL

A series of personal narratives of hunting, Indian fighting, and exploration in the early pioneer days.

Missionary Explorers Among the American Indians
By MARY GAY HUMPHREYS

The stories of the first and greatest of American missionaries to the American Indians, told largely in their own words.

True Tales of Arctic Heroism in the New World
By MAJOR-GENERAL A. W. GREELY, U. S. A.

The true stories of the most heroic adventures on the Arctic expeditions from the earliest explorers to our own day.

The Boy's Story of Zebulon M. Pike
Explorer of the Great Southwest
Edited by MARY GAY HUMPHREYS

"A brilliant story of adventure and achievement"
— *Washington Star,*

Each Illustrated. 12mo. $1.50 net

CHARLES SCRIBNER'S SONS, NEW YORK

ADVENTURE AND EXPLORATION

Trails of the Pathfinders
By GEORGE BIRD GRINNELL

Accounts taken from the journals of Henry, Lewis and Clark, Pike, Frémont, and others.

The Boy's Catlin
My Life Among the Indians

Edited with Biographical Introduction by
MARY GAY HUMPHREYS

"As interesting a story of Indians as was ever written and has the merit of being true." — *New York Sun.*

The Boy's Drake
By EDWIN M. BACON

" Much of the story is told in the words of old records, and interesting old maps and pictures make it still more valuable." — *The Bookman.*

The Boy's Hakluyt
By EDWIN M. BACON

The voyages of Hawkins, Drake, Gilbert, and others, retold from Hakluyt's chronicles.

Each Illustrated. 12mo. $1.50 net

CHARLES SCRIBNER'S SONS, NEW YORK

Indian Why Stories
Sparks from War Eagle's Lodge-Fire
By FRANK B. LINDERMANN
Illustrated in color. Sq. 8vo. $2.00 net ; postage extra

War Eagle is a fine old Indian chief who tells the young people, across his lodge-fire in the long evenings, stories that are likely to have much of the wide popularity of Uncle Remus's tale of Br'er Rabbit and Br'er Fox.

BY PAUL G. TOMLINSON
In Camp on Bass Island
What Happened to Four Classmates on the St. Lawrence River
Illustrated. $1.25 net; postage extra

An exciting account of the adventures in fishing, boating, and swimming of the same four boys who travelled so adventurously in Labrador in "To the Land of the Caribou."

To the Land of the Caribou
Illustrated. $1.00 net

"A rattling good story of the sort boys love is well told by Mr. Tomlinson." — *New York Times.*

African Adventure Stories
By J. ALDEN LORING
FIELD NATURALIST TO THE ROOSEVELT AFRICAN EXPEDITION
With a foreword by THEODORE ROOSEVELT
Illustrated. 8vo. $1.50 net

"An illustrated book with thrills for any boy, grown up or growing." — *New York World.*

The Black Bear
By WILLIAM H. WRIGHT
Illustrated. $1.00 net

"Finely illustrated, informing, and entertaining."
— *Philadelphia Inquirer.*

CHARLES SCRIBNER'S SONS, NEW YORK

BY GEORGE BIRD GRINNELL

The Wolf Hunters
A STORY OF THE BUFFALO PLAINS
Edited and arranged from the Manuscript Diary of
ROBERT M. PECK
Illustrated. $1.35 net; postage extra

The true adventures and thrilling experiences of three young cavalrymen who spent the winter of 1861-62 in hunting wolves on the Western Plains.

Blackfeet Indian Stories
With frontispiece and cover by N. C. WYETH
$1.00 net; postage extra

Twenty-five or more real Blackfeet Indian folk-lore stories are here related as simply and as graphically as the Indians themselves told them.

BY NOAH BROOKS

First Across the Continent
A CONCISE STORY
OF THE LEWIS AND CLARK EXPEDITION
Illustrated.. $ 1.50 net

"For any one who has an interest in adventure and in the hardihood of the pioneer this is a great story." — *Boston Herald*.

The Boy Emigrants
Illustrated. $1.25 net

"It is one of the best boys' stories we have ever read."
— *The Christian Work*.

The Boy Settlers
A STORY OF EARLY TIMES IN KANSAS
Illustrated. $1.25 net

"The boys have great sport killing buffaloes and some trouble about Indian uprisings." — *The Independent*.

CHARLES SCRIBNER'S SONS, NEW YORK